I GREW UP IN WOLVERTON

Compiled and Edited by

Ruth Edwards

A collection of thoughts and observations from the Facebook pages of those who spent their growing years in Wolverton.

To
Vivienne

Regards
Ruth Edwards
Ruth

I GREW UP IN WOLVERTON

Published by Magic Flute Publications 2012

ISBN 978-1-909054-03-5

Magic Flute Publications
Magic Flute Artworks Limited
231 Swanwick Lane
Southampton SO31 7GT

www.magicflutepublications.co.uk

A description of this book is available from the British Library

About this Book

This book owes its origin to the phenomenon called Facebook. A group was started by Faye Lloyd in 2008 to talk and reminisce about growing up in Wolverton and over the years has attracted almost 800 members. It has proved an opportunity for those who once grew up together to re-establish contact and for people of different decades to share memories of what it was like to grow up in a small, 19th century railway town in rural North Bucks.

The group trotted along quietly for three years with a few scattered contributions here and there, and then, in the Autumn of 2011, there was a sudden explosion of interest amongst former Wolvertonians wishing to share memories. The group literally lifted off. In January 2012 it occurred to me that there was a potential hoard of important memories that deserved more lasting exposure than to sit in a digital vault somewhere in the world. I put the idea of a book forward to the group and there was interest. I asked for help and Ruth Edwards came forward enthusiastically (and also bravely) to take on the task of compiling and editing this material. It has been an enormous amount of work.

What follows is a collection of "conversations" within the Facebook group. They will read differently from a dialogue in a play for example because people pick up a thread mid-way and sometimes replies come at some remove from the original point. They are "live". One remark will stimulate another memory. Occasionally things are mis-remembered, and often corrected. Some in the group are good friends, some knew each other in the past and some have become confident enough to exchange their thoughts and opinions with people they have never met and with whom they only have Wolverton in common.

All the contributors to this book spent their growing years in Wolverton before Facebook was invented, before the Internet was invented, and in many cases before computers were dreamt of as part of our daily lives.

So in the final analysis this book is about Wolverton. It is about growing up in Wolverton and sharing the joy of memories of those most intense years. Wolverton is not unique, but it is unique for the people represented in these pages.

We have done some editing to avoid repetition but we have kept most of the remarks to try to capture the immediacy of the interaction. We have tried to organise the material thematically, but it will not read like a narrative. These are mostly thoughts and recollections at random. The comments are sometimes witty and sometimes ponderous; sometimes memory is sharp, sometimes imperfect. Overall the contributors have a genuine affection for their growing years in this small town and this is what we have tried to capture in these pages.

We were also surprised by the sheer volume of material generated by these Facebook comments, and we have left out a great deal simply to bring the book to a manageable size. We will wait to see whether or not a second volume is required. We have come to believe, however, that this book represents a unique record and a unique way of telling the story of growing up in a certain place at a certain time..

There is a spread of age groups represented here; some grew up in the 1940s and contributions extend to those who grew up in the 1970s and 80s and 90s. Memories will span 70 years. Roughly half of that period covers Wolverton, the old railway town and the later half when the town was subsumed by Milton Keynes. Not surprisingly Wolverton retains its own identity and character, and nowhere better than in these pages.

Bryan Dunleavy.

Contents

About this Book.. iii

Contents v

Photographs.. viii

First words 1

1 Diamond Jubilee Reflections 3

   60 Years Ago... 3

   30 Years Ago... 6

   Life in the 1950s 10

   The Best and Worst of Wolverton................................. 15

   Three Days in Wolverton 18

2 Days of Prams, Pushchairs and Play 21

   Nursery rhymes 24

   The Back Alley as Playgrounds 28

   The Free Range Childhood. 33

   Over the fields 37

   The Sweet Tooth... 40

3 We went to school.. 49

   Wyvern 49

   Ink Pots.. 51

   Pencil Sharpeners 53

   Pocket Money 55

   Handwriting 59

   Songs 62

   Country Dancing... 65

   The School at Moon Street... 68

   First Bike 78

   Hammers and chisels 79

   Temporary Classrooms 81

   The New Radcliffe School... 87

   Form tutors 95

   How do I remember that? 98

   School Dinners 99

   TB tests.. 104

   That's not what I heard 105

4 What we did in our spare time 109

Collecting.. 109
Children's TV.. 111
Fishing.. 113
Radio Days 114
Cinema Days (and Nights)... 120
Palace Nights 126
Park Memories.. 128
Springtime 130
Under the arches 131
Swimming Pool Opening... 133
Summer days... 135
The New Pool.. 138
Underage drinking... 139
Top Club Remembered.. 143
Those were the days.. 151
. . . when we were young and stupid 154
5 Notes from daily life 159
Unusual eating habits.. 159
Home made wine 160
Pop 163
Milk.. 165
Chores... 166
Togetherness... 167
Neighbours.. 169
Having a flutter... 172
Premium Bonds... 174
Plimsolls.. 176
A bit nippy in Winter.. 177
Baths... 184
Lifebuoy Soap 185
Noise 187
You mean what?.. 189
6 Around the Town... 193
Survivors... 193
Essam's Shoe Shop 195
Gurney's.. 196
Wavy Line... 200
Green Lane Stores.. 202

Alice Bremeyer..206
Ron Tuckey 206
The Square...206
Greengrocer on the Square...216
Pearks..217
Pedleys 219
Music Shop..221
King's 223
Jersey Road..227
Smiths..231
Prices in 1964..232
The Old Market Hall 233
Little Streets 237
One more conversation 239
Last Words...243
Index of Contributors 245

Photographs

P 1: Oxford Street Party 1953.. 3
P 2: Oxford Street Party 1981.. 8
P 3: The Cricket Pavilion - "The Pineapple".. 9
P 4: The Secret Garden, former site of the Railway Villas............ 20
P 5: Baby carriage, preambulator, "pram"... 21
P 6: June Levitt with pram in back garden 1960............................... 22
P 7: Nursery School 1945... 24
P 8: The water fountain at the Swing Rec. c. 1965......................... 29
P 9: A Wolverton Back Alley, once a favourite place for children's
    play... 34
P 10: "Rhubarb Island"... 39
P 11: The old fashioned sweet jars... 40
P 12: Sid and Iris Davies, shortly after opening their shop on The
    Square in the 1950s.. 44
P 13: Old style school desks at the MK Museum.............................. 52
P 14: Half Crown and Threepenny bits... 55
P 15: The School at the top of Moon Street, built in 1908............ 69
P 16: The School Hall, 1930s... 70
P 17: School Assembly in the 1960s.. 71
P 18: Aerial View of School with additions c. 1965......................... 75
P 19: Raleigh Trent Tourist.. 78
P 20: Radcliffe School Tower Block.. 88
P 21: Palace Cinema on the Stratford Road..................................... 120
P 22: The Empire Cinema in the 1930s. The Post Office is being
    built next door.. 123
P 23: Interior view of The Empire.. 125
P 24: Part of a Football Crowd at a Saturday Afternoon game... 129
P 25: The Viaduct over the River Ouse... 132
P 26: Opening Day Brochure... 133
P 27: Wolverton Swimming Pool in the 1980s................................ 136
P 28: The New Swimming Pool under construction 2012........... 138
P 29: Club Centenary mementos.. 144
P 30: Working Men's Club on Western Road. The "Top Club." 149

P 31: Old Premium Bond 175
P 32: Some shops on the Stratford Road 197
P 33: Formerly Gurney's "Monumental Masons" 198
P 34: Co-op Store on The Square 207
P 35: Early 20th Century photograph of the Co-op on the Square.
.... 209
P 36: Moreland Terrace, east side of the Square. c. 1920 210
P 37: Cenotaph c. 1970 211
P 38: The Market Square c. 1950 213
P 39: Peark's Staff 218
P 40: George Pedley outside his shop c. 1940s 220
P 41: Church Street in the 1950s. 222
P 42: King's Bakery on Church St. shortly before demolition 223
P 43: Winsor and Glave Workshop 229

First words

I once a went a browsing
To see who I could see
And stumbled upon a Facebook page
For those who grew up with me

... I found some lovely pictures
That reminded me of home
I chatted to some people
And didn't feel so alone

'cos when you've moved away from home
You never really settle
So chatting with old Wolvies
Was like putting on the kettle

Photos of streets that were long forgotten
New names and some old faces
Some pics of family members
Reminders of lovely places

A laugh and a giggle
All friendly each and every one
I am happy that I found you
And that "I Grew up in Wolverton"

Sheila Higginbotham

1 Diamond Jubilee Reflections

60 Years Ago

In 1952, the Queen came to the throne. In her Jubilee year we reflect on life in Wolverton 60 years ago. This photograph shows the residents of Oxford Street at their Coronation year street party. They won first prize for the best-decorated street.

P 1: Oxford Street Party 1953

Jill G. Great pic

Ian H. That is Mr. Watts next to Colin Gear, that little lady on the left had one leg much, much shorter, stunted, than the other. I recall her limping around.

Ian H. That is Joy Johnson next to the lady holding the baby and Pauline Durdin as well next to the tall man in the centre

Sheila S. Could the tall man possibly be Reg Tite?

June L. All I recognise on this photo is the little lady. I didn't know her name or where she lived, but we often passed one another in the back alley of Oxford St. when we were out shopping. I lived in Oxford St. from about 1964/65, I know Terry was 6yrs old when we moved to No 62, before that it was Green Lane & Victoria St. with my Mum & Dad while Pete was in the Guards. I knew Colin Gear of course but can't see him.

Ian H. Colin is the boy on the left at the front almost on the pavement with his hands in his pockets June.........I think.

Ian H. Looking again it could be Jim Cobley :-(

Bryan D. Jim was Bedford Street Ian.

Ian H. So was Joy Johhnson but she is on there Bryan.

Pam F. The lady in front is Mrs Butler my Sister in Law's Mum. I think that may be Mavis too about four along from Mrs B. And that is Reg Tite I'm sure.

Bryan D. I've just got home and taken a careful look. Yes he could be Jim Cobley. For one thing he looks a bit too elegant to fit in with my memory of Colin Gear. They could have had a street party on the occasion of the photograph and invited the kids from Bedford Street. I would therefore expect to see, for example, Royston Camozzi. The boy at the front with the bow tie is David Durdin and I think his father Jack "Come on Wolves" Durdin is at the very back behind Reg Tite.

June L. Before I knew him then Ian, he wore long trousers & was a good bit older than Terry.

Mike W. Pam, yes I am sure you are right I've seen this pic before and Mavis pointed out herself and her Mum (who I am told was never without pinny)

Pam F. You're right I always remember her with a pinny.

Pam F. I thought it must be your Mum as she still looks the same as ever. x

Mike W. Indeed she does Pam.

Terry L. I remember that little old lady. She had a built up shoe on one foot, and the tall man I thought Reg Tite too.

Phillip W. The museum would like to copy this photo for the archive is that ok?

Ian H. I have looked again and I have convinced myself it is Colin. I can't see his parents or Anne his sister but Colin was always smartly dressed, he did get a bit dishevelled during the course of the day (as we all did). Perhaps as it was a special occasion his father, who was very attentive to Colin, dressed him with a tie. The way he stands with his hands in his pockets isn't a Jim Cobley pose;-) Colin was probably born in 1939.

June L. In my previous comment I meant to say 36 Ox St & it was 62 Victoria St, sorry.

Bryan D. So right first time then Ian. I think the photo would be the occasion of the street party, which is why they are all in their Sunday best.

Faye L. Brill photo x

Hazel S. Jim thinks its Colin. He was in his school year with Miss Kemp. 1940/41 born.

Ian H. Glad Mr Hyphen concurs Hazel.

Tricia D. Could the little lady be Mrs Clutton, of Jersey Road/Anson Road? mother of Norman, Philip or Colin?

Jackie N. Funnily enough, I looked this photo out over the weekend ! The tall chap is indeed my dad, Reg Tite. The lady holding the baby is my Mum, Kitty with my brother Brian- and the little girl in the front row in a dark cardigan , with her legs crossed (!)-is me! Next to dad, by the cake is Ted Cockerill, who lived next door to us (no.46) and Colin Gear and his parents lived the other side of us.

Pina R. Don't think it's Mrs Clutton, she lived opposite me in Anson Rd back alley.

Bryan D. As you were there Jackie, did you have a street party on that day?

Jackie N. Yes, it was a street party (well we had to share the cake we'd won). Every lamp post in the street had hanging baskets and there were flags etc: across the street. But the best bit (which doesn't show in the photo) were the metal crowns strung across the street at intervals. They were decorated with fairy lights -and were switched on at night from our front bedroom! I think that's why we won first prize-quite ambitious for the 50s!

Mike W. Mum remembers it well!

Bryan D. Yes it did look good. My Mum, who worked hard on the Windsor Street decorations, felt a bit niggled at the time because she felt that Oxford St had an unfair advantage with no front gardens. Even so the prize went to the right street. At the back of my mind I think they awarded a 3rd prize to Furze Way for no other reason than it had just been built. I could be wrong on this.

30 Years Ago

Andrew L. 30 years since I last lived in Wolverton, still feels like yesterday. When I was the same age as my children, 30 years before was the middle of World War 2. Those older folk back then never let on or complained.

Jacqueline G. You can take the Boy out of Wolverton, but you cannot take Wolverton out of the Boy. Childhood is the 'stuff' that dreams are made of.

Bryan D. The sense I got from my parents and grandparents is that there was not a great deal to complain about. There was full employment and a high level of home ownership. There was scarcity but everyone "was in the same boat" so to speak. Am I romanticising the past? Possibly, but I don't recall a lot of misery around Wolverton in the 40s and 50s. No doubt others will correct me?

Chris G. There was no one else to blame Bryan ;)

Hazel S. Those red boxes, wasn't that where telephones lived? You could press Button B and get your money back.

Jacqueline G. They had that very rare quality, Stoicism - the ability to endure without letting it show. Sadly lacking in society today, as the constant bleating, complaining and negativity demonstrates.

Jacqueline G. Thank goodness for the Wolverton upbringing which lets me see my cup always half full!

Bryan D. Ditto, Jacqueline. And we also ate organic food before we knew it was anything other than organic! However, I have to observe that blaming someone else has always been a human trait. I seem to recall some story about Adam blaming Eve for being thrown out of Paradise.

Ian L. It may feel like yesterday in your head Terry...But not in your joints I bet.

Chris G. The comment was tongue in cheek Bryan but you know what I mean, for example how many times haves the ills of Wolverton been laid at the door of Tesco for having the audacity

6

to build a store on derelict railway land. Back in the day we couldn't really blame the fall of civilisation on the likes of Sam & Harry Tuckey. Mind you at Harry's prices . . . . well... ;)

Terry L. The country was still getting over a costly War in human and economic terms, and the memory of how things could have been so much different focussed everyone well into the late 70's.

Jacqueline G. I believe we were all brought up with an ability to 'appreciate' and to 'conserve'. We adored spending time with each other we cared about our neighbours. We delighted in the simple things in life and we were brought up to respect our elders, our surroundings and nature. We all needed the 'community' that we were we all a part of.

Chris G. True, and the world was a much, much bigger place back then and we were much more insular in our outlook. Thinking on it as kids, we didn't have that much to do with Stony and Bradwell was a different world.

Bryan D. As a 1960s progressive, now of some long standing, I have always been in favour of development. Now that I am able to take a longer view, I can see that we didn't get everything right - in fact we got a lot wrong, But heigh ho! If you make change a few things are going to get broken. People have always complained about progress (by which they mean change) but have generally had little difficulty in adapting to it. Almost all the people who condemn supermarkets still push their carts around the aisles once a week. Campaigners for a green planet are usually unwilling to give up cars and refrigerators. Now that I've taken an interest in Wolverton's history I can see that it has always been subject to change and there's no point in trying to freeze a moment in time just because you liked it the way it was. The other week we were talking about newcomers to Wolverton. Well, for them, Wolverton the way they found it is going to be the Wolverton they like. The fact that Wolverton had a Science and Art Institute is of interest, but it has no reality, just as Wolverton's castle hasn't been there for several hundred years and people have got on quite well without it. The shopping High Street is dying in most large towns and cities and even Mary Portas won't save it. In that context, Wolverton as a regular shopping centre has no hope. It does have prospects as an area for specialty shops, but that will take some imaginative planning. As Jacqueline says, the glass is always half full; it's a matter of finding a jug to fill it.

Chris G. And at times trying to stop others from trying to knock everyone's glass over with their own prejudices and insecurities...

P 2: Oxford Street Party 1981

Matty R. Oxford Street, but not sure of the date.

Chris G. Wedding of Chuck & Di, you can just make it out on banner, 1981?

Matty R. Thanks for the info Chris. This pic for Faye

Terry L. I can see my Auntie Jean, Ina Dewick at the end, The Grooms, Jack Durdin's Son and Daughter/in law and a couple of others. I can't think of the name - ooh Rosemary and her hubby.

8

Faye L. Can you imagine trying to have a party in the street now? Where's my house then?

Terry L. On the right Faye , but 3 or 4 houses behind camera...

June L. Reid Watson, your cousin, Terry - little boy holding glass. Jean's next door neighbours. I don't remember their names perhaps dad will, I'll ask him later. I think you've named the ones I remember.

June L. Can't imagine it now Faye. We all knew one another & chatted when we were scrubbing our steps & cleaning our brass Knockers. Ha! Ha! Good old days.

Ron B. Glad you added Brass to that sentence June. lol

June L. That's why I did Ron. lol

June L. It was more important to have friends than money, we gave away to the unfortunate rather than take other peoples belongings like some do these days, that's why it's nice to know we have friends to chat to on our I grew up in Wolverton site.

P 3: The Cricket Pavilion - "The Pineapple".

Andrew L. When everybody was busy hating the Pineapple building, to me that was a piece of Dr Who space station Wolverton to marvel every single day on the way to school. I

9

secretly loved its incongruous, outrageous, spikey, dayglo shape! Was it just me?

Chris G. Nope not just you mate, I tend to like change for change's sake sometimes, and to challenge. Me and Prince Charles wouldn't get on. (The Agora though is a different matter.)

Jacqueline G. YES it was Andrew, Just YOU! Hey that description of the Pineapple sounds familiar, incongruous, outrageous, spikey, Day-Glo ???? OH YES its YOUR HAIR, when you were Tangoed !!!

Andrew L. Right. Now I'm scared.

Life in the 1950s

Bryan D. For a start, there was still rationing, and our mothers had to go to the Food Office in the tin hut on Peel Road to get their ration books, full of coupons which, for example, only allowed you 1/4lb of butter a week. Margarine was the substitute and was mostly unpalatable. Incomes for most workers were between £300 and £600 a year. Most Wolverton people would fit into that group, probably at the higher end, being skilled workers. Family incomes came from one source. You could rent a Council House for 10/6d per week. I remember reading somewhere that the Council wanted to charge 12/6d a week for the new houses on Furze Way, but got few takers and had to reduce the rent. If you had a mortgage you probably paid a similar amount. Each family probably spent about 1/3 of their income on food and 1/5 on housing costs. The rest went on clothing, beer and fags. You could buy a pint of beer for 9d in 1952 - that's about 4p in post decimal currency. There was no central heating and no insulation. Any warmth in the winter months came from a coal fire and all the heat was sucked out by the morning. Hot water? If you were lucky you had a "Burco" boiler which provided hot water on demand - enough for washing up, but not enough for a bath. In that case you had to heat the water in large kettles on the stove. Car ownership was uncommon but just beginning to develop. At this due there might have been four or five car owners in Windsor Street, for example. Some had been able to save enough money for a TV which were small and hugely expensive because they carried a 33% sales tax in the price. The majority of women made their own dresses and mothers darned socks. The pubs closed at 10:30 (10 on Sunday). A lot of people went to church or chapel and most places were full for the Sunday morning service. In like fashion the pub and club bars were heaving at 1 minute past mid-day. On Saturday afternoon the town football club attracted at least 1000 supporters to every home game, a figure which would be respectable for many lower division professional clubs these days, and even the cricket club attracted a fair crowd on Sunday afternoons.

Hazel S. Street lights went out at 11pm, except for a select few at road junctions.

David W. Pub opening times - My mother was upset in 1959 when a neighbour told here she had seen me waiting outside the Craufurd Arms on a Sunday at 11-55am for it to open at noon - brought shame on our family name!

Alan C. I remember in Feb 1958 playing at a friend's house when the radio came on and reported the Manchester United Busby Babes air crash; I have supported Man U ever since. Also following on from Bryan's theme, getting ice cream as a treat from the Co-op and it being wrapped in newspaper to keep cold and then it was eaten straight away. There were a few corner shops that sold sweets. The one nearest us was Whalley's on the corner of Church Street and Windsor Street. There were very few cars on the road and the buses only went down the Stratford Road, so we took over the roads with our bikes

Ian H. Deposits on bottles......................nicked or owned. ;-)

Ian H. Gaslights still seen.

Ian H. Horse drawn milk and bread carts.

Hazel S. Jim says those were the days when A.N. Other used to appear in the football club programme, because it had to be printed before the team had been selected.

Maurice H. Horse drawn refuse carts. Sweets still on ration - if you could get any.

Maurice H. Chicken was a luxury meal, Rabbit was quite popular. Butter was still cut off a huge block in the Co-op in the square and wrapped in greaseproof paper. Cars were a rarity then. Policemen patrolled the streets and gave you a thick ear if they caught you up to anything, or you even looked guilty. Whale meat wasn't too bad, and made a change from Rabbit or horse.

Ron B. Ah the old Vera Lynn favourite. *Whale meat again, don't know where, don't know when* etc

Janet B. Alan you are correct Whalleys was the name of the corner shop on Church St. When I lived in Windsor St., I used to take my grocery order in and Mr Whalley used to deliver it on a Thursday night - no charge.

Geoff Ll. Welfare orange juice, in those small bottles, Virol (malt extract) and cod liver oil. I can taste them now!!

Bryan D. Blimey Maurice I don't remember horse drawn dust carts. They must have changed over to a lorry just before I became conscious of those things.

Ian H. With you there Bryan, mind Maurice is SOOOOOO much our senior ;-

Bryan D. When we were very young we just took things on board as if it had always been that way, so when a lorry drove down the back alley to pick up the dustbins it was hard to believe that a horse and cart once did the same job. Maurice is only a couple of years older so the transition must have happened somewhere in that window. Its like when we went to infants school Ian. I assumed it had always been that way and it wasn't until quite recently that I discovered that the transition to a mixed school at Aylesbury Street had only happened two years beforehand. The lower playground was still theirs. We had staggered breaks so that we were in class when the boys came down and thundered around the playground for 15 minutes.

Hazel S. Jim remembers rag 'n bone men having a horse and cart at the time Maurice is talking about but Wolverton UDC had Karrier Bantam vehicles specially designed for negotiating the tight corners of the back ways.

Barbara L. *Jam Jar Jack* from the bottle dump would collect silver, rags, copper etc for recycling. Horse and cart once shot through gardens in Southern Way. He made a fortune from his little empire. Hammond family - my grandfather

Maurice H. I clearly remember the council dustman coming round down the back alleys with a big horse and cart that went on till the early 1950's. There was also the rag and bone man with a horse and cart but they were at the time not one and the same. As I say Ian, I am a bit older than you, but there was another posting some time back on here that confirmed the horse and cart, I think it was a relative of someone on here what used to handle it.

Janet S. What about the scissor sharpener? He would also sharpen knives.

Ivor S. The Coop in Church Street Jersey road used to have two horses in the stables at the back - used to deliver milk. People used to rush out of their houses as they passed, especially to shovel up the manure. Good for the garden roses. Also the horse used to stop on its own on cue. Nan used to keep chickens in her back garden and feed them on the potato peelings - nice eggs though.

Terry L. Co op milk depot near the Vets where all the milk floats and the big fridges for milk were kept, and I remember milk bottles on a massive machine at the rear of Market Square - can't remember if it was a cleaning plant or actually bottling milk. The Co op Bakery, the Co op coal man and the coal yard just off corner pin. Mr Stobie delivering every thing on a hand cart. And as Maurice said the Rag and Bone man calling out BONE (long delay) BONE - and white dog poo, oh happy days !!

Pamela J. Rag and bone man with his horse and cart.

Brian E. Most houses did not have a telephone then. Some had a 'party-line,' shared with next door. But most of us had to walk down to the phone box with out four pennies. Milk was delivered to the door-step, and unless you left out a cover the birds pecked in the top to reach the cream. It was a world of Bakelite, Meccano and fuse-wire. Usually, plastic items had 'made in Hong-Kong' stamped on them somewhere, meaning, 'This is tat!'

Kazza B. We were only saying his morning, as we drove out of Tesco's car park, that when we celebrated the Silver Jubilee in 1977 all of the shops were closed so if we had run out of anything it was tough luck!!! Told the kids of the days when all the shops in town were closed for half day on Wednesdays and that they were all closed on Sundays too!!! How times change eh!!??? I reckon this Sunday opening and Bank Holiday opening has made us disorganised!!! That's my excuse anyway!!!!

David E. Mr Stanton with his mobile shop with fresh fruit and veg.

13

Pam F. Mr Wright (no relation) in his strange looking trailer selling wet fish.

Janet S. In the summer we had the van on a Friday night selling strawberries.

Jackie N. In the fifties I remember my Dad (and many others) bringing home off cuts of wood from the Works. I think it was "pot luck " what you got - some for firewood, but better stuff could be made into things. My Dad used to show cage birds and made them travelling cages so he could take them all over the country to different competitions. The men pushed a cart, borrowed from the Works, home with their allocation of wood on it - we used to wait outside the Works gate to ride on the cart up to Oxford Street - no *elf and safety* then !

Brian E. Jackie, this is why so many garden sheds and fences were painted in British Railways *blood 'n' custard* paint.

Chris G. Probably much cheaper in years gone by but I can remember it being ten bob (or 50p) a load. I'd still like to know who had all that mahogany bought to build new mail coaches - which never came to fruition.

Hazel S. Cars had to be fitted with suppressors to ensure that television reception clarity was not impaired. Otherwise you might just as well be watching a snow storm at the South Pole.

Edith H. Oh Jackie I remember your Dad having cage birds. I had forgotten all about that. The wood was good though. I used to get a ride back down in the cart, I think. The front or the back side used to come out and all the wood fell out into a heap.

Gary K. 1950s Wolverton experiencing food rationing actually contributed to predominantly healthy, energetic, well-fed kids playing outside leading active lives. And no obesity crisis - I wonder why?

Pamela J. Good wholesome food

Sheila S. Every week the delivery of coal the lorry navigating all those back alleys

Jane B. Ah yes Gary - but do Tiptops from the Corner Shop constitute Healthy Eating? Nnever did us any harm did they?

Pam F. I've just remembered, there was a van come round selling fish and chips too wasn't there?

Pam F. Anyone remember Nibbets. I loved them when I was little, probably why I'm big now

Pat C. Was that Nibbets or Niblets?

Brian E. Nibbets were wheel shaped!

Pat C. Thanks Brian, My favourites were *Cheeselets*.

Barbara L. Bacon and onion clanger, with jam roily poly at other end, remember that? Suet Pud?

The Best and Worst of Wolverton

Phillip W. What is the best part of Wolverton? Or what has been the best part of Wolverton?

Terry L. Agora !!!!!!!

Dave M. The people - end of!!

Colin H. Wolverton!

Terry L. My Dad's cellar was always a good place to be! Refuge and all that!

Dave M. Especially if it was a wine cellar.

Ruth E. The Palace when it was open as a music venue. Happy Days....

Becca H. Loved the path we took through our back fence when we lived in Woodland View. Left and down past the end of Southern Way - on down the side of the field, to play at Braddle Brook. Right to go round the slight bend, past the end of Gloucester Rd (no road beyond the end of the last house tin these days - and well before the Health Centre was built & before Greenleys) then on to Barleys Pond.

Becca H. Now if you are asking for LEAST fave place in Wolverton - Montague's dentist surgery wins it for me Hands Down!!!!

Brian E. I go along with that, Becca!

Sylvia A. Scariest place when I was a kid was the water tower opposite the tennis club at Osborne St. I used to hate walking past that at nighttimes. strange eh?

Helen P. Lying on the grass up the top end of the swing rec. Watching cricket in the summer! The rugby club on a Friday night too!

Andrew L. Wolverton Park was a special place.

Jennifer T. The Pancake Hills, and Canal.

Faye L. Playing by the river as a kid. Watching Santa come down the road on his 'sleigh' when I was little. lol.

Edward Q. The newt ponds over where Greenleys is now!!

Julia B. My old Dad's allotment and associated newt pond. However, thinking back to the amount of hours I spent in the North Western, perhaps it should be my favourite place.

Elaine S. Is that where you met Sheila, Julia? lol

Julia B. Haha, I think Sheila Beales, enjoyed the Pubs in Stony a tad more to be honest! ;)

Sheila B. Yes I spent my fair youth in the pubs of Stony.

John C. The best part of Wolverton is the people who constantly support Wolverton and not moan about it, they just get on with trying to make Wolverton a better place,

Becca H. Whoa thought those two (Bennett & Beales) would become liquor louts later in life! Such innocent, fair and demure little faeries at five! X

Julia B. I have to say Becca H., the only time "Fairy" has been used in relation to my good self, was my old dad calling me a "fairy elephant" xx

Sheila B. What about <u>my</u> favourite place? Wolverton Library, when it was down Cambridge St and where I worked for 10 years. Many a happy time spent in the cellar of the library reading the banned books.

Vicky L. My best place in Wolverton, was the Swing Rec, swimming pool & as an adult The Western, Vic & Craufurd!! Good pubs before the city came alive!!!

Ian H. All those things in my head and heart which I want to share on here.

Julie W. The farm. xx

Richie B. The Agora - roller skating in the 80s.

Elaine S. The Agora! Wash your mouth out!

Anthony Z. Youth club discos and the scout hall discos - Friday and Wednesdays.

Sheila B. I remember going to dancing classes upstairs in the top club. What was my Mother thinking of? I was a fairy elephant in those days.

Becca H. Julia B. - I got called that too!! It was in relation to my micro second career at Ballet and Tap Lessons when the teacher explained to Mum, that even though I "appeared to be quite an agile child", ballet and tap might not be for me.

Julia B. Hahaha! Yes Top Club ballet classes. I must have followed Becca and Sheila out the EXIT door. Mother Bennett gave me a choice - Brownies or ballet class - she couldn't afford both....Her way of removing her chubster kiddie from weekly torture, without being made to feel guilty for all the suet puddings.

Sheila B. My mum told me it was time to leave when the teacher turned up in her welly boots and tried to teach us to dance. Who was the teacher?

Julia B. lol, Don't know, thought you would remember.....Mrs Jaqueman.

Becca H. Julia B. - I feel so much better now knowing I got "binned from ballet" with two of Wolvie's finest!

Janet S. I remember going to watch my friend do tap dancing in a hut near the corner of peal road think the lady that ran it was Mrs Lynn's.

Julie B. Skating at the Agora. Met Stephen Barnes.

Diane K. The old indoor Market and the Pancake Hills.

Ian S. Passadena Café.

Edward Q. I spent many happy hours in the old cricket pavilion with Keith Tull, Jeff Preston over a pint and a game of cards.

Phillip W. And the worst part?

Faye L. Let's focus on the positive shall we Philip?

John Rd. Radcliffe School, the Vic, Glyn Square, St George's Street, take your pick, the Greenleys, Crofts . . .

Faye L. What are the nicest places in Wolverton, that hold most memories?

John Rd. Swimming pool R.I.P.....

Phillip W. If think a lot of the waste land areas are in need of cleaning up.

Faye L. Can we get a bottle of anti depressants for Mr. Webb and Mr. Reed please? ;)

John Rd. I don't do legal drugs thanks you...can mess your mind up more than illegal ones. ;)

Faye L. The streets I lived and grew up in, the river where I spent hours climbing trees and just being a little sod, the swing rec where I would play on the old roundabout till I was sick and my Nan's house, to name a few.

Phillip W. Faye you are being cheeky tonight ;-)

John Rd. It was fun when I was a little kid but soon as I got to 12 an onwards I didn't really stay in Wolverton much - went to other estates.

Phillip W. The nicest places in Wolverton must be the Park and the Square.

John Rd. The Square was more fun before it all got fixed up. We used to race home made karts round them over the rough dirt...was great fun.

Faye L. I used to swing from the trees in the square .....and make prank calls in the phone booths.

John Rd. You mean the old willow trees that were there? Yeah, we used to do that and run over peoples cars whilst swinging off them. Also we used to go into the Agora lift an pull the doors open whilst halfway up on the inside and do bongs. . . .we weren't the only ones coz it was full of grafitti in there.

Faye L. Well I didn't go that far I am talking about when I was 12 or so.

Phillip W. Wolverton holds lots of good memories for me. I think that's why I feel so sad that it's fallen into what it is today.

John Rd. You know the big house with the Hovis sign painted in the side on Church Street. Before it was fixed us lads used to go in there through the cellar grate in the back garden and made it our den...though in the end it got trashed proper.

Linda K. Nicest place probably St Georges Church or Madcap or either of the two Recs! Worst place, easily Glyn Square!

Three Days in Wolverton

John R. I'm sitting on the plane waiting to take off reading the in-flight magazine and they have a section, "3 perfect days in Seattle", which highlights how to see the best bits of Seattle and

18

surrounding areas in 3 days. If you were to spend 3 perfect days in Wolverton, what sights and attractions would make the list?

Chris G. I'd stay in bed days one and two, pop to Tesco day three, then go back to bed.

Wendy C. The Museum.

Jane B Like Chris I'd stay indoors - my front room has better sights than Wolverton town centre.

Kim P. If it was JUST Wolverton - the Rec, the museum, the secret garden, the cemeteries and spend some time walking round the streets looking at the little architectural details on the houses and shops. If the surrounding area - three days wouldn't be enough!

Elaine H. The Museum, the Secret Garden.

Angie A. Holy Trinity Church, stroll along the canal path, riverside walk, museum, secret garden.

Terry L. The Western, the Eastern Paradise, and Maisies...

Sharon S. The road out in 3 directions.

Susan B. My old house, the Recs and walk along the canal in either direction.

Elaine M. 1. Stacey Bushes museum, where I used to get straw from when it was Luckett's farm for my Dad's rabbits. 2. The old bathhouse. 3. The Top Rec where we used to play every day in the summer holidays.

Janice M. When I was there last year I walked along the canal, found the Secret Garden I didn't even know existed, walked along Stratford road for a few mins....

Vivienne B. I wouldn't need three days John, I would sooner have 3 days in Seattle, we often go to Portland, Oregon, 3 weeks isn't enough, and 1 of the best places there is Pioneer square great place.

Susan B. Where is the Secret Garden?

Barbara L. Can't tell u it's secret, only joking!

Colin T. The Secret Garden, is on the left hand side of the road as you're going towards the train station (The old train station) along Stratford road. The wall runs alongside what was Dunlop & Rankins. Where the wall ends is the entrance to the gardens, Hope that makes sense.

19

Susan B. Morning Colin, yes it does. So it's near where the park entrance used to be where we did school sports. I'm coming home in a few weeks' time so I'm going to visit Wolverton to see all the changes.

P 4: The Secret Garden, former site of the Railway Villas.

Deborah G. I did that recently Susan.... didn't take me three hours never mind three days!

Elaine H. Sorry to disagree. We went to the Secret garden two weeks ago. The entrance is in fact on the right hand side of the Stratford Road as you go towards the station. There is a slip road off main road but you can't take the car down. Big metal sign above your heads saying *Secret Garden*. I daresay you can get to it from the Park Steps though.

2 Days of Prams, Pushchairs and Play

Jill G. Who got pushed around in one of these?

P 5: Baby carriage, preambulator, "pram".

Terry L. Me.
Penny G. Me. Also my oldest daughter. We had a green one with silver trim.
Jill G. Me too mine was mainly white with navy.
Pina R. Me too!
Lesley W. Both my daughters
Shell F. I had one for my daughter and my son x
Jackie S. Me too.
Margaret C. My boys. Navy with white inside took it on the train to Northampton many times in the guards van.
Pat B. I had a green one for my boys. My wheels ended up on someone else's pram and Father in laws wooden truck.
Steve B. Me!
Natalie J. I remember mum pushing my sister in one of those and she sat me on the front of it.
Terry L. And there it is!

P 6: June Levitt with pram in back garden 1960

Jill G. Wow lovely pic!

Graham S. Best wheels to make a go-cart from...

Becca H. My 'little' brother Chris had a dark maroon one. May have been a Silver Cross Pram - but I seem to remember it saying something like 'Royale' on the side on a metal fancy writing badge. When the infant school was separate and at the 'bottom' of the school site (i.e. complete opposite end to the main juniors) the Mums used to wait along the other side of the hedge on Church St - and you could just see the tops of the prams if the hoods were up. Mrs Hill would get very angry if children kept craning their necks to look. We used to have to sing a song at the end of school everyday - that started "Now the day is over, night is drawing nigh..... Anyway, I once got slapped on the back of the legs for "impudence" for craning my neck to see if my Mum and baby brother were outside and for changing the words of the song all by myself to "Now the mummy's are waiting outside and Christopher's in his pram....... Didn't scan quite right then, but I knew what I meant.....and I MEANT it ....at the time! (hehehe) This would have been approx 1962/3.

22

Brian E. And, later, they could be converted into go-karts, with the aid of a pallet.

Jill G. I think that's what my brothers did with the pram wheels in the end.

Pat C. Those prams were a work of art, but thank goodness the McLaren fold-up buggy arrived in 73 approx and made things easier to transport our growing family!

Marc H. Blimey I think we all had one of those things built to last for ever.

Bryan D. What I don't see much of nowadays is the little harnesses parents used to strap around toddlers to keep them from running into trouble. They were called reins. Mine were red leather from memory and were later used for my young brother.

Bev P. I had red leather ones! I think there were bunnies painted on the piece that went across my chest. Years later for a brief moment kids in the US were put on wrist straps with telephone cord type things. I was at Disney World and about four kids had run up to a character and got their cords all in a tangle. Thus my little dear got his pic taken first.

Bryan D. I think mine had little flower cut-outs sewn on the front. Society wasn't advanced enough for bunnies in the 1940s – we had to wait for Hugh Hefner. :-)

Brian E. What we do see however is gigantic baby buggies, the size of a mini-bus. They are enormous these days. The old prams that many of us will remember were really not much bigger.

Ruth E. I lived on a farm so no need but I had them for my two. Sarah does not have any for her two and I am a bag of nerves when they are near a road lol.

Pat C. Remember my younger sister's reins had tiny little bells on them.

June L. I had to put reins on Terry when I took him out shopping because every gate that was open along Cambridge St etc Terry was in there, I had a job keeping up with him without the reins.

Chris G. June, me and Ian had to do the same with Terry 20 years later - and that was just getting him from the Craufurd to Church St. ;)

June L. I quite believe that Chris; he was a live wire.

Donna S. Don't believe our Mum used them. I never did. Reminded me too much like taking the family pet for a walk... when my daughter was small we lived in an apartment .. the person directly below us had her child harnessed or reined to a tree.. ever since I saw that I said, "Nope! No way no how...

Nursery rhymes

Donna S. What nursery rhymes to you remember? ... or little songs you would sing?... comes to mind rain go away come back on washing day.... and cant remember it all but something about ladybug ladybug fly away home...
Lesley W. Your house is on fire and your children alone
Donna S. Trying to remember some of the songs we sing whilst skipping or bouncing multiple rubber balls off walls in school playground...

P 7: Nursery School 1945

Bryan D. I'll start you off Donna and then I have things to do.
Little Miss Muffet
Sat on her tuffet

24

Eating her curds and whey.
Along came a spider
And sat down beside her
And frightened Miss Muffet away.
At the time I didn't know what a tuffet was nor curds and whey.

Penny G. One song I used to sing to my children when we were out for a walk was:
"Daisy Daisy Give me your answer do
I'm half crazy oh for love of you
It won't be a stylish marriage
I can't afford a carriage
But you"ll look sweet, a proper trea
On a bicycle made for two "
 My baby is now 39.

Penny G. Two little birds sitting on the wall one named Peter one named Paul.

Sharon S. I used to sing "You are my sunshine!" to Daryl every day no our way home from nursery holding his hand- lovely memories

June L DON'T get me started Donna & Penny I know so many, I can't keep up with it lol

Penny G. There was a little girl who had a little curl right on the top of her head

Sharon S. Right in the middle of her forehead

Pat B. And when she was good she was very very good, but when she was bad she was horrid.

Penny G. How come it is the Mums who are doing this then lads come on?
"Rain rain go away come again another day."
"Pussy cat pussy cat where have you been?
I've been to London to see the Queen.
Pussy cat pussy cat what did you see?
I saw a mouse go up a tree."

Ron B. Incy wincey spider, Can't believe I just posted that

June L. Incy wincy spider climbing up the spout down came the rain & washed the spider out.

Sharon S. Incy wincey spider climbed up the spout,
        Down came the rain and washed the spider out,

Out came the sunshine dried up all the rain,
So Incy wincey spider climbed the spout again

Jill G. There was an old woman who lived in a shoe she had so many children she didn't know what to do.

June L. Georgie Porgy pudding & pie kissed the girls & made them cry when the boys came out to play Georgie porgy ran away.

June L. Little Bo Peep lost her sheep

Jill G. You are my sunshine my only sunshine you make me happy when sky's are grey

June L. Humpty Dumpty sat on a wall, Humpty Dumpty had a great fall. Wee Willy Winkle. Rock-a-bye baby, Don't you cry.

Jill G. Mary had a little lamb.

Donna S. Wee Willie winkie runs through the town,
Upstairs and downstairs in his nightgown...
Little jack Horner sat in his corner.
Little boy blue come blow your horn,
The sheep's in the meadow the cows in the corn...
Hickory dickory dock the mouse ran up the clock.
London bridge is falling down falling down falling down..
lol Have you noticed I don't know many in their entirety?
hmmm

Jill G. Oranges and lemons say the bell's of St Clement's

Donna S. When will you pay me say the bells of Old Bailey.. I love this one ..

Donna S. I do not know say the great bell of bow

Donna S. O.K googled it...
Oranges and lemons say the bells of St. Clements,
You owe me five farthings say the bells of St. Martins,
When will you pay me say the bells of Old Bailey,
When I grow rich say the bells of Shoreditch,
When will that be say the bells of Stepney,
I do not know say the great bell of Bow,

"Here comes a candle to light your bed, and here comes the chopper to chop off your head."
One my mum said to my kids, while holding on to their hands drawing circles... roundabout roundabout runny away moose.. up a

step up a step to his wee hoose (at this point she had tickled them).. and imagine in a Scottish accent!

How about, "I am Popeye the sailor man I live in a caravan with a hole in the middle for Popeye to piddle I am Popeye the sailor man." - another one dad would say..

Jill G. Hey diddle diddle

Donna S. the cat and the fiddle, the cow jumped over the moon

June L. Mary, Mary quite contrary how does your garden grow, with silver bells & cockle shells all in a row.

Donna S. While bouncing on my dads leg......

Ride a cockhorse to Banbury cross
To see a fine lady ride on a white horse
Rings on her fingers and bells on her toes
She will have music wherever she goes...

Little Jack Horner sat in his corner
Eeating his Christmas pie.
He put in his thumb and pulled out a plum,
And said what a good boy am I....

Sing a song of sixpence, a pocket full of rye,
Four and twenty blackbirds baked in a pie,
When the pie was opened the birds began to sing
Wasn't that a dainty dish to put before the king?

The king was in his counting house, counting all his money,
The queen was in her parlour eating bread and honey,
The maid was in the garden hanging out the clothes,
When down came a blackbird and pecked off her nose

June L. Twinkle Twinkle little star how I wonder what you are?

Donna S. Up above the world so high. . . like a diamond in the sky..

Donna S. This old man he played one
He played knick knack on my thumb
With a knick knack paddy wack give a dog a bone
This old man came rolling home..

Pat C. Simple Simon met a pie man going to the fair,

27

Said Simple Simon to the Pie man let me taste your ware.

Pat C. Three blind mice, see how they run.

Pina R. One man went to mow, went to mow a meadow. one man & his dog spot.........

Maria M. Farmers in his den.... farmers in his den....

Donna S. Diddle diddle dumpling my son John,
Went to bed with his britches on.
One shoe off and one shoe on
Diddle diddle dumpling my son john...

Sharon S. Walk around the garden like a teddy bear, atishoo atishoo a tickly under there!

Helen P. In and out the dusty bluebells.

Sharon S. This little piggy went to market, this little piggy stayed at home, this little piggy had roast beef and this little piggy had none and this little piggy went wee wee wee all the way home!

Donna S. Patty cake patty cake baker's man.
Bake me a cake as fast as you can,
Roll it and pat it and mark it with D
Aand put it in the oven for Donna and me .

Wendy C. Skipping song......on a mountain. Stands a lady who she is I do not know. All she wants is gold and silver...all she wants is a nice young man...so come to her????.

.Pina R. two ball.......1,2,3, O'Leary....4,5,6, O'Leary, 7,8,9, O'Leary, 10 O'Leary drop the ball.....

Sharon S. Clapping game song my mother told me if I was goody that she would buy me a rubber dolly my auntie told her I kissed a soldier now she won't buy me a rubber dolly

Donna S. 3, 6, 9. the dog drank wine clap clap...

Maurice W. Hey diddle diddle, the cat done a piddle,
All over the kitchen floor.
The little dog laughed to see such fun,
And the cat done a little bit more.....

The Back Alley as Playgrounds

Bryan D. I have a general question - Did you play in the streets or back alleys when growing up, or both? My own experience was that we typically played in the back alley, although I do recall practising tennis against the Green Lane side wall of our house. But what did you do if you lived above Victoria Street or on Eton crescent? Was it generally considered safe to play on Young Street, for example?

Phillip W. I played in the back alley behind Jersey Rd We went to the park but mainly hung out in the alley.

Peter W. It was always in the back alley. We were allowed to venture out more when we got older and now I come to think of it used to play in the street up on Aylesbury Street West.

Terry L. Back alley mostly, but did have the occasional running or bike race around the block. oh and cherry knocking...

Ian H. We did cherry knocking with a difference, we knocked two doors that we had tied together by the knockers!!!

Margaret C. Back alleys of the little street and the triangle..

Faye L. I dabbled in a bit of cherry knocking mainly further up Aylesbury Street. Ran off giggling like mad lol. Also used to press the buzzer at the snooker club on the Square and leg it ......I have since grown up... Well physically he he x

P 8: The water fountain at the Swing Rec. c. 1965.

Margaret C. That brings back memories of my mum trying to catch us to give us a slap. We use to run round the triangle. Mum was so often pregnant she hadn't a chance.

Ian H. Margaret nearly spat my tea out there mate reading that, nice one!!

Geoff L. Mostly in the Rec or across the fields, Pancake hills, along canal, Iron Trunk, riverside, broad waters.

Kim P. Usually the Rec because it was right behind the house. We lived on the corner of Victoria and Stacey and there was too much traffic by the 70s for us to play in the road.

John C. Where was Young Street, was it a little street?

Margaret C. Yes it was John at the back.

Jean G. Played in back alley between Green Lane and Victoria Street. Rode bikes round streets too, when we were allowed.

Elvia W. I can't believe you played there I used play in Moon St I used live there.

Jean G. Really! wow what a small world I lived in Green Lane from 1974 to 1985.

Donna S. Had a friend that lived on Green Lane..... Helen Clark.

Elvia W. I was in Moon St from 1969 till 1986.

Jean G. We moved in in August 1974, loved that house!!

Andrew L. Back alleys, but we had the big lawn next to the Tin Hut which we gradually took over. Never in the road unless we were on bikes.

Diane K. Alleys of the little streets but mostly the green in front of our house in Young Street we used to stand at the fence and watch the works lads play football in the yard.

Pina R. Played in Anson Road back alley or in Eton Crescent. Some of the Eton Crescent lot used to come to the alley as some of their gardens backed onto it.

Anthony Z. Football up Top Rec in morning, fields in the afternoon.

Sheila B. Played in the Cambridge St., Windsor St. alley way with the Earp family's he Clarridge family, Carter family and the Knight family and I had the best shed in the whole street!

Edith H. Used to play in Gloucester Road. Remember when a car came up the street we used to have to put the skipping rope down but used to lift it up as the car was going over it. Not sure why we

30

did that. We also used to play marbles in the gutters and someone had to stand to make sure the marbles didn't go down the drain. We also used to play hop scotch on the pavement.

Alan C. Used to play mainly in the back alleys, we also played soccer in the. Junior School Playground before we graduated to the Top Rec. We were also always on our bikes racing around all of the streets. Used to practice tennis and cricket against the workshop wall and sent many tennis balls into Bob Dunleavey's garden!!!!! We then used to climb over a couple of walls to retrieve them.

Bryan D. How did you manage that Alan? He lived in Eton Crescent!

Alan C. I always thought he lived at 53 Stratford Road.

Bryan D. I knew what you meant Alan but it was my grandparents (Moore) who lived at 52 Stratford rd. After my grandmother died in 1956 my grandfather was on his own and in 1963 my parents moved in, which is why you associate the house with Dunleavy...My father was Fred by the way. His younger brother Bob was better known to a few generations of school kids for obvious reasons. He lived at 179 Church st and 2 Etonian Crescent. Either way your undoubted tennis ball smashing skills would have been challenged.

Pina R. Bryan D., was Bob Dunleavy's wife slim with dark hair?

Bryan D. Pina, my uncle's wife never had dark hair as far as I knew - unless the colour came out of a bottle. She was naturally ginger - a sort of mousy blonde and then grey. She worked at Sellicks - Wolverton Motors. She died just before Christmas, a few weeks short of 90.

Alan C. Thanks Bryan, I thought my memory is failing me. We timed everything and usually collected quite a few balls at one time. We went across the Dunkley's and the Osborne's (I think) but only when the Osbornes and Dunleavys were known to be out or away.

Ian H. When did your brother buy the Windsor St house Bryan if I may be a tad impertinent? (which as you know is not my nature!!!) I always associate that house with you and your family.

Bryan D. Yes that was the house we grew up in. I think my parents purchased in in 1942 after I was born. They were living in Chiswick at the time because my father had been seconded to

31

Sperry's for the duration of the war. So I suppose my arrival (I was born at my grandparent's house - 52 Stratford Rd) prompted them to do something about housing, which was apparently scarce. We lived there until 1958 when my Mum and Dad took over the New Inn and the Windsor St house was rented out. Richard got married in 1971 (just celebrated their 40th wedding anniversary) so that's when he took over title. I think it was valued then at £3000 and I got half - out of which I was able to get on the Canadian property ladder. I think Richard and Kay lived ether until 1980 when he got a job with a company in Kings Lynn. So they sold the house and moved up there. Unfortunately his new company went belly up and within a year was back in MK, living in some place called Heelands.

Natalie J. Mainly Gloucester Rd and Woodland View streets as we were living at top end of Wolverton. Used to walk down the alleys to school though, or when at Radcliffe through the Top Rec.

Jackie N. I lived in Oxford Street and we used to play in the alley. In the summer holidays we would put on a play in someone's garage. or do crafty things like Plaster of Paris models (remember them?) We also used to roller-skate down the alley from the top by the water tower.

Vicki L. I lived in Oxford St. The Alley between Cambridge St & Oxford St was my stomping ground - Hayfields, Neal's, Chambers, Grooms, Levitts, McGee's, Lewis's, Last names the younger generation so missed the Hayfields & Neals!!! Days of elastic, skipping, singing, dancing & hide & seek. -:)

Maurice H. Yes Bryan, I did too. In the back alley, we would play footie, cricket, learnt to ride bikes, al sorts of tag games, then we would go down the park, football ground, bowl ground, by the station and play in the bushes and under the grandstand, and we also had a den under steps that went down to the canal opposite the station. How the hell we never fell in the water as we swung round the fence I will never know.

Tracy S. We used to play in the Rugby Field, by Gloucester Road and over the fields by the newt pond - before Greenleys was built!

Steve A. Loved that old pond, did you ever build a raft?

Chris G. We were lucky a chunk of our childhood spanned the time the Gurneys left Stacey Hill Farm till a lot of the building started on the land round Wolverton, brilliant time to grow up.

Phillip W. Wish I was round at that time.

Jennifer T. We played rounders hopscotch etc in Windsor St.

Steve A. Greenleys and Stacey Bushes building sites were an excellent playground as well.

Tracy S. Probably my brother Wayne's would have tried something to float on the water, he was always up to no good!

Jackie S. I came at the very beginning of the building so I do understand about the freedom of messing about in the fields and up by the farm etc. I made sure my two daughters had the same at the beginning of their lives.

Ian H. Were you really, really round Phillip W. or just a little bit ....plump? ;-)

Jon P. Cambridge Street Back alley, between Aylesbury Street and Buckingham Street, used to bump into the Bunkers, Russells, Hennesseys, my neighbour Mark Rose. I remember the house in Aylesbury Street that our back gate backed onto was empty for a while. And the garden wall had half fallen down so as 6-7 year olds we decided to remove a few more bricks with a hammer from my Dad's garage, only to be grassed up to the police by a certain Mrs. Blackwell. Had the shock of me life when got in from school to see a policeman in our front room wanting to ask me questions!! Criminal damage Sonny!!

The Free Range Childhood.

Bryan D. Moving on from yesterday's post, I find I am often tempted to represent my childhood as much freer than children enjoy today. Of course, everyone of my age agrees, but was this really the case?

My early years were spent very close to home and then I was able to play in the immediate back alley - in my case a short block between Windsor and Cambridge Streets.

As I got a little older, say about 9, that freedom probably extended further down Windsor St and to the recs. Once I reached 11, the whole of Wolverton opened up to me, although there were some areas I steered clear of because there were territorial guardians who were quick to chase off outsiders. Once in my teens those boundaries we're only limited by the time it took to get back home for meal times, this being the rigid law of the times "Don't be late!" Others may have had a different experience, but it appears to me that the parental reins were gradually loosened as I grew older, and that our childhood was not as "free" as we are tempted to present it.

P 9: A Wolverton Back Alley, once a favourite place for children's play.

Ruth E. I always felt during my childhood I was given a free rein of the fields at Puxley and as I got a bit older the surrounding. villages, there were never the threats that there are today. My brother and I often walked to Tathall End on our own at aged 9 and 11, me the older one trying to lose him on the way lol... So although we felt free our parents knew that as we wandered those fields one of our family was around them to keep an eye on us! My big problem was getting home on time as a 14 yr old coming from Pury Youth Club. I always found something to keep me a bit longer only to be met by an irate older brother sent to fetch me.......

Chris G. We grew up in the years between a lot of land being compulsory purchased and the building of MK starting up. We had acres and acres of disused farmland to play in, a great time. And as long as we turned up when we were told our parents gave us pretty much free rein to wander off for miles.

Pamela J. My childhood was freedom I was allowed to roam the fields, swim in the river, and roam around Stony and Wolverton, but then my Gran brought me up and she was all ways too busy to keep a check on me.

Richie B. Same as Chris. Pretty much allowed out all over and early teens was mostly spent down Old Wolverton, the canal and used to bike for miles with the old Wolverton gang.

Penny G. As much freedom as long as I was home for my meals & not got too dirty as I used to play with my cousin Michael. We used to cycle all the way to Cosgrove on our bikes along the canal to visit my Aunty & Uncle who ran the Barley Mow. We also played out in the streets & back alleys playing. Cherry Knocking was a favourite also *tin ay acky*. Who remembers them?

Colin T. Bryan, Good morning, Very much the same as your good self, On Sunday we were washed, dressed and off to Sunday school on the square, then home change in to scruff clothes, we were allowed into the back alley (Church St) until Mum or Dad called us for dinner, As time went on we was allowed further afield. But like you said we sure as hell made it back at meal time's,

Pat C. Spot on there Bryan.

Pamela J. Agree with you both never be late for meals OMG

Terry L. Same as Chris Gleadell, My parents gave me free rein travelled miles from a very young age!

Ron B. Was too tired to play after climbing up and down chimneys all day. lol

Bryan D. Nickname Sooty?

Penny G. Ron B.it sounds as if you come from the Victorian age where they sent little boys up chimneys lol

Chris G. Oh no Penny, he's much older than that ;)

June L. Terry doesn't know this but I was hiding in the bushes seeing where he was going, the little bugger.

Colin T. Hahaha Now you got Terry thinking,.....Was Mum really watching me lol

Marc H. June you can stop following him now he's a big boy now!

June L. I wasn't only watching Terry I was keeping my eye on all of you that were in the same gang.

June L. Do children play skipping in school playgrounds these days? We were able to have a long skipping rope across our street so a little row of us could jump in & out. Better fun than sitting playing Xbox (whatever they are) on your own, too much traffic & people now, spoilt a lot of fun for the kids to play outdoors these days, they are talking about children not going out to play on the radio this morning.

Lynnette M. They do June in the school I work at boy's and girls.

June L. That's good, plenty of exercise then Lynnette. Haven't got a school here in Wicken or shops come to that, just a Pub.

Lynnette M. No shops no school just a pub, oh poor you!

June L. I do love it the way it is because it's so peaceful, hardly any traffic only when people are driving through to go to work etc. & the horseback riders, that's lovely, I just wish there was a village shop that sold fresh baked bread, milk & dairy produce, home grown fruit & veg. That would be perfection for me.

Margaret C. Children are not safe anymore. We used to play outside, and in the fields for hours, no worries, now with so many weirdoes about parents can't take their eyes off a child...it's so sad June, we had so much fun.

Lynnette M. We used to play out in the street and go off over the fields down the river and then back for tea and if my mum went out she would leave the door unlocked. That changed when the rent lady Mrs Herbert got mugged.

Jill G. In the summer hols we used to make up a packed lunch and go out for the day and there was always someone that knew where you were. Everyone always looked out for one another, sadly not anymore: (

Lynnette M. Children today only want to play computer games we used to make our own fun skipping, elastic two balls, roller-skating, cycling, bulldog, tag, tiniake - all good fun.

June L. Yes we really did have fun & it didn't cost our mums & dads hardly anything plus normally one person only working.

Lovely thought to know our mum was always at home whatever time we got in for our Tea.

Over the fields

Ian H. It wasn't just street games we played as children; Wolverton in my childhood was encircled by exciting places to play. Who can forget the steam trains hissing and blowing their clouds of smoke and steam as the trains passed beneath, then the "Braddle Brook" where, when the water had been flowing you could find patches of water cress. The hedgerows full of hips, haws. berries and birds nests, not forgetting the "double hedge", which goes back centuries, and where the best blackberries were found. The disused Quarry just outside Stony (a half an hour walk across fields from the White Gates) where we used to scramble and slide to the bottom then crawl and struggle back up to the top then throw stones at the rusty old debris at the bottom acting out some medieval battle. Or going over the viaduct looking down at the fish and reeds bending with the current then darting through the trees and coming to the "broadlands" with those deep cold water filled quarries being careful as you walked not to step on the peewit(plover, lapwing) eggs that were laid on the bare ground. Sometimes a trip to the bottle dump to look for old bottles with glass stoppers (Alan Rolfe found one!!) or sticking your arm down one of the rabbit holes in the Warren. Some boys even put thin wire snares hoping to catch something. Just a bit further away down the gated road outside Haversham (bike ride) you could find ammonites and belemnites fossils from centuries gone by (RIP Richard Harris who showed me these treasures) All these things without a watch and we still got home in time to eat. Bon appétit.
Edward Q. Ian do you remember the Ha*ppy Morn* at Old Wolverton.
Edith H. Oh yes Ted very well.
Ian H. Good afternoon Edward (Teddy) We've written quite a bit about the *Happy Morn* on earlier threads who could forget it eh, or those elegant elm trees in the Rec just before it?

Edward Q. Yes Ian and the *Pancake Hills* with our dirt track bikes (no brakes) of course.

Ian H. The trains beneath were at the Blue Bridge. The lad who "showed" me fossils was Richard Harrison not Harris. He was an only child and before he moved to Western Rd. He lived in the pre-fabs in Bradville (next door to Colin Hale's family.) He died after an accident in Newport Pagnell swimming pool tragically.

Edward Q. Used to go to Newport on the Nobby Newport train.

Edward Q. Ian, many of my weekends were spent motor cycle racing as I used to go with my brother John and Tony Monk (who actually achieved 3rd place in the Isle of Man Manx Grand Prix). Tony was a Gloucester Rd Boy !!! Lol

Ian H. All great lads up there, all of them!!! Especially Dennis and Pete who were just a little different but nevertheless lovely, honest human beings. In fact Wolverton kids boys and girls were a grand bunch.

Chris G. Anyone remember Rhubarb Island by the weir at Wolverton Mill?

Julie K. I remember rhubarb island and spent many summer days messing about in the river there, looking for bull head fish in the stream, climbing up the weir and sliding back down on the mossy parts, being careful not to fall in the deep side. An older friend had a canoe and we used to paddle up and down the deep side. I would not do so now as I'd be too scared. We would spend the whole day there, taking a picnic, only going home because we were hungry or it was about to get dark. Then we would walk home to Stony tired out, but hoping it would be nice again the next day, so we could do it all over again.

Bryan D. Great post Ian. Happy memories indeed!

Ian H. 'Tis a pity we can't "see" memories, the upside is we wouldn't need words if we did!! Thanks Bryan.

Steve A. Ian thank you for mentioning the quarry at the southern end of Stony Stratford I can remember it vaguely and had almost convinced it was a figment of my imagination.

Gareth G. Regarding the quarry at Stony. Used to regularly walk over with mates and my Jack Russell. Remember lovely summer days playing there. Always wondered what the long mound of earth adjacent to the quarry was, seemed as though it housed

...something beneath it due to pipes coming out of the top and looking man made. Us kids always used to believe it was an air raid shelter. Would love to know what was under that mound. Can't see the quarry or the mound on Google maps. Any info?

Chris G. That'd be the 'Giants Grave' Gareth. Quarry now filled in and Tudor Gardens (I think) houses now on top.

P 10: "Rhubarb Island"

The Sweet Tooth

Ian H. How about the sweet shops in Wolverton!! Bews, (was Howe's before) and most of the grocery shops had them as well. The one that took over Woodwards, think they came from Derby, had about twenty local lasses working there part-time. Must have been a tax evasion job!!

Shirley V. Do you mean *Terry's* Ian? Kay and Rex Smith came from Mansfield. I worked there from 1973 to 1980 and then went back in 1989 until Kay and Rex sold the shop in early 90's.

Ian H. That's the one. They came when I was just a young married man in the very early 60's. When I came back in the late 70 to live with my parents they were still there. I seem to think Rex had a stroke a while after. Kay came from the same area as Barry Church's wife.

Shirley V. Rex had heart problems. He had a triple bypass at some point. Can't remember exactly when. As far as I know he suffered a heart attack not long after they both retired in the early 90's. Kay went back to Mansfield to live with her sister. Sad really that they didn't have a long retirement together. They were a hard working couple.

P 11: The old fashioned sweet jars

40

Deborah G. I worked at Terry's at the weekends in the early 80s. We worked long hours for low pay but was great fun ... all the regulars visited, particularly on Sundays, for their usual stock up of weekly sweets.

Shirley V. Deborah, do you remember how busy it was on Sundays? It was packed from morning until early evening when it closed. You're right, it was long hours and low pay but a right laugh at times.

Deborah G. I certainly do remember. Worked for hours without a break - had to try to grab things to eat - which Kay and Rex ensured we paid for - behind the counter between serving. You are right though - it was good fun!

Vivienne B. I remember Kay as she always found time to have a bit of a chat, when you went in. lol x

Julie W. Did you know they never holidayed together, because they didn't want to leave the shop xx

Vivienne B. I didn't know that, that's what I would call commitment to your livelihood, not sure about what it says about the marriage thing though. lol x

Julie W. They were a funny old couple, and quite rude as I remember. xx

Sue L. I loved getting my sweets in there, it's not Terry's anymore is it? I've not been on the square for a while.

Vivienne B. Odd, I don't remember either of those two things about them, our minds are strange things with what we remember, or not x

Vivienne B. Hasn't been Terry's for years!!!!

Julie W. To be honest if I had to get sweets I always went to Davies. xx

David Wm. I always went to Davies.

Kim P. I usually went to Davies for sweets bought from the jars behind the counter (at least after the old market closed down) but Terry's for the ha'penny sweets you picked yourself. Before the Co-op opened in the Agora my mum used to get a lot of her tinned goods from Terry's because you could get stuff from them that nobody else had like tongue and faggots :) Terry's tinned tongue sandwiches... yum! And they had a small section way in back where they had those kiddie colouring books where you just

41

washed the pages over with a wet paintbrush and the colours magically appeared on the pages. I think I had every single one of those they ever sold.

Andrew L. I went to Terry's when it was open while everything else was shut - Sunday and early closing day I think it was the only place open for a handful of blackjacks and fruit salads or a pack of spangles to destroy my teeth.

Dave B. I used to bag up potatoes for Kay 'n Rex :) Back when a Qtr of Cough Candy cost a fraction of my pocket money.

Kim P. I hefted a few bags of potatoes there in my time too though I confess I didn't manage to stick it out very long :)

Pete B. The Owners of Terry's used to tell me they lived in a big house in Alderton. Funny really as years later I moved here and its quite a little house. ha ha.

Dave B. I bet as a nipper it looked bigger mind :)

Dave B. Alderton's a lovely place mind. I remember it being on Time team once.

Pete B. ha ha , yes .. I was the digger driver. And the jousting and archery were played out in our paddocks.

Mark B. My wife Paula (Rawles) used to work there too serving behind the till and weigh out veg for people.

Liz T.I worked for Kay and Rex for 3 yrs. Had a great time.

Deborah G. I worked at Terrys for a couple of years at weekends. Was damn hard work with no breaks and minimal pay but was great fun - lots of friendly regulars vising for their weekend sweets!

Liz T. Yeh I started just Saturdays then went to nearly every day after school and the weekends. It was hard work, the kids wouldn't do it now but I enjoyed it there

Julie W. Josie, who used to work there, works at he treatment centre now xx

Dorothy S. That's going back just a bit ha aye......:)

Kim P. She must have softened up by the time I worked there 'cause you got a ten minute break after about 3 or 4 hours, and you could make yourself a cup of tea upstairs, if you had time!

Margaret C. Kay asked me if I would like a little job there when I was home for a year in 1970. They were really nice people, I was working there when the money changed – decimalization. It was awful. Poor little ladies didn't know what to do -- all bent out of shape about it, ha! Kay came to visit us when we were stationed in Germany. I wonder where they are now?

Ian H. Geoff Woodward (his parents had the sweet shop on the square) had sweets in his pockets, he could unwrap them, silently, and get them in one rapid gesture into his mouth during class, and no-one was any the wiser he thought!

Bryan D. This post is interesting to me because it shows how certain images of places get fixed in our mind when we are young and also how things change. When I was growing up the shop was Woodwards. Around 1960 (Geoffrey Woodward will be able to give precise details) Mr. Woodward retired and the shop was bought by the Beckwiths - an elderly couple with one son, Terry. Accordingly the shop was re-named "Terry's". Terry Beckwith was about 30 at the time, possibly older. I don't know how long the Beckwiths stayed there, but obviously not many years passed before this Rex and Kay took over and became well-remembered by the next generation. They obviously chose to keep the name of the business. However, that name has gone now and the present generation will remember it as the Polish Mini Market.

Geoffrey W. Well Bryan, as I recollect we left the shop in approx. 1957 and moved to Radcliffe St, my father moved to Stony Stratford soon after (long story). It may be interesting to some that in 1947 the chimney situated on the Masonic Hall building, being a storey higher, fell down onto the front of our shop, It landed on my parents bed, a couple of minutes before they went to bed, otherwise my brother and I would have been orphaned. 1947 was a year to be remembered by the amount of snow that fell. I remember that the front doors and windows of the houses in Buckingham Street were completely covered by the snowdrifts. For those old enough to remember, 1947 and 1963 were made memorable by the weather. Incidentally, there are many more stories I could recount connected to The Square, but fear that they may be of little interest to current subscribers.

Vivienne B. I Remember 1963

Len E. That winter of 63, we had a fish pond in the garden and my father took cine film of somebody taking the dead fish from the frozen water, after that it got cleaned out and turned into a splash pool for us children.

43

Geoffrey W. It was also the year of the death of the commercial use of narrow boats on the canal. Most of them went into administration or simply ceased trading as their boats were trapped in the ice for some weeks. Those were the days when every house had a pair of ice skates in the house to use on the frozen canal **Bryan D.** On the freezing of the canals, I recall a story once told to me about my great grandfather William Webster, who kept the Red Lion at Leighton Buzzard. One week at the end of the 19th century the canals froze up, isolating a number of barge families at Linslade. In those days they weren't paid until they completed the job; there was no welfare, nor were they the responsibility of the parish. However, they were hungry and destitute, so William Webster, who used to do weekly hog roasts for the farmer's market, organised a big cauldron in the street outside, filled with vegetables (he was also a market gardener) and meat donated by farmers and offered free soup to the bargees and their families. **Ron B.** Sid and Iris Davies in their shop.

P 12: Sid and Iris Davies, shortly after opening their shop on The Square in the 1950s.

Jill G. When sweet shops were real :)

Ron B. yep Jill.x

Jill G. We have a little sweet shop in Newport and the sweets are far nicer out of a paper bag. x

Mark B. A quarter of sweets in a paper bag that's the way! Oh an remember how many black jacks or fruit salads you got for a penny, and then there were 10p mixes and you always got extra strong mints in there too.

Jill G. God that means I will have to go up the High street tomorrow and get some army and navy now :)

Brian E. Four Blackjacks or Fruit salads for 1d.

Celia R. There was a shop in Margate that sell their sweets from jars. I think it is still there.

Kim P. He was much older by the time I came along so he was always Mr. Davies to me... brings back good memories seeing his face again.

Ron B. Still see him and Iris most weeks Kim. Lovely couple

Kim P. Glad to hear they are still around! I always remember him being a very kindly man whereas Mrs. Terry across the road frightened the pants off me :)

Ron B. They are not in the best of health, but love to come over to Stony for a drink on a Saturday

Barbara L. Multi coloured sherbet, oh yes the tongue told its own story after eating it.

Ian H. How about those big glass bottles of sweets you could buy by the 2oz or 4oz for a tanner!! Acid drops, barley sugars, mint humbugs, Pontefract cakes (liquorice), blackcurrent & licorice, aniseed balls, fruit mixture, cough drops.......loved them. No wonder Wolverton had so many dentists Lesley !!!

Margaret C. I loved Pear drops and Rhubarb and custard sweets..

Ian H. Butterscotch.... Callard & Bowsers . Not in jars though' and not a tanner!!

Deborah B. Mmmm. Rainbow sherbet - the fingers used to change colour.

Margaret C. Can you remember they use to put sherbet into paper done as a cone. We use to get a really hard liquorice stick to dip in it as well.

Deborah B. Yep I remember that. Yummy.

45

Vicky L. Cough candy & Herbal tablets.

Ian H. Remember those liquorice "twigs" that you chewed and chewed and chewed and chewed and chewed then put them in the sherbet powder 'til all the paper bag got soggy!

Helen P. Who remembers orange triangle jubblies? Used to get them frozen from Pantlins in the summer and walk up the rec. Mr Virco the crazy rec keeper...like a Beano character!

Brian E. Helen, we used to buy those Jubblies from the Victoria Stores most mornings, and keep them, opened, in our desks. They were hard to balance so they did not spill. During first two classes we would raise our desk-tops and surreptitiously dip our fingers in the juice & lick them. By morning break, we had orange fingers. They cost 4d in those days, 1964/5. Didn't they come with a free plastic straw?

Kim P. Clove candy in paper twists from the sweet stall in the old market hall - there were lots of different flavours but I like the clove one - hard candy made in long thin sticks they broke up with a little hammer.

Andrew L. The Post Office in Anson Road, had the main counter straight in front as you walked in, and wonderful sweets counter on the left. Behind the sweets counter they had the old fashioned jars from which they would weigh you out a quarter pound in a paper bag. The front window was full of toys and they sold caps for the toy guns.

Ian H. What about the shop opposite the Co Op bakery in Aylesbury that sold "stink bombs"?

Ian H. Now and again, not very often, my mum gave me two bob to go and buy six fancy cakes from the bakers. I always went to the Co Op, although East's sold cakes too. I remember vanilla slices, jam doughnuts, those coconut dome things, small iced bakewell tarts with a cherry and those white iced sponge cakes with a little bump on the top which when you bit had some cream AND a piece of pineapple.............oh and those thick stodgy slices about three inches thick (my brother reckoned they were made with the left over stale cakes). Any more favourites?

Brian E. My father always regarded cream slices as a treat, and we often had cream horns and Eccles. You cannot find Eccles anywhere these days, except nasty supermarket ones. I even asked at Greggs.

Pat C. Stodgy slices were Chester cakes made from leftovers, my Dad loved them in those days, called them Killer cakes. ok if they were a bit moist.

Ruth E. I make my own Eccles cakes now I am a retiree. My Dad loved them from Hazeldines.

Ian H. I used to like them warmed up! And the Eccles!!

Helen P. My Dad's homemade bread pudding, or cakes from Hazledines in Stratford on a Saturday.

Sheila B. What about Japs? Don't see them now.

Jackie S. My downfall is custard doughnuts. I have a local bakers that makes all of your fave's Ian, unfortunately it's all fake cream and icing so they are not as nice, just sickly. I used to go to Hazeldines and later George Ort at MK city centre.

Terry L. I am afraid I indulge a little too much in the cake department, my good lady being an excellent baker and all that, but with a job that involves picking up cakes most nights as well! Danish pastries too with Lemon filling and icing on top, and Butterscotch ones with Pecans sprinkled on, and Yum Yums with Apple or Custard. I am sure they do Eccles cakes too but have never been keen on them!

Jackie S. Terry, Danish with lemon is best frozen. Maple and Pecan to die for.

Brian E. I was working at Blue Star garages on the M1 at Newport when we changed to decimal currency. A week-end student job. I agree Margaret, it was awful. We all carried those little card converters, but they did not help. The big problem was when the conversion came to a different figure to what was displayed on the pump. The new half-penny was actually worth something then - abolished now!

Margaret C. We were young then Brian..ha!

June L. I still keep to Pounds & Ounces, Inches Feet & Yards Miles & Pints if I can.

Vivienne B. I was working at Associated Octel when we went decimal, I was sent on a course to Ellesmere Port for a couple of days, very nice hotel as I remember, but I have to say I find cms

47

much easier than feet and inches (its probably because that's what I work with know)

Jennifer T. I'm with June on this. £'s shillings and OLD pence, I was in the maternity ward having my youngest at the time

Jackie S. I agree with Vivienne, so much easier when everything in multiples of 10.

3 We went to school

Over the lifetime of the older contributors to this book the schools underwent many changes. The Boys' School on Church Street became an Infants School after the war and the Girls and Infants School on Aylesbury Street became a mixed school, with the "seniors" downstairs and the "juniors" upstairs. The Wolverton County School on Moon Street became a Grammar School at the same time. In 1956 the Technical School at the Science and Art Institute merged with the Grammar School. In 1958 this became formally known as the Radcliffe School. This school moved to a new building at the west end of Aylesbury Street in 1960 and the Wolverton County Secondary School moved to Moon Street. Later the Radcliffe became fully comprehensive and the Moon street school became a Middle School, renamed Bushfields. The older schools between Aylesbury Street and Church Street became primary school renamed Wyvern. The memories on these pages cover all of these schools during different eras and the conversations tend to roam.

Wyvern

Vince C. The building on the left is Windsor & Glave's old woodshop. I lived in Jersey Road and my house backed onto this school. We used to play in the school when it was shut and used to get chased by the caretaker Mr. Sherwood, he lived in Peel Road, although we used to hear his motorbike so had plenty of time to leg it.

Faye L. lol Looks much better in this pic than now I think

Kazza B. Oh yeah Vince. Talking of Peel Road, what was the building in Peel Rd, (where the new houses were built) think it was a wooden pavillion??? remember playing in the brick buildings to the back of it with Terry Lambert, Rhona Bradburn, Julie Wallace, etc

Kazza B. I remember being sent to Windor & Glaves to collect paraffin for our bathroom heater!!! (God it used to stink)!!!!

Vince C. I used to get free wood shavings from W&G for my gerbils.

Terry L. Yep free shavings too for my Rabbit Snowy....

Vince C. I used to have great fun playing around that old building. I think it was owned by a religous group. The brick building was an air raid shelter. It always stank of wee as it was regularly used as a toilet. I think in its heyday there was a tennis court at the back of the building, which was overlooked by a veranda. We used to climb under it and found some old from early 1900s pennies once. There used to be snooker tables in there too. When it was being demolished we managed to get in and have a look around. It was a magnificent place when I look back but at the time we really treated it quite badly. Kids eh, no respect for property! Funny you mention Terry - his brother once set off a sugar/fertilizer bomb on the old tennis court. You'd get sent to Guantanamo for that these days!

Jon P. Great school Wyvern. On my first day, I didn't like it, so at playtime I sneaked out and wandered along Aylesbury Street. Two old ladies found me and took me home. Uproar followed. !! If it happened nowadays it would be big news. By the way that's my Mum waiting by the gates! Ha Ha!!

Bryan D. The building on the scrub land at the bottom of Peel Road (sometimes known as the *Tin Hut*) was the Food Office during the war (and after). This was where you got your ration books. Rationing finished in 1952 I think. After that either the Wesleyans or the Methodists used the back part for a billiard club. We used to climb through the window on Saturday afternoons and help ourselves to free games of billiards and snooker. Some of the rooms were used by the Secondary Modern school as additional classroom before they moved to Moon Street. I'd forgotten about the tennis court Vince. I don't ever remember it being used.

Georgina S. I know I'm late replying to this photo but to Vince Clinton that's my Dad your talking about. He is still about but not on his motorbike anymore. lol

Dave M. Your dad was a nice bloke, let me use the school workshop once to repair my motorbike.

Chris G. Our Dad was the caretaker for a while in the early 60's. We lived in that same house at 36 Peel Road.

Alan C. In my day the Junior School was upstairs and the Secondary Modern downstairs. On cold winter days when icy in the Juniors playground at play time we use to make a slide and try to get it as long as possible. We were always in the Junior playground after school playing football, usually with a tennis ball.

Ink Pots

Ian H. Remember those little white, lipped, ink pots that were inserted in holes in your school desk, the blotting paper, and that big pencil sharpener that the teacher had on his desk. What about those tiered, wooden pencil boxes with a sliding lid? Then there were the pens with wooden handles like a pencil and replaceable nibs! If you were lucky there was a fountain pen, what a luxury, which you filled with Quink ink from a bottle, blue or black, by pulling back carefully a long metal strip encased in the side of the pen which depressed a rubber sleeve inside to allow the ink to be sucked in by air pressure, what joy! Talking of pencils Elaine Hayfield was a wonderful sketcher and Ferdy Old won a prize for the best handwriting. A bientôt.

Ruth E. I remember them. I think I was Ink Monitor at one time a very elevated position lol R emember my first Parker Pen , a fountain pen. In fact I used a fountain pen for many years after I left school.

P 13: Old style school desks at the MK Museum

Lesley W. Do you recall the ink bombs that were flicked round the classroom. Screwed up blotting paper dipped in the inkwell?
Donna S. Oh! the dreaded ink blots... buying India ink to refill my pen... and the never ending don't know what I did wrong blots on my paper.... and I miss those pencil boxes...
Brian E. A Parker Cartridge pen cost 5/9d, and was way beyond my means in 1965. Then, an Aunt gave me two shillings, and another relative half a crown. So now all I needed was 1/3d, which was more within my grasp. Then, one dreadful day, I was playing near a pond near Castlethorpe, and when I pulled out my hanky my two precious coins fell out and rolled down the bank. Plop! Plop! I scrambled around in mud and water for the rest of the morning, but never found them. So I continued using a 'pitchfork' type pen, dipping it in the inkwell thereafter. I have never got over that loss! Ball point pens were banned at Moon Street School in those days.

Ian H. Talk about "couldn't rub two pennies together" Brian, I am quite certain how many people, including some way back then, don't/didn't realise the poverty in Wolverton that existed.

Hazel S. Ink wells were a disadvantage to left-handed people - always on the wrong side!!!!!!

Ian H. Didn't have a "proper" pen then Hazel, bet you had a wooden pencil box though, AND a rubber!!!!!!

Hazel S. Sure did!!!

Ian B. The days before calculators when you used log tables or the guessing stick (slide rule).

Brian E. Oh my gosh yes. All those lessons with Mr. Dunleavy looking at log tables and sines.

Alan C. What about rolling the pencil under your feet, the noise really annoyed Miss Davey!!!!!!

Jill G. Still got the old pencil box :)

Toni B. Ooh! scratchy ink pens setting my teeth on edge thinking about them--- loved biro when they came in.

Pencil Sharpeners

Becca H. Just a random thought really..... Does anyone remember those big pencil sharpeners that were clamped to a desk or table in junior school?

.**Deborah B.** Yep I remember those well at Wolverton Junior School.

Jill G. I used to sharpen my pencils just for the sake of it :)

Becca H. Hahaha Jill - so did I. xx

Steve B. Yes indeed! Used to be great for crayons too, but strangely got bunged up quite quickly whenever I tried!

Dave M. Could reduce a new pencil to a stub in 30 seconds.

Sue L. I'm with Jill on that one, I used to sharpen my pencil for the sake of it; it fascinated me - when I was young (obviously)!!

Becca H. Oooh - I now have a hankering for one!!

Jill G. You can get electric ones now much quicker Becca ha-ha x

Chris G. Electric pencil sharpeners??? That is the devils work!

Becca H. I still think I'd like one with the manual turn handle Jill! In my mind's 'ear' I can hear the sound it made!

Jill G. Yes a nostalgic sound :)

Brian E. And, the blotting paper & ink wells we used.

Steve B. Blotting paper! I had all but forgotten it! And didn't Stephen's black ink make a wonderful mess when you accidentally tipped a bottle over?

Brian E. I still use a fountain pen. But a decent one, not like we had at school.

Len E. And the day at junior school when you made the transition from writing with a pencil to a pen.

Susan B. Remember the sharpeners well, I knocked my ink well over a couple of times, not used a fountain pen since I left school, Steve used one for the first time at the registry office yesterday.

Pete B. QUINK.

Ron B. Your little finger always had an ink stain. Well mine did.

Dave M. And for the naughty ones a bit of blotting paper dipped in ink and a rubber band was a wonderful weapon.

Len E. Dave, an early form of paint balling.

Pat C. None of you are old enough to remember writing with quills? One of my best Christmas presents many years ago was a fountain pen with a broad nib.

Dave M. Earliest I remember was those wooden ones with the nib on the end. Although we did make one from a feather as part of a lesson once.

Len E. Pat thought you went to school in the days when you wrote on a slate. (No offence) :)

Pat C. No offence taken Len, did hear you roofed your first house with those slates, and when it rained, yours, Ron's and Colin's ink ran down and ruined the paint!

Chris G. I can remember some bright spark making 'cigarettes' out of the shaving from the sharpeners and tracing paper. Didn't last long and gave you an instant singe to your fringe!

Pat C. Putting shavings into, was it hollow old elderberry shoots cheap fags?

Brian E. At my school in Mexico, a blackboard was installed in my classroom to replace the whiteboard, so I changed from smelly markers to chalk. The difference was incredible, no more marker stains or smells. Other teachers began asking for the old fashioned boards. Nothing wrong with the old ways sometimes. Plus, chalk does not dry-up in the middle of a sentence.

Pocket Money

Becca H. Remember feeling really rich as a child in the early to mid 60's with thrupny bit in my pocket!
Robert G. Still got some.
Becca H. Still got quite a few Victorian and George pennies and halfpennies and a couple of farthings.
Pat C. Used to go up to my Aunt's corner shop in the 50s. Her side window was devoted to sweets, penny sweets, 4 for a penny, the gallon glass jars. I used to help her make ha-penny ice lollies, good egg cup size and 1p lollies small beaker size. Used to fight with my sisters over the sixpences in the Christmas Pud!

P 14: Half Crown and Threepenny bits.

Brian E. Nice, chunky coins. Especially the half-crowns.
Ian H. Where was this Pat, it sounds magical?

Pat C. Walsall, Staffs Ian, needless to say never minded going up there for a week or two in the holidays. When she retired she came to live with us in Bucks.

Ian H. You a Saddlers fan then? From now on you can be Bescot Pat ;-)

Pat C. Always have been Ian. My uncle used to take me to home matches, gates of around 11,000 then. If they got a good player Birmingham or Wolves used to buy them.

Len E. Thrupny bit!!!...is that not rhyming slang for something? Ron might know :-)

Brian E. A kind of Mockney slang, Len, as in, "Cor, she had a nice pair of thrupny bits!" Sort of thing Sid James might have said.

Becca H. Yeah Len and if Ron doesn't know I'm sure he'll make something suitably salacious up!

June L. I bet Ron will know what your *ape nee* was!!!

Becca H. Long as 'e don't expect me to talk to 'im about me 'tuppence' June - then thats fine!

June L. Yes it is slang (your *Thrupny Bits*) Don't forget the S.

Faye L. I got some old Victorian coins somewhere and a florin.

Becca H. I got a couple of florins too. Not really worth anything yet unless a date in demand but worth keeping for now.

Faye L. Mine's so old most of the date and such have been worn off.

Josie O. pre 1946 it may be worth more for the silver content.

June L. Mothers use to say to daughters when they were going out, Keep your hand on your halfpenny (thus-pronounced hayp-nee) sorry I spelt it ape nee before Becca.

Ron B. Aha, Thrupny bits, now you are all expecting me to say something rude. Why I cannot imagine? I used to catch the bus from Stony to Corner pin in Braddell, and it used to be Threepence return. *(Sits back to await further abuse.)*

Chris G. I remember *On the Buses* well Ron and even Lothario Jack didn't mention thrupenny bits when talking of clippies Ron. It's all in you're mucky mind. ;)

Becca H. Here we go....just cos Ron's been challenged again.....it always makes him worse. Why don't I EVER learn?

Ron B. I was going to remark on you having a thrupny bit in your pocket. But thought better of it Becca, dear.xx

Becca H. First wise decision you've made in a long time Ronster!

Ian H. Not many went to Braddle from Stony (or Wolverton come to that) you must have been on a "cert" Ron;-)

Ron B. Going to my Gran's Ian.

Brian E. How much pocket money did we get? I got 6d; six old pence a week. I only started to get this when the man who had repaired my father's garden fork asked me to tell him it was ready. He stopped me the next day and asked if I had delivered his message. When I said I had, he said, "Good boy, you will have to ask your father to increase your pocket money." As soon as he came home that evening, I said, "Dad, what's pocket money?" I could tell he was annoyed that someone had been putting ideas into my head! I was about 5 then, and I have often wondered if I should have sued for back-pay!

Jill G. I got pocket money but can't remember how much as it depended what dad could afford as I was one of 8 kids.

Len E. Zilch!!!!, but didn't seem to go without things. :)

Celia R. I can remember getting half-a crown when I was 15.

John R. Same as Len, the only "real" pocket money I had was the pay I got from my paper round.

Len E. Me too John, was paid about 60p week.

Pat C. Got mine for various jobs, sweeping yard, trip to shop etc.

June L. I don't remember much about pocket money, I do remember my Nan taking my brother Pete & I with her each week to the little Post Office when she drew out her Pension. She would then buy me & brother Pete 2ozs of boiled sweets each. Pete would crunch & eat them all at once & I would put them in my bedroom drawer to make them last all week lol.

Bryan D. I can't remember if I ever got pocket money. My Mum and Dad would buy treats every now and then (and more on the then side than now). I don't think I had any income until I started working for it, like clearing out the weeds from some old lady's garden for 6d. When I got a paper round, then I had real income, most of which I saved to buy my first bike.

Penny G. I do think it was the post war years for some as we didn't have much money I got 5/- a week for doing a paper round from woods in the High St in Bradwell.

Bryan D. Child exploitation Penny! We were getting 11/6d in Wolverton.

Penny G. Well the ride up the hill was a bit too much as I had done it twice in one day when I was at Moon st as I went home for dinner lol.

Ruth E. Think I had sixpence to buy a saving stamp with probably got to spend it all at Xmas maybe, no money until I started collecting eggs' on Holes farm for the princely sum of 14 shillings for 2 mornings work in 1964....

Faye L. I had £2 every Saturday from my granddad.

John Rd. Not much as I was grounded a lot of the time.

Brian E. When I was a boy; late fifties, early sixties, the word 'grounding' was not known in this context. It just did not exist as a parental option. I suppose this may be partly the ubiquitous American influence, and partly down to the fact that we had nowhere special to go anyway. Neither could we be deprived of phone rights, as very few people had one in their home, and the home PC had not been invented. (Good old Bill Gates!) Being sent to bed early was an option I suppose.

John Rd. Phone or PC?? I am not that young buddy ;) I never got them things till I was around 13 by which time I didn't get grounded anymore.

Brian E. We never even had calculators when I was 13! Or videos.

John Rd. I had a mega drive and a bicycle....bikes are much more fun that for sure. ;)

June L. Someone bought me a Calculator but I never use it. I want to keep my brain cells in working order.

Andy M. Circa1963 2/6d, Half Crown, each week!

John Rd. What's that in today's money then? Around 20 odd pence?

Chris G. 12.5p John

Penny G. I didn't now how to use a calculator till I was in my 30's then struggled to understand the workings. I still use paper & pencil I can see what I am doing. 2/6d John is approx 12p. as 10p as we know it was a 2 bob bit. 6d was no longer used and that was turned into 2 & half pence it took some of us a long time to get our heads round it all when decimalization came in.

Pat C. Anyone remember the times table in their classes up and down? Now it's the march of the machines. My 9yr old granddaughter is teaching my son-in-law how to use his first Smartphone.

Len E. I can remember the class as whole shouting out the times tables like some sort of mantra.

Bryan D. And what did I find the other day? Instructions for using my slide rule. They were probably made obsolete when the pocket calculator came into being in the 1970s.

Chris G. Someone tried to teach us how 'simple' they were to use. Was that you Bryan?

Bryan D. Ha ha! Not at that time Chris. I think calculators (which had just appeared with 9v batteries which used up their juice in 5 minutes) were banned in school. Banning new technology is usually the first response of schools. Biros (ball point pens) were banned on the grounds that they would spoil your handwriting. Slide rules were not permitted until you got to the 6th form - and you know the rest.

Handwriting

Chris G. I can remember when they finally allowed biros for everyday use. Ken Speaks nearly went and threw himself off the Iron Trunk. To placate him for a while we still hand to have italic handwriting lessons and the once a year writing competition still.

Pat C. I got the odd frown from teachers because I was left handed!

Bryan D. It was a tough old world for left-handers in our day and earlier. My father was naturally left handed but was forced to write with his right hand. As a result he was quite ambidextrous and I would notice him often using hands interchangeably - with a screwdriver, for example.

Terry L. My Pop is a leftie....

Len E. I'd give my right arm to be ambidextrous. :)

Pat C. Playing cricket late fifties it was pointed out to me that, I threw the ball with left hand, bowled with right hand never realised myself.

June L. My brother Pete has always bat with his left hand in cricket & he is right handed.

Bryan D. Oddly enough that was also true for me. I always felt more comfortable holding a cricket bat as a left hander, and the same later with a baseball bat and golf club - -yet in every other respect I am right-handed.

John R. I managed to smash my fingers in one of those caravan doors that open at the top and the bottom when I was learning to write, so I never did learn to hold my pencil the "right way" because all of my fingers were taped together for about 3 months. I hold a pen between my thumb and index finger - seem to do just fine.

Sarah K. I'd forgotten about the handwriting competition - I remember the bulb competition and every time I smell Hyacinths I think of Mr Speaks - oh the good old days

Constance O. I remember the handwriting competitions.

Brian E. Mrs Peglar gave me a writing exercise paper to improve my hand writing, I was supposed to copy the letters. After about a week she asked me about it, and I said I had lost it. Those who knew Mrs. Peglar can imagine the result. She hit the roof! One of her gripes was that it was her own personal property I had been so careless with.

Janice M. I am a leftie, pain in butt sometimes! where I work we have many kids that's are lefties in our class.

Deborah B. Anyone remember 1970 Wolverton Junior Shchool. We were taught Italic handwriting with the special italic ink pens. There was a writing competition copying a poem Seven Lonely Poplar Trees. It made the local newspaper under the heading I think called 'Children Can Write Well Nowdays'. There was a picture of me with my two pigtails - I was ten at the time. God I am know showing my age. I have a photocopy of the article but it is not a very good one - I would like top get hold of a good copy anyone know how I could do this?

Jane B. I was always well jealous of your handwriting Debbie as mine was total rubbish - still is - and I remember you getting in the paper - ooh, what I wouldn't have done to get my piccy in the old Wolverton Express.

Deborah B. I was quite proud of that myself at the time. But it took so long to do.

Tracy S. Jane you never cease to amaze me - how do you remember so much.

Deborah B. She has a better memory than mine - have trouble in remembering yesterday. But if someone prompts me. then it helps.

Jane B. As to getting a decent copy - leave it with me and I'll have a chat to the Librarian next time I go down there - they have items on microfiche so will enquire as to whether or not I could get you a copy - might take me a week or so but I will definitely get back to you asap.

Tracy S. Deborah, do you remember when we used to walk to school together across the rugby field and our knee-high boots?

Deborah B. Ha ha yes I do - soooo funny looking back at it now. I thought I was so cool with my skinny pins.

Jane B. Ha - I can remember things from 40 years ago - but ask me what I had for tea yesterday and I'd struggle !!!!!

Ian S. I remember Janet Stephenson's hand writing being very good in that competition.

Deborah B. I still have the certificate that I won!

Chris G. Ken Speaks was obsessive about italic writing wasn't he?

Deborah B. Yes he was - had to be perfect height and perfect formation of the letters or you had to do it again!!

Elaine P. Bless Mr Speaks, I still have my Writing Certificate from Bushfield :)

Debbie H. Who remembers the McCorquodales' painting/drawing competition? I always got 2nd place...God knows who got 1st.

Patsy G. I think he just finished off my handwriting completely!! could never do the italic stuff! :O)

Chris G. Yep Mr. Speaks loved handing out his little certificates too didn't he, be it handwriting, pottery or growing three hyacinths in a bowl for Xmas.

Julia B. Bless. He was such a good man.

Constance O. That is funny, I was just talking to my son-in-law about that. They do not even teach that any more. But I still write letters in ink, not with the ball point pen.

Chris G. Yep he was a good man Deborah and still always spoke if he saw you in the street, thirty odd years after teaching you.

Songs

Ian H. Songs at junior school. I often sing the old Molly Malone, Early one morning just as the sun was rising, What shall we do with the drunken sailor, Barbara Allan etc. I believe it was Miss White who was the teacher. Anybody any souvenirs??

Ian H. Not forgetting a few years later "Gaudeamus igitur, Iuvenes dum sumus..." especially for Bryan and others like us.:-)

Vicki L. My eyes are dim I cannot see, I have not got my specs with me!!!!

June L. Quarter Masters Stores Vicki, my great great uncle wrote it during the war, it started (there was butter butter sliding down the gutter, in the stores, in the stores)

Ian H. Army duff, army duff, soldiers don't get half enough!

Pina R. Remember Molly Malone also a song about 'riding on a donkey' which Miss Georgeson explained to us being a song about the oil 'donkeys'....

Bev P. 'Hey ho away we go, donkey riding, donkey riding".

Ian H. Bryan was your father a baritone of some local repute? In my reminiscences I see him in dinner suit complete with bow tie. There were a couple from the Stratford Rd that played the violin and chamber music, perhaps he gave local concerts with them. Excuses if I'm" doolally" with my reflections.

Maurice H. How about.....Have you met old Lovell with his wooden pick and shovel, digging up potatoes on the turnpike road, it continued for about 6 verses in similar vein to the old lady who swallowed a fly.

Andrew L. If Hanslope Spire, was 10 times higher, I'd take off my shoe and jump over it. Hanslope Spire is very visible from the upstairs north facing windows at Wyvern School. Anybody else ever hear that rhyme about Hanslope Spire?

Ruth E. Yes I have but I thought it was <u>hat</u>! Taught it to my children.

Hazel S. Heard that rhyme a few times!!!

Ian H. I believe it to be the highest in north Bucks, may be wrong on this. Olney seems quite steep(le).

Ruth E. Also visible from my house at Puxley...

Marc H. I've been up the spire when I was in the village never thought about trying to jump over it LOL

Alan C. Ian H. my Dad, Norman Cosford played the violin for years, we lived on the Stratford Road and he used to play in some orchestras and dance bands. In fact he has only just stopped playing in Chard and Taunton. He did not like the driving anymore. He is 91.

Bryan D. And you might also have been thinking of Elizabeth Clark who lived at the western end of Stratford Rd. She used to strengthen the school orchestra at performances, usually coming to one or two rehearsals before the event.

Ian H. That could be the lady Bryan. Her husband was a short bespectacled balding man. If so she also came to the junior school to comment and judge on the performances of our little" shows" They lived near Pedleys/Bews.

Bryan D. With no great claim to being right on this - since my memory is no longer the precision instrument it used to be - I thought she was married to Brian Clark (not our contemporary Brian Clarke). He did have glasses but also hair. He played the cornet, I believe, in the band. They were probably both under 30 in the 50s.

Ian H. They were a "refined" couple Bryan somewhat rare but not unknown in our day. ;-)

Becca H. Riding on a Donkey!!! Times I have tried to remember the words of that! (and often wondered why) lol. I remember it starting "Were you ever in Quebec.......? " Another one I loved was about "Sweet Polly Oliver" .... it started "When Sweet Polly Oliver lay musing in bed, a sudden strange fancy came into her head" ....It was a sad and tragic love story, She cut her hair, and I remember a line "she dressed herself up in her dead brother's clothes....." Basically she went off to pretend to be a bloke to find her love who had gone off to war (I think) but I seem to remember it didn't end well. Was she a latter day tragic heroine - or today would she be seen a bit of bunny boiling stalker? I can't remember the full tale and my memory may not be that accurate on this one. I do remember loving the song - in the same lessons we did Riding on a Donkey in that little separate classroom then known as the music room at Juniors. Same room I got a bollocking for coming into school with my school violin broken from falling off the wardrobe (where dad Gleadell had put it to keep toddler Chris Gleadell's mitts off it - then I dropped it and it bounced all the way down our Woodland View stars. OMG - for a confident and usually quite happy go lucky child - that day at the time seemed it would be the worst in my life! I arrived at school a palpitating, hyperventilating chimp! Sad day as it marked the end of Becca 'Ya Hoody Menuhin's string quartet career. Never been able to look a bloody horse hair bow since without shuddering.

Ian H. I find Hephzibah (Google it if in doubt :-))Hemmerman more appropriate somehow. :-)

Bryan D. Good story Becca. I think most musical careers are like political ones - they end in failure. For most of us it's an early exit. My piano playing and clarinet playing years ended circa 1958 - not as spectacularly as yours but probably to everyone's benefit.

Becca H. Ooh - liking your work Ian H. Heph' is good! Had I grown to larger proportions with this middle age lark, I may have been naturally nicknamed 'Hepher' though. However despite being a lass known for fairly constant grazing, I unfortunately never managed to accrue much in the way of winter insulation and am still quite a lean lamb really!

Chris G. I remember things differently Rebecca. Wasn't the violin put on top of the wardrobe after several neighbours (and a few local cats) complained. I do remember an impromptu street party being held when they heard you'd dropped it.

Becca H. Bless you Chris for sharing your albeit cloudy an inaccurate account of events dear little brother. The impromptu "street party" you make mention of was in fact a "WAKE!" to mourn the passing of an opportunity Wolverton had fleetingly had within its grasp to nurture and produce a musical genius!

Helen P. Casey Jones *Steamin' and a Rollin'*. Had to sing a solo at the Raccy. Never got over it.

Maurice H. I mentioned an old song "Have you seen old Lovell", Memory came back that in our class around 1950 ish, we always had a titter when we sang that song, because there was a tall lanky lad in the class by the name of Lovell, who was always being teased because he was a little bit slow on the uptake of things. I sometimes wonder what happened to him? The words of the song went something like this

Have you seen old Lovell with his wooden pick and shovel digging up potatoes in the turnpike road, Have you seen his wife with a broad bladed knife peeling the potatoes in the turnpike road. etc etc.

Brian E. A favourite of mine was 'Westering Home.'

Country Dancing

Ian H. Come on own up who enjoyed it, or not? As part of school lessons of course.

Maryanne L. It taught me to count to 8!

Constance O. I liked it :)

Hazel S. Remember going to Wolverton Park Country dancing and all the schools in the area taking part. We danced the 'Gay Gordons', 'The Dashing White Sergeant' and 'Strip the Willow' and our parents were quite happy about it!!!!

Ron B. Am I the only man that's going to admit to liking it. Anyone remember Mr Pastry doing the Dashing White Sergeant. Brilliant. Must find a link on you tube.

Pamela J. Maypole dancing in Wolverton Park

Ron B. Drew the line at that Pamela.

Ian H. Ron get Mr. Pastry on. He was as soft as a brush a bit like Eggo!!!!!

Hayley D. Liked it, one of the few things I enjoyed at school.

Pat C. Circassian Circle?

Steve B. Definitely! The waltz as performed by Janice Forman and my good self would have impressed the 'Strictly' judges!

Angie A. Hated country dancing - still do.

Sarah K. I liked country dancing - Ian Slaymaker was my country dancing partner,

Stephen C. Hated it. With respect to Eileen who was my partner.

Julie W. Loved it xx

Wendy C. I remember country dance to this - return to django - the upsetters. lol..

Chris G. Was my favourite subject at school closely followed by needlework and poetry?

Matt. N. I remember doing it as well at Wyvern. Somewhere there are some embarrassing photos of me doing it. I think we wore blue checked neckerchiefs.

Ian H. What year did cookery start getting taught to lads?

Elaine S. I loved it. In my day we used to have a Country Dance festival down the park.

Pamela J. Yes I remember that well. Good afternoon out and no school.

Terry L. Loved country dancing so much that I often indulge in a quick "turn single" followed by an "honour" in me shed, wearing nothing but me knitted woollen hat and me old wellington boots. big up the Do-si-do !

Mike W. Country Dancing was awful. Just a way of publicly humiliating the ugly kids. I still remember the look of disgust in faces of classmates who had to dance with the ugly one.

Richie B. Loved it the Cumberland Reel the Gay Gordon's used to swing Jackie Batterick around an then let go lol.

Becca H. I preferred the Cumberland Sausage Richie ! x

Ron B. Ooh err.

Becca H. Why, oh Why, oh Why do I never learn. I had just got Ron back in his outdoor Kennel too! x

Ron B. Take me for a walk first please.

Becca H. No Ron - because I'll only end up picking up your trail of innuendos en route!

Ron B. Better bring a big bag then Becca.

Steve B. Ah the Gay Gordon's! How could I forget??

Becca H. Back on the thread subject - I loved Country Dancing. I wasn't the most coordinated of children though - but I valiantly tried to make up for it with (over) enthusiasm. I seem to remember being partnered with a lad called Peter Doyle - who would often look simply bewildered when I would REALLY try to get into it - and somehow find myself ricocheting down to the other end of the hall (by myself). I also remember the teacher shouting over the music "Knees DOWN Rebecca Gleadell!" as I tried so hard to do the sideways steppy skippy moves and my knees somehow came up to meet my elbows. My memory is that at the time Peter Doyle was simply too delicate a child for my seemingly turbo charged attempts at country dancing. I really wanted Pete Beale as my dancing partner - but on reflection, I think the teacher made a good decision not to pair us, as together we probably would have had the potential to cause a collision on a par with the Corrie Train Crash!

Becca H. Durham Reel anyone?

Terry L. Becca, I think you may mean chassé, instead of "Sideways steppy skippy moves"

Becca H. Hahahahaaha! (get YOU with you proper dancing words!) I thought that meant summate to do with the body / frame of a car or motorbike. Now if they had said THAT to me and Pete Beale we might paid more attention!

Becca H. Awww I love that - I want to go and do it now! Notice none of those ladies have a knee anywhere near an elbow or their own forehead throughout. It also reminds me of our mum! She tried with me a good few times as well at dances when I was really young in her homeland of Scotland. The people always smiled - but not one dancing 'scout' approached us to sign me up! xx (I'm just looking at the tutor bit on the vid now Terry - to see if there is any potential in a 'comeback' for me - a second chance! That's all I need! xx

Terry L. Sorry after watching that vid I had to nip out to me shed for a quick Strathspey. Trouble is, with just me knitted hat and wellies on the security light came on halfway across the garden, and the unexpected sight frightened Mrs Smith next door to death!

Becca H. Taking into account your shed preamble - then watching the vid, I have to say I can hardly breathe for laughing. The image in my head is either insanely hilarious - or downright unhealthy for a middle aged woman!

Linda R. Does any one remember going to Wolverton College and having to dress up in long dresses for the evening cant remember what the action was went to a couple of these?

Becca H. I had to go a couple of times in my mid teens with my Mum and Dad to a Bowls Club (I think) dinner dance there Linda. Anyone on here who knows me will tell you it would have been hell for me to have to dress up in a long posh frock - so I can only assume it was a punishment for some sin. Mind you Mum and Dad (David and Kitty Gleadell) were very impressive waltzers on the dance floor - but of course I would never have said that to them then - as a 'disgruntled for simply being there' teenager!

Brian E. In 69/70 I was at Bletchley College which was part of Wolverton FE college. We had dances, but I never heard about this long dress business. One time we had what we called a Super Ball at the Wolverton site. Rod Stewart was booked, for £40, I think. But in the weeks before we booked him and the night of the do, Maggie May went to number one in the charts. So, he demanded £400 instead, which was way beyond us. In their place we booked a then little known band called UFO. Supported by local bands Hackensack & Hot Cottage. (Did anyone here go?) UFO at that time wore Bowie style make-up. We found out later they laughed at how much we paid them that night, before they went on to become an International metal band. I still resent Rod doing that to us though, as we had already silk-screened the posters.

June L. I did wear long gowns for dancing, but most of us did in the 1950's. Because I lived in Essex in my early Teens we use to go Ballroom Dancing at the Lyceum, Tottenham Court Road in London & wear Ballroom Gowns. The massive dance floor had a Large Silver Ball hanging from the high ceiling sparking as it spun round under dimmed lighting.

The School at Moon Street

Nahida K. Where was this Secondary School in Wolverton?
Terry L. Moon Street.
Nahida K. Oh really? I went there.
Chris G. Nahida, it would have been Bushfield in our day.
Susan B. We had our first year here then we went up to the Radcliffe, good exercise for the day from Jersey Rd.
Nahida K. Yeah I remember that. We walked it.
Tricia D. Moon Street! Lots of memories - particularly of taking a day off and getting caught out. My teachers should have realized

with St. George's Crescent being so close that we might have bumped into a teacher or two!!

P 15: The School at the top of Moon Street, built in 1908

Kevin S. Is that the old hall?

Bryan D. It's kind of an odd feeling to see that again. Every morning we would all troop into the hall and line up by form in rows in front of the platform - first year at the front and 6th form at the back. When we were assembled, Harold Nutt would come in and go to the piano, followed by Pop Eyles, Zillah Full and the Boss. The other teachers would sit at the sides. None of the pupils had chairs, so if we had to sit down it would be on the parquet floor. The usual format was announcements a hymn and a prayer. At Red House assemblies we would sing "Gaudeamus igitur" (Let us therefore rejoice) to a tune written by Brahms or somebody like that. The honours boards listed all those who had achieved County awards. These were scholarships for those who were university bound, a system that existed prior to state funding. After the war state scholarships were introduced. Scholarships were still awarded in the 1950s but I expect that it had petered out by 1960 because every university entrant was state funded. The right hand board had a few more names on it in the 50s, so I would expect Terry

69

that this photo would again date to the 1930s. I wonder what ever happened to those honours boards? Nostalgic days!

P 16: The School Hall, 1930s.

Terry L. Did I tell you that my Uncle was caretaker there? Do you remember Frank Chippy Watson ?

Bryan D. Yes I remember Chippy very well and I posted a photo of him and some tales that I recall a little while back. He was a very genial chap and quite popular with the boys, a number of whom would hang around his little office attached to the Canteen during breaks and lunchtimes, to listen to his words of wisdom. He and Fred (the grounds man) would have their tea and possibly cigarette, although I can't remember whether he smoked or not.

Terry L. Fred Watson was my Granddad, he took over for a while when Chippy went to the Radcliffe..

Andy M. Stage was the other end of the hall during my time, 1963 to 1967

Brian E. Right Andy, when we were there the windows would be to our right in Assembly.

Terry L. I have just noticed the piano Bryan now you mention it, it kind of blends in! Pop Eyles was he the teacher who Died whilst I was at Moon Street in circa 1971, I thought his name was Popeye Elliott?

70

Brian E. Yes Terry, Mr Elliot, unusually for a teacher he had 2 nicknames. Popeye, and Jumping' Jesus!

Andy M. Mr Elliot drove a Riley Elf as I remember.

Brian E. Yes, a green Riley. One day, about a year after I had left school, I broke down on the way to Bletchley, and he stopped and kindly gave me a lift in. However, he clearly did not remember me from being in his RI class for 4 years and had no idea who I was.

Ian H. The Hall! Morning assembly. Oh the black gowned teachers and head. Smaller in this photo than I "see" it in the past, fabulous photo' this! Thanks Terry. Keep them coming!!

P 17: School Assembly in the 1960s.

Brian E. I have not been inside Moon Street for over forty years, but I hear the hall now has some kind of mezzanine and steps, creating another floor under the ceiling?

Donna S. looks so tiny .....

Ian B. I seem to remember the stage being at the other end of the hall when I was there.

Andy M. Ian. Yes it was!

Donna S. Which school had the raised stage, curtains across it etc where we put on school plays?

Sylvia A. Radcliffe wasn't it

Donna S. Probably but this was the elementary school Sylvia I am thinking of ... I remember big windows on the right when you stood on the stage, it was raised not a platform like the one in this pic just cant remember if it was one on Aylesbury street or Bushfield..

Chris G. By the time Bushfield came along a new hall had been built as you came in the main gate, I guess this was converted to something else, library maybe?

Bryan D. From the period of this photo Donna the only two proper stages were at the Church Institute (Madcap) and the Science and Art. The Church St and Aylesbury St schools had raised platforms. If they had (or have) stages, they must have come later.

Andrew L. Chris, yes, this became a library with a mezzanine at the end the pictures were taken from and domestic science cookers under the mezzanine. Completely unrecognisable from this picture.

Ian H. When was the Scout Hall built Bryan that had a lovely stage. Remember doing a few "turns" on it in the day:-)

Bryan D. I had totally forgotten about that. I do remember sleeping on the stage at some weekend "camp". Probably got rained out.

Hazel S. The Wolverton Works Canteen had a stage big enough to feature the Festival of Britain Pageant in 1951 and many local bands played there during past years. Harold Nutt had several concerts there too. Left or Right turns Ian tell us more!!!

Ian H. They were the "Gang Shows" Hazel . Keith Webb was our Ralph Reader:-) Also wrote and played with Geoff Woodward a few "Bugsy Returns" sketches, all good fun tho'!!!

Brian E. When we put on plays, we rehearsed at Moon Street, but used the Radcliffe's stage.

Pina R. Donna, Aylesbury St school had windows to the right of the stage...

Hazel S. Do you remember the Top of the Town Shows Ian - Comedian Ted Lune came one year - Wolverton Youth Club members performed as did the Roger Kightley Trio featuring Roger on piano, Bill Atterbury drums, Peter Gill on bass?

72

Ian B. There used to be a stage in the hall next to the congregational church on The Square I'm sure I saw Brian Tight and some magician putting on a show there.

Ian H. I don't Hazel I had perhaps married by then!!!!!!! I do remember however the Xmas Pantomimes in the Science and Art Hall. Chambers' wife was Cinderella one year and very pretty too I may add! Not forgetting of course the Top Club stage!!

Hazel S. She still is Ian I saw her about a fortnight ago.

Alan C. When I was at the Grammar/Radcliffe school when it was at Moon Street the girls came into assembly through the door that you can see it the picture and the boys came in the opposite end

Bryan D. I think that's right Alan, but when we were in the classrooms off the hall did we go outside and come back in?

Brian E. Correct Alan, the doors in this photo were known as the 'girls' doors,' leading to the so-called girls stairs. In point of fact, it did not matter which stairs we used. Bryan, I assume those pupils in the downstairs classrooms went straight in hall? In fact, to go outside, you would first have had to enter the hall.

Hazel S. Bryan, wasn't 'Gaudeamus Igitur' exclusive to 'Red House' and sang in the school gymnasium assembly every Thursday? (Jim Smith)

Ian H. It was a Red House (mine) song Hazel in brackets;-)

Bryan D. That's right Jim. I've sung it so many times that I can still remember all the words. I might even be able to translate them too! :-)

Bryan D. Actually, now that I'm at the senectutum end of life I take more heed of "nos habebit humus"

Ian H. Blimey Bryan cheer up mate I know Chelsea won but come on....... ;-)

Alan C. My memory is that the boys always had to use the same stairs and doors and were not allowed to use the girls stairs. We did not have to go outside. I also remember the deputy head (I have a memory lapse and have forgotten her name Miss.......) coming into the classroom and the girls have to kneel at the front of the class and their skirts had to just touch the ground!!!!

Brian E. I can recall our form being told to stay behind in hall after assembly. The girls knelt on the floor, and the boys stood in a

73

row behind them. Mrs Peglar checked the girls' skirt lengths, whilst Mr Llewellyn looked to see if the boys' hair was above the collar. Mine never was, but those of us told to get a hair-cut were never checked afterwards to see if we had. I think this was just a formality, as I never heard of anyone being hauled over the coals regarding hair, or skirts.

Brian E. Alan, in my time, although we had 'girls' & 'boys' stairs, no one actually observed this rule. For instance, when we were based in room 10, we just went down the girls' stairs for assembly. The staff room was on the girls' landing, & the headmaster's study on the boys'.

Alan C. Brian, I cannot remember ever going down the girls stairs, but that is not to say that boys did not, I do know that when we went to the new Radcliffe School on Aylesbury Street there was no separation at that time, which is when I was taking more interest in girls anyway!!!!. We also had to wear indoor shoes then to save the wood floor in the new hall. Assemblies were held every day led by Harold Nutt on the piano with gusto.

Ian H. Miss Fuller I think Alan , Zylah.

Hazel S. Miss Full, Ian.

Ian H. Do you know that is what I typed at first but on reflection thought it wrong. It must have something to do with my memory of her" fuller" figure no doubt:-)

Bryan D. Zillah Full. In my Mother's time (c 1930) she was the Games Mistress and the school photo shows her with black severely cut hair and a gym slip. She was pretty fierce with the girls as Alan suggests. I remember one occasion when I was passing through the girls' lobby and one girl came in out of the rain wearing one of those clear plastic scarves, which were quite new at the time. Miss Full ripped it off her head and gave her a right telling off. "I told you never to wear these things etc." The girls will probably have more stories to tell.

Ian H. I remember the severe hair style and her very ungainly way of walking very unfeminine. One of the Kemp sisters (Junior School) had the same misfortune.

Bryan D. And they both lived in Stony Stratford - if that has anything to do with it.

74

Gill B. Yes Bryan D. Zillah Full was very strict with the girls regarding our uniforms. We were made to kneel on the floor to check that our skirts were the correct length, but as soon as Miss Full had gone we would roll the waistband over to shorten the skirts back again.

P 18: Aerial View of School with additions c. 1965

Bryan D. It looks as if this shot was taken just after the Gables tower was built, so it shows the old County/Grammar/Radcliffe/County Secondary before additions. The pre-fab canteen and Chippy Watson's domain can be seen on the right and the bike sheds. Now I don't ever remember taking my bike to school and I am left with the impression that if you lived in Wolverton you weren't allowed to ride your bike to school. I'd be interested in other people's recollections of this.
Terry L. I think you are right Bryan, as Nicholas Atter had to leave his bike in the back garden of a house in Victoria street, and he lived in Church St.
Brian E. Tom Whinnet lived in Stacey Ave. visible behind the school. Doesn't the alley look wide in this?

David Wn. 1953 - You could cycle to school and park in bike shed if you lived in Anson Rd or any street west of it. Strangely we kept to these rules!

David Wn. A rare photo indeed - goal posts on "A" pitch !

Brian E. Most of the cycles came from Haversham and Stony, in the days when it was safer.

Terry L. Well N Atter lived West of Anson road, far end of Church st ?

Ian H. I parked my bike at my gran's house 24 Victoria Street;-)

Bryan D. The Atters purchased my grandparents' house at 179 Church St., so he should have qualified under the "Anson Road Rule".

Chris G. Funnily enough Bryan the teacher who took over from you, Mrs. Thomas, wrongly informed us we couldn't ride our bikes to school so we used to leave them in the Bancrofts garage alongside. She saw us one evening going home and took us to Mr. Garner the next day who informed her there was no such rule. She didn't get the slipper though. ;)

Brian E. If you take a look at Moon Street today it is totally blocked with parked cars. Just a narrow passage up the middle.

Alan C. I believe there was some sort of rule but I always rode my bike to school from Stratford Road, and all my friends did as well,. I do not think we were ever checked. Also continued to ride our bikes to Aylesbury Street West when the new school was opened there. I remember one snowy day six of us were riding our bikes to Moon St., somebody, to this day we do not know who, aimed a snowball at us and we all went down like a pack of cards with pedals through spokes etc, did not go well with our parents, and our parents did not allow us to ride our bikes to school for a few weeks after that.

Penny G. I lived in Braddle & rode my bike to school & went home for dinner so I had the station hill to go up twice in one day also parked my bike in those bike sheds

Geoffrey W. I didn't know your Gran lived in Victoria Street, Ian

Bryan D. When I was cleaning my bike last night I remembered that some people used to tie pieces of leather inside the hub to keep them clean, and as kids we would find an old fag packet in the street, fold it, and wedge it between the forks, so that when it hit the spokes it would produce a satisfying clatter - until it wore out.

Terry L. I Remember that too Bryan, some looked like little miniature belts on the hubs, and we used old playing cards held on with a clothes peg....

P**enny G.** I think only the boys put those silly cards on there bikes just to make a noise as the saying goes "Boys & Toys" lol

Chris G. Anyone seen the new Halfords advert yet? Kid rides past with a playing card pegged to his spokes. Think they've been reading this site ;)

Bryan D. There you go Penny. They're still at it. Boys will be boys!

Barbara L. Little things pleased little minds then.

Lynn A. Mr Speaks taught Cycling Proficiency. Passed with flying colours.

Pete B. Playing card and clothes pegs in the back wheel was my first motorbike !

Vivienne B. I went to this school it was known as the Secondary Modern then. It was for those of us that failed our 11 plus, lol. If I am correct there was a white building further down the field on the right as you look at this picture, where there was a further 2 class rooms, we use to do R.E in there. I was there for 2 years, then we moved to the Radcliffe as it became a comprehensive school, that was a hard life.

Julie M. Sorry to be a bit thick but is that Wyvern or Bushfield School? Went to both but cannot get bearings.

Vivienne B. It's Bushfield now.

Julie M. Thank you. I don't normally add to these but was interested. Apart from growing up in Wolverton I don't seem to know many on this site but do find it very informative.

Vivienne B. I not sure its informative, but as I am born and breed in Wolverton, and still living here, I have found quite a few people that I went to school or lived near on here, so its been interesting and brings back lots of good memories

Lin G. I was just wondering Julie Maxey if you are related to Juliet and Jeffrey Maxey who were in my year at school, I was Linda Nicholls then.

Andy C. I remember being told off by the policeman who was running the cycling proficiency test at Wolverton Juniors before

77

we had even started the test. Only found out after he had passed me that he had observed me riding "no-handed" along Anson Road as he drove to the school to prepare for the tests. I would clearly never make a master criminal. :-)

Julie M. Yes I do remember you. Jeff is still about.

Lin G. Ah I see you are Juliet now Julie. I wondered if it was you. I like my name short as well. Last time we met was a school reunion at the bathhouse I think. Aanyway nice you are on here as well.

First Bike

Barbara L. Do you remember your first bike? Solid rubber tyres,

felt every bump but 3 wheeler great fun, could stand on the back if you didn't have your own, go-carts best, not much control, remember crashing a few times, oh well now its all Play Station.

Brian E. Scooters were pretty good too. I used to scoot miles on mine.

P 19: Raleigh Trent Tourist

John R. I had a red MoBo Scooter with yellow wheels. I was envious of those kids who had the upmarket model with a thing attached to the back wheel that they could push up and down to make it go. I had to use my right leg!

Becca H. Don't know if you will remember John but we had the same MoBo scooter as you and also the MoBo red and yellow go-kart/pedal car. We have an old B&W photo somewhere of Chris round the back of the house at Woodland View sat in the pedal car thingy.

Becca H. He was only 37 at the time - oh no sorry he was 2! x

Sheila B. I had a tricycle with a thing like a bread bin on the back.

Penny G. My first bike was called a fairy bike I got it from Mr Smith in New Bradwell in the High St., when his shop was at the front of his house. I was 5 years old. I still remember as it didn't

78

have the stabilizers on & I ran into the back of Mr. Munday's car, who was the local taxi service then. He lived in Harwood St. on the corner of North St.

Pat B. My first bike I had when I was about 9. It was painted blue all over. I think my uncle must have found it on a dump and tried to make it look smart.... My first new bike was in 1958. A Raleigh Trent Tourist.... Still riding it today.

Hammers and chisels

Bryan D. My education was mainly academic, so I was rarely taught anything useful at school. However, today, as I was chiselling out space for the hinges on a door frame, I realised that without learning this at school I wouldn't have known how to do it. (And yes, the door hangs perfectly. Thanks for asking.) So I can thank Peter Lowe for that piece of practical knowledge and others of my generation would have learned similar skills from Bill Coxhill. Now, if only I can find a use for quadratic equations . . . . .

Jackie S. Knew what you meant Bryan. Don't worry computer dyslexia affects any age group.

Chris G. Never dun eny gud, eye blaym meye teecher att Bushfeeled skool, Mista Doneleavevee.

Ian H. Geoff Woodward built a canoe in woodwork which we paddled in on the Ouse at Haversham Richard Lockwood (remember him Bryan) made a gorgeous low oak table and I failed miserably trying to make a simple book end "thing".

Ian T. Having studied physics after the Radcliffe school, I am now cursed with seeing many things in life as equations. Now I come to think of it in some instances it really helps!

Bryan D. Yes I had my share of mortice and tenon joints that rattled, and I remember, when it came to making dovetail joints that I hit on the expedient of filling the spaces with glue and sawdust. Still I did learn some things, and I have been able to call on this knowledge from time to time over 60 years. Having said that, if you want any cabinets built, don't come near me!

Pat C. I banged down a wood chisel to tighten the blade as I had seen TEACHER do, the blade flew out hit said teacher in his upper back he turned round to see what had hit him and turned white! We came to a mutual agreement that I would do college cross country during double woodwork!

Bryan D. Ha ha! It's amazing we survived, being let loose with saws, chisels and hammers at the age of 11. 'Elf and safety probably wouldn't allow it today.

Pat C. To this day I can't cut a piece of timber straight, I preferred mechanical challenges.

Pat C. Plus spelling challenges!!

Bryan D. All down to a flying chisel. ;-)

Ian B. I think without realising it algebra helped me throughout my life but never did find a use for that flat table and blue engineers ink. I suppose it depended on the career you took after leaving school.
Who said "take away everything you were taught and what remains is education".

David Wn. Either all the door frames in my house "out of square " or was I just crap at woodwork. Pedro owned an impressive black Wolseley 4/44; made up for him not being qualified for the "black gown" club

David Wn. Bryan, did you ever find a use/application for "The Laws of Thermodynamics" or were they just there to make the exams more difficult to pass!

Bryan D. Yes, it meant that I could understand, and laugh at, the Flanders and Swann song about the Laws of Thermodynamics. That's entropy man!

Bryan D. Or you could apply the 2nd law to Liverpool's season David, or to Wolves Ian ? Sorry guys, I do feel your pain (I think). :-) :-(

Ian H. You know how to hurt Bryan! We shall return, as the Wolves motto says "Out of darkness cometh light"

John R. I remember Cedric Parry telling me I was particularly good the 100 yards hurdles - while that was useful during athletics meets, I have yet to find a use for the specific skills of hurdling in my everyday life. It really looks out of place leaping over gurneys and other obstacles in the hospital!

Len E. Yes, winning an Egg and Spoon race in junior school has really stood me in good stead.

Pat C. Lads could I be so bold as to ask which soccer team Bryan supports?

Ron B. Ian, they have the best team in London tomorrow.

Bryan D. Arsenal, since 1948. Go on, have a go!

Ron B. Ooh to ooh to be ooh to be a gooner. I was told on a regular basis that I was for the high jump. Never did get in the team though

Ian H. Fantastic "FRENCH" manager, n'est-ce pas!!!!!!

Bryan D. Vraiment. Le patron est pur genie!

Pat C. I hope there's no charge for these French lessons!

Ian H. Just a pint of "Porter" will do Pat, remember you from way back!!!!

Pat C. Bad news for Liverpool tonight their goalie sent off.

Ian H. Carroll just scores 2-3 !!!!!!!!!

Pat C. Well done the Pool!

Ian H. Good game (free link on the net) ,lovely bubbly, who's for the drop with the mighty Wolves hope QPR are there!!!!

Ian T. How in the blazes did this conversation go from carpentry class to soccer? I was so looking forward to discussions about pencil boxes, the smell of hot horse glue and the curses of kids as they cut, grated and smashed their fingers or otherwise tried to maim themselves!

Pat C. You can blame the original "poster" for changing the subject from Thermodynamics to soccer!

Temporary Classrooms

Bryan D. The view from "A" pitch! The concrete pre-fab on the left was put up after the war and accommodated the fifth form in the years I was at the Grammar School. There were two classrooms. I suppose the wooden building was a later addition.

Phillip W. There is no trace of these buildings now

Chris G. I can remember those concrete classrooms being full of junk when we moved to Bushfield, there was all manner of things in there, old sports equipment and oddly stuffed animals, birds and fish in glass cases which all went to the tip probably,

Ian B. Spent my 5th year in the building on the right 64/65.

Chris G. I've a feeling they were done up for some use when we first moved there Gary. A few of lads helped Ken Speaks move all the junk to a skip before the decorators moved in.

Deborah G. One was used for French lessons when I was at Bushfield!

Ian B. I may be wrong but I have a feeling the girls used to have needlework classes in one of the two rooms on the left and remember doing RI in the other. Do they still do those at school these days?

Terry L. Think they had a Terrapin building later just beyond the wooden building, as I remember Popeye Elliott reading lovely poetry to us as we looked out over the school fields and across the railway line....

Terry L. Actually it might have even been that wooden building on closer inspection!!!

Andrew L. Yes Gary, Mrs Pennington had the class in the prefab. In my 4 years in that school I don't think I ever set foot in that prefab.

Kazza B. I remember attending some sort of holiday club in those buildings........ Happy days!! Xx

Brian E. The two classrooms were 13, typewriting room, and 14, Mr Elliot's form room. The single Terrapin at the end was Room 15, the 5th Form room. As Bryan remarked, the view is taken across 'A' Pitch. Football in winter, athletics & cricket in summer.

Brian E. We did Maths with Mr. Dunleavy in Room 15!

Dave P. I was a pupil in the 'Horsahut' as we knew it around 1980... This is the first pic I have seen of it. The little building on the right was gone by then... Thanks for bringing back the memories....

Ian H. Talking of Bryan's uncle, as well as teaching in the school he also gave gardening lessons. He once famously told my mate Trevor (Link) Hobson "Hobson boy! Did you know bees have hairy arses"!!! During one such lesson, according to Link that is.

Brian E. This photo must have been taken after 1970, when The Gables was nearing completion. The boys are both wearing maroon shirts. Up till 1968, boys wore one of two shirts for PE. The orange and maroon stripes of Northampton Town for football, and white with two Olympic style hoops, in maroon, for athletics. So this must have been taken when trendy new MK names were in vogue, and it became Bushymeadow or something!

Chris G. Nope it would be Moon Street still Brian, we didn't move into the new Bushfield till long after the Gables were finished and as a middle school there was no colour requirement for PE kit.

Becca H. I think we were the first year to not do 11 plus and the first lot to go to Moon Street for the two years before we went to Radcliffe. My lot started at Moon Street in Sept 68. Our first classroom was the temporary classroom that backed on to the wall that surrounded the neighbouring garden/orchard. Pete Beale and I once got caught nicking apples over the orchard wall. Pete must have begun his charm offensive at a very early age because the pretty French teacher accepted his explanation that we "fell" over the wall - that was actually taller than us! AND ....she never told Mrs Fitch or Mr Gee. Most house team sports only had teams differentiated by team colour "tabards" that you put over your head and tied at the sides. At the time I hated the maroon of my house which was Cheshire, after Leonard Cheshire

Brian E. Yes, that makes sense Becca; naturally you wore totally different uniforms and kit post 1968, after the changeover.

Becca H. Yes Brian - we started off from the outset with the Radcliffe uniform. Those who started in 68 were also the last lot that had the option to leave at the end of the 4th year at 15. The game of rounders was very popular then too. It was usually played in an area at the back far side of the Home Economics Classroom. Also remembered that last single classroom furthest away from the main building and separate from the two classroom hut. At the front of the classroom to the side of the teacher's desk was a big cage with a heater / boiler in it. It often broke down and we sat freezing and classes were often distracted by the caretaker coming to sort it out, I remember we had an Italian girl from Braddle for a while in our first year called (I think) Marissa Bordoni and she was never cold when the rest of us were. We did French in the hut next door, finding it hilarious for some reason to come out the front exit door of our classroom and turning left instead of right, then clambering round the back of the building, to go right round to get to just next door.

Brian E. I remember the boiler being down a few years before that. We were in one of that group of Terrapins, and Mrs Peglar had us all jumping up & down and clapping our arms to get warm. I guess that would be a reason to send the kids home today.

Becca H. I think a lot of good things have evolved over the decades to protect kids and make their lives easier perhaps safer - but I am torn between that sentiment and the question of whether we have (in many but not all cases) inadvertently produced less resilient and less resourceful young people.

Gareth G. The concrete building on the left was my old form room in 1966/7 when I was in the 3rd year Popeye Elliot was my form teacher. If anyone was ever slippered by Popeye they will know that his guilt at having to punish a boy would force him to say "This will hurt me me more than it will hurt you boy" I heard those words along with a few classmates quite a few times, but not as many as Martin Beale. The one on the right was a terrapin building in my day and used to be used for typing.

Gareth G. Hi Brian, yes I remember the name but can't put a face to it. I went on to finish up in 4PB in the terrapin buildings at the

side of the woodwork huts. Mrs Woodward was our form teacher. Only had 8 months to serve though finished at the Easter 1968 as I believe I was amongst the last cohort of kids to be able to finish at 15 due to the comprehensive system being implemented when school leaving age went to 16, how lucky was I ;-).
Don't know why but thought you were from Hanslope or one of the other nearby villages.

Brian E. Gary, were there two Gary Griffiths at that time at Moon Street? We had a GG in my class. The one I am thinking off got on the bus at Linford Turn. Yet you were living at the club weren't you?

Becca H. Hi Brian Eakins and Gareth Griffiths. Actually the last cohort to be able, legally to leave school was my year - many of whom left at 15 in 72. I was one of the rest of us that opted to stay on for the 5th form - thus leaving in 73. I thought this was the case - so checked it out on Wiki and this is what I found:
The Raising of school leaving age (often shortened to ROSLA) is the name given by Government to refer to changes regarding the legal age a child is permitted to leave compulsory education, usually falling under an Education Act. In most countries, the school leaving age often reflects when young people are seen to be mature enough within their society, but not necessarily when they are old enough to be regarded as an Adult.
In England and Wales, this age has been raised numerous times since the introduction of compulsory education in 1870. The most recent Raising of School Leaving Age occurrence was on 1 September 1972, following preparations which began 8 years prior in 1964. [1] This increased the legal leaving age from 15 to 16, leaving a gap year of school leavers who, by law, had to complete an additional year of education from 1973 onwards.
(I.e. from the academic year that commenced in 1973)

Gareth G. I stand corrected Becca; I bow to your informed knowledge on this occasion. I think I may be confused in that maybe early leaving (Easter) was may be abolished that year. I think you could only leave then if you had an offer of work which as I remember I had to show evidence of. Hope all is well with you :)

Brian E. Quite correct Becca, up to 1973, staying on for the Fifth Year was an option. Gareth, most students left at the end of the Summer Term, I was not aware of any who left after Easter. For want of anything else, most boys were virtually guaranteed employment at the Works in 1968 in that happy time of full employment.

Gareth G. Hi Brian, yep you got your head round that one OK. Gary Griffiths was a mate of mine later on not so much at school, when we both went out with the Watson sisters from Buckingham Street; he lived either on Jersey road or Anson Road and had a sister Lesley. As you rightly suspect I was Gareth Griffiths, also known as Gary or Griff and lived in the Top Club on Western Road.

Becca H. Yep all is well with me Gareth thanks. Only thing you should bow to is my skill in the speed with which I can click on Wikipedia! I think you are right about the Easter leaving thing too. I remember some of the girls in mine and Chris's sister year having to have a letter from their parents too to say they agreed with them leaving school. Was also wondering if that pub on Rolleston is still standing. Did you marry a local girl? How are Dawn, Clive and Keith and their families? A whole generation and then some has passed since I saw you lot.

Ian B. Hi Gareth. Were you in the same year as my brother Phillip? I feel I should know you but can't pin it down.

Gareth G. Hi Ian, I knew Philip well but the year above me as I remember. I also knew Marilyn who was in my year she was a constant escort when I was going out with Sheila Trew, she introduced me to The Beatles Sergeant Pepper which I wasn't really into but Marilyn used to bring it with her everywhere we went and it grew on me.

Gareth G. Hi Becca, yep the Major Oak is still there, Dawn Keith and Clive are still all fine I pop down to MK for the odd weekend about 3 times a year, Keith still lives in Nottingham and is now on his third marriage. I married a local girl who I was seeing when I gave you the lessons on that Honda 50. We have twin girls who are 30 now and have 4 kids between them and both have another on the way. Divorced from the first wife, although still friends. Married the love of my life in 1998 and have 3 step kids and 3 step grandkids so 9 grand kids between us come the summer, so 2 generations since last we met.

Andy M. Gareth. I was in 4PB, left summer 1967. I seem to remember our form teacher was a Miss Brown. Remember being in the terrapin hut, adjacent to the woodwork shed.

Gareth G. Hi Andy, I was the year following you. I do remember Miss Brown. She was Welsh and with my name I was a bit of a favourite of hers. When I was in Tom Whinnet's class in the first year, she was my history teacher.

Becca H. I remember Mrs W. turning to address the class falling right inside a glass display cabinet and 'showing her own wares' in 1968! As soon as we saw the only thing that was hurt was her pride - everyone spent the rest of the lesson chewing their lips really hard trying to keep the giggles in. As soon as we were outside the lesson a tsunami of guilty laughter made a wave across the yard!

The New Radcliffe School

Deborah G. On my recent 'tourist tour' of Wolverton I snuck into the Radcliffe and took this pic. I was amazed that 30+ years after I had left ... everything looked the same - even the paintwork!

Tricia D. Well 'snuck in'! lol

Deborah G. I did feel a bit 'naughty' Tricia ... didn't get caught though. Took my picture and ran for it. Guess being back in school makes you feel like that!

Andrew L. I did the same recently, didn't think of taking a photo though. I intend to get back inside the building soon.

Tricia D. Lol....funny x

Vivienne B. I've been inside a fair bit. Believe me not a lot has changed, and that's since I was there. lol

Andrew B. Going up to the top floor to registration everyday wasn't fun, especially when the bus was late. It looked grotty & out of date then. But one of the best places to go for a smoke, was almost were this photo was taken from. Didn't realize myself that it was 31 years ago when I left the Lower Sixth. Bet it hasn't changed on the inside.

Marc H. Looks like they got new windows.

Susan K. I visit the Radcliffe school on a regular basis. There have been a few minor alterations but essentially the inside of the buildings still feel the same. It is very strange, I go there as a professional but still feel like I am a naughty school girl when I am walking around during lesson time!

P 20: Radcliffe School Tower Block

Patsy G. I have done Zumba in the main hall a few times recently and believe it is the same paint!!

Elaine H. Anybody else want a visit? I go there everyday so would show you round.

Pete B. Ha ha, after 40 yrs ... couldn't wait to get out, now would like to have a look. lol

Elaine H. Perhaps we could have a 'group' tour.

Faye L. I was ecstatic when I finally left Radcliffe. lol

Wendy C. We called it Colditz...lol.

Stephen W. Our form class was the top floor in that block. It's no wonder we had a PE teacher as our form tutor haha!

Deborah G. Fortunately I was in the 'sporty' group in those days Stephen. Stairs were not so bad. Wouldn't make it every morning now!

Jane B. Debbie - but did you walk on the grass? We went to a Reunion there a couple of years back and I wouldn't let Brian walk across the front lawn in case anyone saw him !!!!!!

Terry L. Trees are taller but expect they would be 37 years later! Lord is that how long it's been?

Richie B. I'd love a tour.

Len E. My classroom top left.

Terry L. Lessons from Mr Tibbles in that one Len. We hid in the cupboards one lesson; can't remember the outcome... Probably another visit to creepy's office ...

Pina R. Had a quick walk around a few years ago. Looked the same to me only seemed a lot smaller than I remembered!

Nick C. I left in 1965.....went back in 1970 and first words I received were 'You owe for some photographs',,...not 'how are you?', 'what are you doing?' Never went back again!

Jacqueline G. I was there too very recently with a special ex pupil

Matt N. I had history on the top floor. My most lasting memory was Mr Clayton threatening to throw a student out the window. He actually picked a student up and walked to the window with them. It was to illustrate how events would change over time. This fuelled my interested in history to this day. Fantastic teacher.

Ralph C. We dropped golf balls from the top floor so we could get the elastic out of them to make catapults. Then Len Brooker and another would sit on the chairs and a piece of A4 folded paper would be launched at the blackboard. They nearly got the French mistresses hand one day. She was not impressed.

Phillip W. I hated that school.

Lynette M. Life for me at the Radcliffe was not good. I hated it. Couldn't wait to get out.

Phillip W. My art teacher at Radcliffe told me I was not good enough to go to art college and R. S. at that school was so crap I used to go to sleep in the class.

Wendy C. You rebel!

Phillip W. That not the worst thing. When I was asleep I got sent out and given detention for throwing paper around. So I ripped up the detention slip and said I was asleep, then walked out and left the school for the day.

89

Phillip W. Wendy C. can I ask how did you recognise me? It's been a while since I have put me as my profile pic

Wendy C. I didn't. I saw your name when I saw the woman you were speaking to. lol.

Phillip W. Ok cool. I was going to say I am not good with names or faces and I didn't wanna seem rude by not remembering you from any where.

Wendy C. No probs.

Phillip W. I was made by A4E to go to library to job search on Fridays so all I do is go in job search for hours and the leave. I never stay the whole time as I have other stuff to do.

Wendy C. First time I'd been...

Phillip W. Don't know how long I have to go for. I can't wait for the day when I don't have to do it. I can stay at the museum all day on Fridays then.

Wendy C. Are you in the shop?

Phillip W. Nah in Cellar scanning Wolverton Works cards.

Julie T. Used to go into this building for Mathis and English with Mr. Tibbles.

Nahida K. The building looks the same. Yes I used to go into this building for Geography.

Brian E. Younger members here won't remember The Milk Snatcher! Or indeed, free school milk. Today we have ludicrously over-priced so called energy drinks! To supplement the milk, we also had Jubblies of course.

Kim P. Brian how funny I was just talking a couple of days ago about the free milk we got (not Radcliffe years of course but we had it at Wyvern), miniature glass bottles, foil tops and paper straws... Did we get free biscuits too or did we have to bring our own? I can't remember.

Kim P. I was probably in one of the last years to get it as I was 8 when the Milk Snatcher got in.

Jackie N. I was among the first group to go to the Radcliffe - have visited since (with Bushfield pupils) and as everyone says, very little seems to have changed. I remember they were so proud of the new floors that we had to buy some slipper type shoes to wear as indoor shoes to try to preserve the highly polished look!

Nahida K. Yeah Kim Remember having free milk before morning break and sometimes after break, Those were the days. Now at present time what happens? Still get free milk?

Ivor S. Mr Morgan was the head and he had his office on the ground floor just to the left of the door.

Elaine H. The Head's office is still in the same place

Donna S. Think I had geography class in here and for some reason I do believe a music class. Can't remember teacher's name but all we had to do was compliment her on something she was wearing and that was all she would go on about . Didn't learn a thing - oh and math class...

Len E. Similar thing with Mr Hanley, just mention the RAF and he would be regaling us with his wartime memories. It was more like a History than a Maths lesson.

John B. Remember our history lessons in tower block with Mr. Whittock . Lovely man! Used to bring sweets in and share them. Not all teachers were like him. lol

Len E. Ahh, Mr. Whittock. I got on well with him. He had hands the size of shovels. You didn't want them crashing down on the desk in front of you.

Kim P. I think the only lesson I had in the old tower block was German. Had very few lessons at Morgan until I went into 6th form. Unless you count hiding in the recording studio when I was supposed to be in chemistry.

John R. Just to show how old I really am, I spent my first three years in the "tower block". I remember looking out of the top left window during the 2nd Form, which probably explains my lack of academic prowess during my time there. The only thing I really remember was that we had a religious education teacher, I think it was Mr Hay, who really used to struggle to get up the steps, and always arrived in class exhausted and spent the first ten minutes of every lesson recovering.

Alan C. Just a bit older than you John. I was in the 5th form when Radcliffe moved to the new school. I had no lessons in the tower block but remember that Cedric Parry used to be on the top to watch and make sure that we completed cross country runs that went over the fields towards Stony. Also we had to wear soft indoor shoes so as to not damage the wood floor. I remember as well that Harold Nutt's grand piano was rigged so that when he struck the first chord with gusto the top came crashing down. Morgan went a bit mad over that!!!!

Deborah D. Wow my house was Charnwood My daughter was in the tower blocks!! ... Where does time go?

Andy S. My form room was at the top of the tower block (Windsor) makes me tired just looking at it?

Vicky L. My house was Windsor in the tower block. Form tutor, Jesus looking Mr Taylor!!!

Vicki L. Now who can remember Windsor house head of year??? I was always sent to him!! But cannot remember 1980 - 1984 :)

Andy S. Ha ha I remember Mr Taylor. My form tutor was Mr Kay but I can't remember the head of Windsor?

Vicki L. Mr Kay was a teacher of mine too!!

Vicki L. Think head of house was Mr Whittaker or something!! Tall, stocky man!! Can see him now tutting at me!!! Not sure of name though?

Julie P. I started working there today!! I didn't attend it though as I come from Twickenham originally!!

Sarah K. Blimey there's a blast from the past! As you said happy days, that's the very tower block we used to throw eggs out of.

Andrew N. God that is one ugly building, and how old do I feel? The brand new Orchard Hall that I went to isn't even standing now.

Vicki L. I feel old as remember being in the terrapins, while it Orchard was being built. Our year was separated. Half went over to Orchard. Others, including me, were left in Morgan!!!

Andrew N. Yes but we still spent half the day crossing over for lessons in Morgan.

Vicky L. I only had about 2 lessons a week in Orchard!! Mainly passed it, doing Cross Country Bleugghhhhhh!!!:)

Sue L. Am I the only one who actually liked cross country? I much preferred it to gymnastics stuff they tried to get us to do! Xx

Eddie H. I was on first floor in Tibbles class then went over to Orchard and used to come over for woodwork with Mr Palmer and Engineering but in 4-5th yr was a very naughty lad and was in unit for over a year situated in art block next to Mr Blaine I think , Vicki you no that area as was wear ur Harrington was graffitied on

.... Oops never lived it down, and got 6 canes from Mr Johnstone ouch!

Sarah H. I loved Cross Country but then I was a weird child ha ha. I was in Ashdown House - anyone else there?

Eddie H. I was in Sergeant before it changed due to Orchard being built then Kielder.

Deborah D. Yvette didn't you hang about with David King?... I remember your name??

Deborah D. Who remembers Mr Henshaw (Charnwood) ... He thought I was the best student in the school ;)) lmao..

Geoff B. Oh no top floor of the tower block was my home room.

Ed C. The school results coming out of Radcliffe is one of the lowest in the area shame.

Julie P. Edward - don't know where your getting your information from but Radcliffe has just had a very good Ofsted report and is better then a lot of the schools in the area including Elizabeth Woodville School. The school has completely turned itself around.

Lisa H. Ed, wrong again !!!!! My kids are steaming along there, A* all the way !!!!!!!!!

Ed C. I am glad Julie if it has. Wasn't having a go but if you say is true then credit to the school WELL DONE!

Lisa H. Donna, I remember him, he had no idea how to control a classroom, I remember once he was in a right mood shouting and had tears in his eyes, coz we were all laughing so much.... he stomped out hyperventilating

Sam W. Am I the only person who for the life of her cannot remember what house she was in! For some reason Windsor rings a bell, but then so do most of them!

Vicky L. Anyone remember Mr Miles - Career adviser - He said I would make a great comedian ~ Hmmmm:)

Vicki L. Eddy Hayes. I indeed remember that area!! You were a very naughty lad, ruining my Harrington jacket!! That wall you always hung about was outside, where you were placed!!!

Becca H. Not saying all schools (including the Radcliffe) and teachers are perfect and faultless, and some may lack committed and clear leadership and support for teaching and non teaching staff. However, ALL schools are under immense pressure from

Government, OFSTED etc. to not only meet the demands and challenges of their pupils/students and their families, but also to administer a whole raft of paperwork and target led documentation these days that simply didn't exist in earlier decades (i.e. the 60's, 70's and much of the 80's). Society and its needs have driven many changes, without that being matched by equitable resources. Many teachers work long hours after work and at weekends marking and preparing and dealing with other issues they simply can't accommodate in the normal working week. Set in this context, it sounds like our Radcliffe needs all the support and motivational congratulations it can get for turning things round and demonstrating this with better and very encouraging results. I don't live in the area now but spent all my childhood and a bit beyond in Wolverton and still visit regularly and have strong family and friends ties to the area and always will and the Radcliffe needs all the support it can get to retain it place at the educational heart of the Wolverton Community. Exam results are not the only indication that a school is or isn't fulfilling its vital role in young peoples lives and sometimes target led, academic only measurements can blur the picture we see from the outside. Well done though for the recent results!

Vicki L. I personally couldn't think of a worse career than being abused by nasty feral kids in some area's - xxx

Senior school kids I mean!!!

Becca H. That's what makes me mad when people slag off public service workers. I have worked in the Public Sector for over 30 yrs and when people outside Social and Health and other public sector work drone on about how easy we have it - pensions tra la la la. I say walk in our shoes and have our jobs then you can have our pensions. Majority of Health and emergency service and public sector workers report they have on more than one occasion been verbally and sometimes physically assaulted, sworn at etc. and its seen by some people outside these jobs as 'par for course' ?? xx

Vicki L. Window cleaner just came £12 for 10min - Now that's a good job eh?

Becca H. Go halves with you for the ladders then Vicki ! x

Ian S. 90 people allegedly working in the council on £100,000 per annum. This can't be right can it? That's 8 quid for every 10

minutes work 52 weeks a year - a lot more than the poor window cleaner with no pension or holiday pay.

Vicki L. Ah but window cleaners, get free porn, cups of tea & fresh water!! Now that's works perks!!!

Chris G. Okay Vicki you've convinced me, you hold the ladder, I'll climb ;)

Becca H. Eeewwww Vicki Levitt! That just made me remember those AWFUL films - Robin someone or other in the 'Confessions of a Window Cleaner .... Ugh!

Ron B. Ask with Becca and before you ask, I did not watch them or appear in any of them.

Becca H. Not even a 'bit' part Ron ?

Ron B. You couldn't leave it could you?

Becca H. I could not let it could I? (Reeves and Mortimer made me say this).

Vicky L. Chris how long will I have to hold the ladder? I get bored easily!!

Chris G. Just till I stop peering through the window, sorry I mean just till the windows are clean Vicki ;)

Ron B. I spend a lot of time up ladders and have never seen any porn, where does this happen Vicki, will have to give them a quote

Jacqueline G. You lot are so funny...its priceless...I am not turning the telly on tonight I am going to stay tuned in here !!!!!

Paul B. Back to Radcliffe. Anyone remember the gym being burnt down just before exams. Would have been about 1983.

Ron B. Convenient that.

Vicki L. Yes Paul. We were all outside watching it burn!! My brother was one of the firemen ~ who fell through the roof ~ all took a sharp in breath ~ then he popped up. Two cheers!! It was someone in my year, that set fire to it!!

Eleanor C. Yeah, I'd just started at Radcliffe (about a week or so) when the hall burned down - loved having a week off! Sarah, I was in Ashdown, Mr Andrew's form.

Form tutors

John C. Just for fun, those of us that went to the Radcliffe, name your form tutor, what they taught and which hall you were in. Mrs

95

McIvor (for 2 years, Miss Beardsworth for 2) both taught French and was in Orchard hall

Donna S. Only at Radcliffe almost a year. Form tutor Mr Whitlock... know I had him for Religious Studies. Can't remember if anything else... and we were in one of the well I call them portables.

Jacqueline G. Mrs Blagden, Mathematics.

Jacqueline G. Mrs Harry in 6th form.

Sue L. Mr Heatley, Applied Science and Technology, Orchard Hall.

Julie W. Mrs Reen, Art I think and Mr Goosey, geography. xx

John R. As I am ancient, I went to the Radcliffe pre all of this hall business. My last year I was in 5R4 and Maureen Varley, who taught Geography, was our form teacher.

Jenny D. Mr Marston was my tutor, taught English. Orchard. Had Mrs Smith for French who was head of Ardon. Great teacher. Rip x

Donna B. Mr Clark he taught technology Morgan hall ;0)

Colin T. Becca., Angie.........HELP lol, I remember 10...2....4 Friday afternoon as it was going home time xxxx

Heather B. Mr Hodges - French...Orchard Hall...Mrs Smith Head of House. Arden...fantastic Teacher...also taught French...always made me say Onions!!!!

Elaine S. You would love it even more now then Colin as they finish at 3 pm lol

Sue L. Poor Mr Hodges I wonder if he is still there? We gave him merry hell in class.

Billy L. Mr John, Geography teacher. The proper one and only Radcliffe, not that excuse they've recently demolished!

Gary Cr. Mrs Jean Blagden, 2S1 taught Maths I think? Only had one hall when I was there!!

Julie B. Mr Stewart S2S Orchard hall Salcey House English teacher had bingo head hair. I think he still teachers at the school.

John C. Miss Smith was a great head of house, was in a state of shock for a week when I heard she was killed by the double mini roundabouts near Orchard. She was pregnant too. Got confused when I read the story in the papers as they used her married name, I think it was Mrs Grewcock.

Andrew L. Mr Ashley, Mr Buckle, Mrs Platt, there were several, I went 2R2, 2S5, and then I went to Roberts on the Square and got glasses and went 3R1, 4R1, 5R1.

Jean G. Mrs Smith when I was in 4th and 5th year, French, Mr Miles, Science when in 3rd year

Sheila H. Pickle Harrison was my form tutor. My house was Sergeant.

Mike W. Form Tutor, Mrs Ward. She was a Maths teacher, but not mine; I was in the slightly thicker set. Orchard hall, Arden house.

Elaine S. Mrs Ward known as Mrs Pepperpot!

Mike W. Thought it was Mrs Bun Head?

Sheila B. Martin Gee, maths and p.e. But no Orchard/Morgan in my day.

Cate P. Anyone remember Mr Henshaw, Windsor house. Think he started teaching about 5mins before I started at Radcliffe. Lovely chap though, Shrewsbury town fan I seem to remember.....

Faye L. Mr Stuart, science year 8 and 9 Morgan hall, Miss Davies , geography year 10, Morgan hall and Miss de Souza , art year11 Orchard hall xx

M. Udhus Mr Smith, taught Maths, Morgan Hall.

Lee Ann S. Mr Pucci - what a legend!

Graham S. Agree Lee-Anne what a great teacher. Went on a few ski trips with him.... He also did great morning assembly :-)

Brian L. Mr Pucci, Windsor House & he taught French. He only retired a couple of years ago. As Leanne said a legend. Told awful jokes too.

B. Kelly Mr Cox (Batman), Maths, Rutherford

Julie L. Mrs Marshall (Morgan Hall) can't remember what she taught.

Julie L. I was also in Burnham House

Sue Mr Lawrence History teacher Orchard hall.

S.Annal Mr Clayton, think he was Geography, Kielder, then Mr Ainsworth, Biology for the last year.

Sally C. Mr Lawrence History 2nd and 3rd yr., Mr Miles? 4th yr., Mr Ainsworth Science 5th yr. - Keilder Orchard Hall

Chris G. Sticks Burton, physics.

Steve B. My 1st year in 1966, Miss Davey, great Maths teacher, bit of an old sweetie too...I was later in Sargent House...way before Orchard/Morgan Halls

Colin H. Mr Llewellyn ... Rutherford House.... Tuat mee Ingleesh.... Oh yeah and how to smoke!!!!

Lisa H. Mr.Raw, taught Geography, Ashdown house in Morgan

Shirley V. Mrs Shewan, English.

Sue C. Sally I can only remember Mr Lawrence and Mr Ainsworth, 3rd and 4th years are a blank!

Stephen M. Mr Smart.

Craig P. Mr Kaye cracking fella always smelt of old Woodbines :)

How do I remember that?

Pina R. Can anyone remember any sayings or verses they were taught to remember things. The two I remember are - 'Richard of York gave battle in vain' - to remember the colours of the rainbow & in maths we were given the word 'bodmas' to remember the order in which to do our arithmetic - 'brackets over division, multiplication, addition & subtraction'......

Ron B. I before E except after C.

Andrew L. SOHCAHTOA

Colin T. Twiselton Get out of this class face the wall & put your hands on your head.......Me being a naughty boy......Again xxxx

Pat C. 30 days hath September, April, June and November, all the rest have 31 except February which has 28 and 29 in each leap year.

Jean G. Never Eat Shredded Wheat, to learn where points of compass were

Graham T. Some people have curly black hair through persistent brushing—Sine = perp over hypotenuse, cosine = base over hypotenuse; tangent = perp over base.

Pat C. Remember, Remember the 5th of November, gunpowder treason and plot.

Maria M. I remember Sue Sawkins In Bushfield said this one: *Big Elephants always use small Exits* - to remember how to write "Because."

Penny G. Lazy fox jumps over the hedge" I think that was what it was as it supposed to be all the letters in the alphabet

Hazel S. *The quick brown fox jumped over the lazy dog.* That used all the letters on the keyboard.

Ian B. We used to run a test tape to test the comms/printers. "THE QUICK BROWN FOX JUMPS OVER THE LAZY DOG'S BACK 1234567890" the idea being it tested every character and upper and lower case.

Hazel S. Should have been 'The quick brown fox jumps over the lazy dog'. It has been a long while since I learnt this at Mrs. Holland's in the Wolverton Road, who gave shorthand and typing lessons.

Maurice W. TOACAHSOH

Pina R. Explain what they mean Andrew, Maurice, & Graham!

Maurice W. Sorry, Tan=Opp/Adj, Cos=Adj/Hyp, Sin=Opp/Hyp

Andrew L. I was at a race meeting and I noticed the name of a racehorse was Sohcahtoa, and I couldn't work out why the name was familiar, so I thought about it for a minute and remembered the Bushfield trigonometry lessons.

Andrew L. Oh, and Sohcahtoa was 25/1 so I backed him each way and he placed for a nice little payout. :)

Chris G. Was the jockey Douggie Sackett Andrew? He loved that bloody word.

School Dinners

Bryan D. These should be the most forgettable meals of my life, but somehow the impression is a deep and lasting one - watery mashed potatoes served in a scoop, grey industrial-tasting tinned peas, tapioca pudding (frogspawn) with a dollop of jam in the middle, boiled cabbage with a bitter taste, meat that may have been sliced off the bottom of a carpet. . .. . and other delights . . . .

Julie W. God, tapioca bane of my life! xx

Becca H. Liver thicker and tougher than the sole of a Doc Marten's boot.

Sue L. Oh my am I the only one who loved all the dinners they cooked at school, spam fritters, liver and onion, chocolate sponge with chocolate custard, sponge with strawberry flavoured custard, ooh I am salivating just thinking about them ;-)

Dave M. Can't have been that bad, there was always a long queue for seconds!

Sue L. Yes there was always a long queue for seconds usually with me in it for pudding lol.

Richie B. I loved them specially the meat balls we called hedge hogs and of all the puddings tapioca was one of my favourites.

David W. Nothing wrong with the "Northern" delicacy of " tinned processed peas" - an essential part of Fish, chips & peas !

Len E. Nice menu Sue...but not on the same plate :)

Hazel S. I worked in the kitchen at the Radcliffe School up to when the County Council finished the school dinners. The dinners then were really good nothing like we had when we were at school Bryan.

Bryan D. I had recognised that things had moved on from the 1940s and early 50s when diet was generally restricted anyway. Yes we ate everything because we were hungry and growing and we were trained to eat everything on the plate. That lesson I got early at Nursery school when I refused to eat some seaweed (or whatever it was) and was punished by being denied "afters" and being made to stand facing the wall for the playtime period.

Gary K. At least they were nutritiously balanced - not like the rubbish youngsters eat these days. I can't remember many obese kids at school either, which would have been down to the fact that they were all eating proper food and playing outside rather than sitting on their bums all day.

Steve B. "Concrete an Custard". The weekly treat!

David E. I remember being naughty deliberately at lunch time because you got put on Mr Garner's (the head masters) table, guaranteed large portions and always first for seconds (in the junior school).

Karen C. The treacle sponge at Wyvern is still one of my fondest food memories! Bryan. You're lucky if you had actual mashed potato - our generation only ever had 'smash.' Sue, do you

100

remember the cheesecake from Orchard Hall school dinners? Yum or what??

Jill G. I liked the school dinners, most of it anyway. Silly really what sticks in my mind is the lovely homemade salad cream they made I have never tasted anything like it since.

Margaret C. I don't know what we would have done as children without our Free school dinner and our daily bottle of milk..

Chris G. Baked beans and mashed potato, still the best comfort food.

Nick C. I loved school dinners too.................For my last year, my dining companions were Dave Pakes and 6 young ladies !....I always had enough to eat, as the ladies were figure conscious.................plus two added bonuses. I was friendly with one of the school cooks, and our table backed onto the staff dinner room, so that was good for extras too, coz they always finished before us !.......well I WAS a growing lad !

Margaret C. WIGWAMS....Chris if you add sausages..lol

Janice M. I remember desert one day was gooseberries, I had never had them so got them. Disliked them immensely was made to eat them and then threw up everywhere lol

Becca H. Dinner queue was a place you got to look at the boys from older years you had a crush on - while they were standing still! No additional comments please Steve Baker!

Steve B. Becca, as if! (and by the way I remember that clearly!)

Bryan D. Yes they were real spuds Karen. Your Dad and I were raised before they invented artificial food - although processed peas, margarine and Camp Coffee were already a step in that direction. Treacle sponge eh? Probably made with Lyle's Golden Syrup. Can you still get it?

Andrew L. Bushfield used a stacked tray made of white plastic. Sort of oval shaped with recesses for the food, cutlery and beaker. No separate plates. These were stacked near the entrance, collected on the way in while we queued for the hatches. Used to get mashed potato served with ice cream scoops.

Bev P. At the infants school they used to bring the food to the tables on trolleys and we would all go "Ooooooo" at the same time when they brought it out. Did anyone else think the custard sometimes tasted of hairspray?

101

Steve B. Bev you all went "Ooooooo" in harmony? Probably why your custard tasted of hairspray. You must have been worth it:)

Brian E. I know people make jokes about this, but I always enjoyed school dinners. After a cursory check that our hands were clean we used to troop into the dining hall at Moon Street and sit down at tables set for eight. It was always meat/pie/fish and two veg, with many different puddings. Mrs. Rolls was the lunchtime supervisor, it was she who said Grace, and kept us relatively quiet. As Bryan mentioned, it was always real spuds and fresh veggies. In the Fourth Year, my friend & myself rushed to take control of the top or spare table; this was to take up the odd numbers. But we still had dishes of veg. meant for eight. This was considered quite a prestigious table of which to be monitors! After dinner, some boys hung around the back door to the kitchens. Tom Winnett would emerge with his hands full of whatever dry pudding was left over and distribute it. This would be washed down with the luke warm left over bottles of school milk. We in our turn would then carry the crates out into the alley behind Victoria Street for collection. School dinners were ok by me!

Pat C. I had school dinners in Wolverton so I had more soccer time. Girls used to give their frogspawn to the boys. Any seconds? Was a most asked question, mid fifties.

Jackie S. Andrew, I have an ice cream scoop just for that purpose, although I don't use it very often. My daughters and grandchildren have had great pleasure over the years in having 'ice cream mash'. Never has any lumps though.
I used to love the iced sponge with coconut on top, with pink custard.

Bryan D. Pink custard! Served in large metal jugs. Amazing!

Alan C. My memories from the fifties are not pleasant, and completely in line with Bryan's original post, it took me years to get over the watery potatoes and the boiled cabbage, I complained so much my parents allowed me to go home at lunch time. One other memory is the warm milk in the small bottles that had been left outside the infant school all morning, I could never drink it

Pat C. Never liked the chocolate sponge, still don't. Never liked peas until Wolverton school dinners. Peas were tasteless and I was hungry so that problem was solved.

102

Richie B. You lot were too fussy I didn't get to this size refusing food.

Chris G. A friend said a few years ago about kids not eating this and that nowadays that we're of a generation that if he didn't eat what was put in front of you, you didn't eat at all. Probably all the more true for the generation before.

Richie B. That's right Chris none of this making them separate meals either although I did turn my nose up at stuffed sheep's heart that wasn't a school dinner though.

Bryan D. Sheep's head? Brains on toast? Tripe? Not that I've ever ventured into this territory but I did hear of some who did.

Richie B. Ooh I've had tripe from Lancashire and the meat pies and I love faggots lol.

Brian E. Because my own father had been brought up with the austerity of Cockney London & the war years, he regarded many things, such as bananas as treats. Not regular diet. Of course he would not have even seen a banana during and after WW2. So, his main reply to us when we asked for something like a banana was "only if you have a slice of bread with it." This of course ruined it's appeal to me. A slice of bread made it a 'proper' meal, and not an unnecessary luxury in his eyes.

Jill G. That's as bad as eating the tin fruit with bread and butter

Brian E. Not only frogspawn, we had dog-sick and drainpipes as well didn't we. But, the days we had fish in batter along with beetroot & chips (the only time we did have chips) were wonderful. No left-over's that day!

Pamela J. I remember the Americans coming to Stony and we shouted to them and they threw gum to us but we never got fruit.

Len E. Jill, you have reminded me of a childhood treat...dipping b&b in the juice from a tin of fruit and Carnation milk.

June L. There were plenty of Yankees where we lived at the time, we use to say "Got any gum Chum?"

Pat C. Forgot about gum used to get it thrown at us as convoys passed through Tingewick early 50s.

Jill G. lol Len yuk I my hubby Nigel said many times that he had to have this as a kid and warned his mum never to subject our kids to it.

J. Parker Pink custard, ummm.

103

Len E. Ha-ha, Jill we never had to have it, our mum rolled her eyes when we ate it :)

Jill G. My poor hubby had to he was told it will fill him up he never forgive her for that.

Ruth E. I loved my school dinners mind my Auntie Edie was one of the cooks so knew the food was going to be good....

a few seconds ago.

TB tests.

Ian H. Anybody remember those TB "scratch" tests at school? You had to wait a bit to see if your body had responded to the scratch correctly, seem to remember if the little spots went a bit red you were OK. A friend of mine(from a poor family) failed the test and he had treatment!!

Ruth E. I had them can't remember what age, maybe 11? Mine must have been OK cos I am still here, although Aunty Grave had TB in the 40's I think?

Pat C. I think reported TB cases are on the rise again.

Ian B. It was the Mantoux test. If you had a negative reaction you got the BCG vaccination if it was positive it was an indicator that you may have been exposed to TB and further tests were required.

Janice M. As I had the BCG I am not allowed more TB tests as it will always come back positive and the area gets to be so big and painful, like an allergic reaction

Marc H. My mum had TB in the late 1940s - took two years out of life type thing. I heard there are some cases on the increase.

Janice M. My mom's step mom had TB too....took quite a while to get rid of it.

Jennifer T. I had the BCG vaccination. My Mum had TB in the late 40s then again in the late 50s she had 3/4 of one of her lungs removed, and lived till she was 70.

Ian H. Jennifer, didn't she have a smoke too, or was that Mrs Ellis?

Jennifer T. She smoked till the 60s, we were not so clued up then.

Ian H. I seem to remember cadging a few off her, good old Eva XX

Helen P. I never did have mine!!

John R. I have to have a TB test every year because I work in a hospital and there are an increasing number of patients that have TB. I get a reaction every time, not because I have the TB antibody, but I have an allergy to the preservative used in the test. Itches like mad for about a week.

That's not what I heard

Becca H. Mishearing things...... I remembered today (for no apparent reason ..... as is often the case in middle age!) being sent to the often formidable Mrs. Fitch by Mr. Gee for giggling in class and looking out the window too much. This would have been 1969 at Moon Street. On arrival at said Lady's Court Martial Chambers, she asked me how I would describe my behaviour and attitude???? However she didn't give me a chance to even attempt a mumbling answer she said in her loud voice "Because I would describe you Rebecca Gleadell as a runt!" OMG How shocked was I??? Wouldn't have expected even her to call me that! Anyways, I was made to stand and think about my attitude and behaviour in the hall by myself until lunchtime, at which time she came and simply said "GO! and don't let me have to speak to you about this again this term!!" That afternoon Mr. Gee called me back into to class and asked me what Mrs. Fitch had said to me. I bit the inside of my mouth so hard it bled a bit as I was desperately trying not to laugh really what she had called me. So taking a deep breath and looking firmly at the floor, I said "Mrs Fitch said she would describe me as a runt". Mr.
 Gee looked like he was going to fall off his chair in shock! He clearly didn't believe me and walked out telling me to stay where I was. He was gone a few minutes and came back with his hand over his mouth - and looking back now as an adult I think he was trying not to laugh. He had been to see Mrs. Fitch and apparently she had called me 'ERRANT' and not 'a runt' at all!!
Jane B. Ha Becca - but I can understand it as Mrs Fitch did talk a bit "posh" and sometimes it was a bit difficult to tell exactly what she was saying !!!! Mind you - could have been worse - if it had

been Richie in there then "runt" would probably hae been terribly misheard !!!!!!!!

Jane B. *have* NOT hae - God, I'm turning Scottish !!!!

Becca H. It's Kitty G winding you up when you are out playing with her kids Jane - that's all! x

Pete B. You were a little ERRANT . But I was a RUNT .. or near offer.

Becca H. Runt Rage was the way forward in them days Pete xx

Colin T. I was a good Boy......So there, I use to take Miss Fitch a little bag of currants in each day, Then Miss Fitch said Colin have I upset you, I said No, Why, Miss Fitch said you have stopped bringing me a little bag of currant & I did so enjoy them, I said that because me rabbit died.......Think about it ?

Susan N. Colin tears are streaming down me face cant stop laughing.

Penny G. Colin Twiselton you are as bad as Ron Baker

Ron B. Oi

June L. Did you tell Miss Finch you loved her as you handed her the Rabbits Currants Colin? xx

Terry L. Fitch Mum Fitch ! Xx

Colin T. June, I did not know what LOVE was in them days, I thought it was for stirring me Tea lol........Think about that one as well xxxx

June L. If I want to put Fitch Terry I WILL

Colin T. Brilliant June! You tell him. Terry, your Mother has Spoken

Pat C. June, if you had put Fitch as per last post you would have been correct and Terry would not have had to chastise you!!

June L. It didn't take me long to work that out Colin, be careful you don't scald yourself.

June L. I didn't want to put Fitch, I'm use to being Chastised xx

Terry L. Finch Mum Finch.

June L. Who's Finch?

Angie A. I was sent to Mrs Fitch once by Mr Oakrind (not sure if spelling correct) for chewing gum in Chemistry. She used to have some red and green lights or something on her door - if I remember correctly and if red was on she was engaged and you weren't allowed to knock the door - red was showing when I got to

106

the office so I wandered aimlessly back to class to tell him I couldn't see her, and he said he was going to take me there after class but when the end of lesson finally came I sneaked out quietly with everyone else and Mr Oakrind forgot all about it thankfully. suppose I was lucky he didn't hurl a blackboard rubber at me as he frequently did if you weren't paying attention. !!!!

Jane B. The French teacher John-Pierre Rasle once threw a blackboard rubber at me - but I moved to one side, it whizzed past my right ear and hit David Wallace on the side of the head !!!!!

Ralph C. My brother Bernie was sent to her often enough worst thing was if we visited our Gran she already knew about it they knew each other.

June S. Angie mentioned Mr Oakrind. I remember him. We used to look at smoke thought the microscope so many times just so that he could have a fag during lesson time! He liked to have the girls in the front row so that he could look down our tops from his stage, and I remember ducking as he whizzed the blackboard eraser at someone. Wouldn't get away with any of that now!

June L. That's always been a thing with teachers throwing the blackboard eraser that happened in my day. They also hit you on the knuckles with drumsticks or hit you round the face with keys in their hand. Not very nice, can you imagine what kids would do these days.?

Terry L. Flinch Mum Flinch !

Brian E. This did not really happen at Moon Street. Mr. Dunleavy used to throw our Maths book to us, not at us. But that's about all.

Ron B. Ah Mr Oakrind. Had a bit of a thing for Miss Marshall in the next door classroom, which conveniently had an adjoining store cupboard.

Pat C. Terry, at the extreme risk of incurring the not inconsiderable wrath of your mother, is there a Spec Savers near her? After reading this post I have finched, sorry fitched, sorry flinched and will apologise now saucy June, sassy June. Got it now, sorry June.

Ron B. Pat, you will be at the back of the class facing the wall with me and Colin if you're not careful.

Pat C. I suppose there's worse places to be, I'm quietly confident the Bucks/Kerry charm will work or am I digging a Colin-Ron-Len hole for myself?

Pete B. I was once queuing to get into class and Mrs Fitch asked why I wasn't at school the previous day and I said I was 'watching telly miss' she lifted me by the hair and took me out of line and asked again to witch I replied I watched the investiture of Charles as prince of Wales at Caernarvon castle, she made me write an essay about it that day. Afterwards she told me I had probably learnt more that day watching TV than I had all year .

I also learnt that as I wasn't to become Royalty I better get off me ass from watching telly and work to make it in life ..

June S. Re Brian's comment above, Oakrind was my chem. teacher at Moon St! You were either lucky or a very good boy ;-)

Brian E. June, this was prior to the 68 change. Sounds like things were different after that.

June L. I was working in my garden just a while ago, Buddy was out there with me playing, I threw a little ball for him to run after which he did, I shouted out to him Fitch Buddy Fitch instead of Fetch.

Becca H. Have to go now and top up the feeders for Goldfitches June xx One of them is really small - in fact only a couple of itches high! Xx

Becca H. Only joking Terry - just take what I say with a pitch of salt luv xx

Pat C. Becca you are a Fitch sorry witch!

Terry L. I saw a Gold flinch this morning, There no such thing as a Gold Flatulent !

Ian H. One of the best teachers I had the privilege to be taught by was the Rev Peter Gravett (a Methodist minister from Olney) who was an English Lit teacher at Wolverton College. Great man.

4 What we did in our spare time

Collecting

Julia B. I collected stamps when I was a child......What did you collect?......Do children/grandchildren collect stamps these days?

Chris G. Football programmes.

Ian H. Footballer pictures from ciggy packets Julia, not mine by the way I didn't start 'til I was about 14!!!!!

Dave M. Bruises mostly !!

Richie B. Never did collect any thing as a kid nor been one for hobbies. Seem to like collecting men and vodka bottles now though :)

Pat C. Carried on with stamp collection inherited from my mother. When we left UK in 64 had to give away my Hornby 00 train set mounted on a folding table and my 72 Dinky cars. You will note I remember the number to this day!

Julia B. The Hornby set + 72 Dinky cars would be worth a small fortune now. My friends hubbie, aged 60, collects them still. The fact that you remember that you had 72 is amazing, must have hurt!

Jill G. Brooches I have been collecting them for more years than I care to remember, I frame them

Richie B. Oh you would have loved mums brooches. Sadly Marl gave them all to the charity shop something she regrets now in hindsight.

Stephen C. Jimi Hendrix LPs

Bryan D. My son had quite a good collection of Star Wars figures from the late 70s (paid for by Dad of course) and in the early 90s when they became collectible decided they would be worth a year's university tuition. However, before he could cash in on his collection, his mother (my ex) had concluded they were so much junk and had given them away.

John R. I got a stamp collection. My Nan got my into it around 15 years ago, though to be fair I don't think I have added to it in around 10 years, still got a few books and a load of unsorted loose ones. I was mainly just after pre-decimal British ones...will get back on it one day though.

Ian H. My mother's second husband had a good collection of Toby jugs.

Ron B. The Post Office are restricting the sale of stamps at the moment. Before the price rise I might add.

June L. I've still got my Stamp Album I had as a child, I have Pete's too.

Helen P. Marbles! used to break my heart if I lost any to my mates so stopped playing!

Becca H. Old Pennies and halfpennies - still got quite a few

Julia B. N.B. Now have a very good collection of junk!

J Steensel Had a beautiful stamp collection. My mum even bought me a huge leather Stanley Gibbons album for one of my birthdays, but because my ex father in law had given me quite a lot of his stamps which were in boxes. My husband took the whole collection away from me.

Becca H. Jackie - he should have been made to pay you 'stamp duty'! x

Steve A. Bubble gum cards, Joe 90, UFO, Captain Scarlet to name a few.

Becca H. And as previously 'sibling scrapped' on here about - Man From U.N.C.L.E cards! ha-ha x

Steve A. Yeah I think that really left its mark Becca.

Becca H. Ha ha - Clipped 'him round the Kuryakin for that one Steve - but would never leave Napoleon to go Solo! x

Steve A. Ha ha, trying to think of a witty word play for Waverly but it's too early.

Terry L. A comprehensive and varying collection of cardboard boxes that all fitted inside each other like a Matryoshka doll ! but we were happy...

Becca H. Lucky you Terry! I had a set of those too - but mine was the earlier imaginary set - I simply loved them! X

Maurice H. Stamps, Cigarette Packets, Matchbooks/boxes, Anything that looked interesting

Pat C. I see Becca collected pennies/half pennies, I was old enough to collect farthings!

Ron B. Groats in my case Pat.

110

Ian H. I had quite a few arrears;-)

Bryan D. Train spotting which is a collecting activity.

Pat C. Only train spotting I ever did was in Wolverton as I fished during one summer holiday in the 50s.

Mike W. Tried stamp collecting, only marginally less boring than fishing.

Children's TV

Becca H. For those who lived through and loved the 60's ! x PINKY & PERKY

Constance O. Now that is a flashback

Colin T. I will take your word for it Becca, I am not old enough to remember these

John R. That was top flight BBC entertainment for us kids. Who needed "mind enhancing chemicals" when we had singing pigs doing covers of Chubby Checker!

Donna S. Becca well this explains a lot .. lol I am amazed we are all "normal"' lol

Becca H. Yeah - and that's without taking into account the 'Tufty Club', Tingah and Tucker and Mr Piper! x

Becca H. Twiz is fibbing again Miss Cummings!

Jackie S. Does anyone remember The Time Tunnel?

Len E. I liked Muffin the Mule....before it was a criminal offence.

Becca H. Blimey Len have you become Ron's deputy at Innuendos 'R' Us !

Colin T. Becca......I Love Yoooooooo, lol Ok so I remember A little bit lol xx Tufty Club Now that is one I loved, That was in the Infant School along Church Street, was the head mistress there Mrs Brown xx

Len E. Ron is a hard act to follow...but I'll do my best.

Donna S. Mrs. Brown you got a lovely daughter .....

Becca H. I seem to remember the Tufty Club was something to do with Road Safety? x

Ron B. Len, It's hard keeping it up, I must admit.

Constance O. How about Andy Pandy?

Ron B. Magic Roundabout.

111

Becca H. Oh for goodness sake! here we go again into "Don't Get Many of Them to the Pound Missus" mode with Da do Ron Ron and his Eccles Cake Accomplice! x

Donna S. Bill and Ben, Magic Roundabout, Andy Pandy, Blue Peter, Crackerjack

Ron B. Now shut your face missus, titter ye not!

Steve B. Still got my Tufty Club hanky somewhere! (along with my Man from U.N.C.L.E membership card...and er.. my James Bond Beretta!)

Becca H. Shame about Len really, cos as the Hollies once said- "I love Jennifer Eccles

Becca H. Retaliation mission complete - cos Ron will not be able to stop humming that Hollies song for hours now) hehemwhahhaha x

Len E. Becca, believe it or not I went out with girl called Jenny, good job that we did not marry.

Ron B. Or wolf whistling

Becca H. No Len ! Really? - Mind you now you've said that Ron will be saying he once dated a girl from some obscure village called 'Ruby Tuesday' x

Becca H. Just nicked this wee snippet off the Net. *1961 - The Tufty Club for under-fives was launched. More than 30,000 books about road safety were issued to parents.*

June L. When I was pregnant with Terry, my Mum, who was a dressmaker, made me a maternity dress designed like Pinky & Perky dresses. It was red & white Gingham lol, . Does that tell you anything?

Becca H. OMG June - that could have made you have a little piglet or Heidi tablecloth instead of Terry! x

Marc H. Trouble is I can remember the twisting pigs from Crackerjack wish that would come back.

June L. I was waiting for that Becca x

Becca H. Oh dear June - I may be becoming a tad predictable as a result of hanging out too much on here with Ron Baker! x Lol x

Ron B. Oy, I'm still here. Off to the pub now, I will know if you talk about me.

Marc H. Anyone remember Supercar another Gerry and Sylvia Anderson show?

Pat C. Anyone remember The Flowerpot Men and Little Weed? they would have been replays of replays in the sixties!

Constance O. I was watching The Flowerpot Men this afternoon on You Tube.

Pat C. Don't see any mention of Sooty and Sweep, or Sesame Street which helped my young ones to count by interacting with the programme, 1 2 3 4 5 6 7 8 9 10 then 10 9 8 7 6 5 4 3 2 1 etc

Ron B. Flobadobalop

Pat C. Hello Bill, Hello Ben. Or was it Hello Ron Hello Len?

Becca H. Liking your style Pat!

Lesley W. What about Muffin The Mule !!!!!

Becca H. See Len's comment further back in the thread Lesley x

Becca H. It was really difficult Lesley, keeping Len and that other Bad Lad Baker (Ronaldo) in order yesterday x

Lesley W. You do a good job !!!!

Becca H. Ta Luv x hehehe x

Ron B. Snigger

Fishing

Bryan D. When I lived in Canada I went fishing in the Northern Lakes with a friend. He told me a story about his one-time visit to England, where he watched a fisherman beside a canal catching very small fish and putting them into a keep net. He remarked, "Where I come from, we put fish that size back in the water." He got this response, "Where I come from we learn to mind our own business!"

I spent many a happy hour on the banks of the canal or river Ouse catching gudgeon, dace, perch, roach, the odd bream and occasional pike. Anyone else with memories to share?

Chris G. Used to go piking under the Iron Trunk. It was the only kind of fishing that interested me, no patience to look at a float all day. Never did catch one mind, all my mates did.

Pat C. Down the steps at the Bradwell end of Wolverton, fishing for perch and anything else that would bite. Crossing off the numbers of trains that passed off my trainspotter's book. Mid 1950s.

Ian T. My Father made me a fishing rod out of an old WW2 tank antenna. It had short sections and a wire threaded through them all with a spring that pulled on them. It folded up to about 2 feet long to carry it but to open it all I had to do was to take it out of its bag hold one end and kind of throw the rest away from me. It would snap straight all on it's own. It was rather heavy but I used to sit by the canal near the Galleon for hours and hours using bread and cheese for bait and catching the odd perch. Later in life my love for fishing lead me to sturgeon, shark and salmon fishing around San Francisco from my cruiser.

Bryan D. I imagine fishing rods are made of glass fibre these days but in the days of my youth the rods were bamboo with a split cane top section. One old chap gave me an old rod made of rosewood. It was a beautiful piece of craftsmanship and probably worth some serious money today.

Radio Days

Terry L. Saturday Mornings in the 60s and 70s always brings back special memories for me, being around the house or out in the garden with windows flung open and the radio blaring away, Listening to Jimmy Clitheroe, Ed Stewart and Arnold and "Ello Darling" songs like *Puff the Magic Dragon*. What songs, DJ's or radio Programmes do you remember, or was I the only one listening to the radio on a Saturday ?

Ron B. *The Runaway Train*. My grandson loves it

Pina R. The charts on a Sunday evening, I think it was on Sundays. Trying to tape the songs onto the old cassette tapes & the DJ would always talk over the top, lol!

Jill G. The radio was always blaring at home when I was a kid and still is when I visit them. Loved the charts on Sunday Pina.

Ron B. Still listen to Brian Mathew 'Sounds of the Sixties' every Sat morning.

Terry L. And me Ron, and Johnny Walker does sound of the 70's.

Julia B. The Navy Lark!

Marc H. Terry we always had a tranny on the go in the 60s Saturday morning and the various pirate radio stations we could find on the big radio set. Just remembered last Saturday I sent a text in to Justin Dealey on BBC three counties radio that I was on the platform with my tranny listening not really the best thing to say the these days!!

Terry L. There's a bit of Dawn and Tie a Yellow Ribbon on the end of the eye level clip. Remember that being a hit whilst at the Radcliffe.

Len E. Sparky's magic piano was one Ed Stewpot played often on his Saturday show.

Pina R. Terry, I'd forgotten about Eye Level - that was the tune to the programme 'Van der Valk' - used to like that programme!

Jane B. Loved "Junior Choice" with Ed "Stewpot" Stewart - two of my faves were "One Wheel on my Wagon" and "Hello Muddah, Hello Faddah" - oh - and "Theme from a Teenage Opera" (got it on CD now - well excited) - great memories xxx

Nick C. Living in lodgings in Luton in 1966, with radio permanently on Pirate Radio London ....wonderful Big L

Sarah K. *The Laughing Policeman* and *My Brother* were two more favourites on junior choice.

Sarah K. I also remember *Little Boxes*, which is now being used for an advert!!

Celia R. I remember Sundays with Jimmy Saville guessing what year the song was made and who sang it. Iit was on at 12 o'clock.

Chris G. *My Brother* by Terry Scott, *I am a Mole and I Live in a Hole* by the Southlanders, and *Right Said Fred* by Bernard Cribbens.

Chris G. Also on a Sunday, Family Favourites, seem to remember it had some kind of forces link up, Roger Whitaker played for Marj and Dennis in BFPO 40 from Cybil and Reg in Sutton Coldfield.

Sarah K. Jane, *Hello Mudda* is called *Camp Grenada* :-)

Sarah K. Ron, my Dad went to the same school as Brian Matthew. He must be getting on a bit because my dad would have been 84'

Chris G. *'Gilly Gilly Ossenfeffer Katzenellenbogen by the Sea'.* Children song sung by Max Bygraves.

Marc H. LOL good one Chris, Max Bygraves.

Sarah K. I've just looked Brian Matthew up on Wikipedia and he is 84 in September - he must have been in the year below my Dad.

Marc H. *The Ugly Bug Ball* when I was a kid, every summer the Disney Channel would play the movie.

Ron B. *You're a pink toothbrush.*

Chris G. *A Windmill In Old Amsterdam* This is doing my street cred wonders ;)

Ron B. MAX BYGRAVES - *'Fings Ain't Wot They Used T'Be'* - *You need hands.* Bernard Cribbins, *"Hole in the Ground".*

Ron B. Round the Horn: "I'm Julian this is my friend Sandy. "Kenneth Williams. Brilliant.

Marc H. And the other one was *Gossip Calypso* from Mr Cribbins. Julian and Sandy do what they do best, so perg yourself, sit back and enjoy this...

Jill G. Tony Hancock's half hour

Ron B. *The Blood Donor.* "That's nearly an armful!" loll

Jill G. Hahaha and the radio ham

Ron B. Love it. Should all be on You Tube Jill.

Jill G. Yes it is Ron I would put some on but don't know how to put it onto this site

Nick C. Oooh Ron.................yes Eth ! .... ' Take it from here'

Ron B. Bloody hell Nick, That has followed me all my life. Thanks mate. lol

Nick Carter heh heh.

Marc H. Blimey I am a radio ham myself and use to get ribbed about the Tony Hancock sketch.

Terry L. Chris , fond memories of World Wide family Favourites, I always imagined the recipients being in a desert somewhere or by a crystal blue sea eating there Sunday roast and Yorkshire pudding, Ah the magic of radio!

Terry L. Ah it was two way family favourites! The time in Britain is twelve noon, in Germany it's one o'clock, but home and away it's time for "Two-Way Family Favourites".

Ian H. Used to love the Billy Cotton Band Show (wakey wakey) and Forces Favourites with all those BAOR addresses. Pete Murray was also a good listen he always seemed to have decent guests.

Gary Cr. I used to like Fluff Freeman on Sunday with pick of the pops 'hey there pop pickers'

Julia B. pmsl....Crying, listening to *Puff the Magic Dragon!*

Nick C. I used to like puff !

116

Chris G. I used to like that other comedy bloke on the radio, started all his programmes 'Germany calling, Germany calling!'

Ian H. Haw Haw Chris ;-)

Marc H. If I mention 'Puff the Magic Dragon' it means a bit more to people these days!

Barbara L. Put all my records on the window, melted in the sun.

Ian H. They had some cracking plays on the radio too. I travelled an enormous amount in the 70's and I think it was Radio 4 that had "Afternoon Theatre" on about 2 to 4 in the afternoons.

June L. I liked listening to Radio 4, Plays, Woman's Hour, even some of Mrs. Dale's Diary way back & Jim her husband.

Ron B. I think we should adopt the Archers theme tune as our National Anthem Dum di dum di dum di dum , dum di dum di dum dum. Plus all the immigrants would learn it really quickly, and even Wayne Rooney would be able to sing it at internationals. Great to march up and down to. Go on you know you want to. Think I have had too much sun.

Len E. Ron, I think you're giving Wayne Rooney too much credit. :)

Pat C. I was a bundle of joy worked every Sat 60s, 70s, 80, most of 90s. Happy Days, actually they were! Great to see all those old programmes mentioned again, lot of my favourites in there.

June L. Have you mentioned Henry Hall's Guest Night & Workers Playtime, was Down your Way Radio or TV?

Nick C. It was radio June.....Henry Hall 'here's to the next time'...and June ..I'm also worried about Jim !

Ruth E. Our radio was always on for the Archers on Sunday morning then two-way family favourites the boys were in the army then pick of the pops and in the evening Sing Something Simple. Used to like the Navy Lark and Round the Horne and in the week Wilfred Pickles Workers Playtime he used to say "give them the Money Mabel" I think?

Len E. Remember Listen with Mother. Weekday lunchtimes?

June L. Loved Sing something Simple, I've got a CD of them or maybe Cassette.

Ruth E. I often find myself humming those tunes June and I sing the children to sleep with them ...Old age great stuff...

117

Marc H. Ron, I spent 25 years as a Radio 4 listener and then found I could not concentrate and came to BBC local radio. The Archers and would you believe women's hour were my favourite programs

Ron B. Cutting edge Marc. love it

Marc H. Just think before breakfast TV, we woke up to john Timpson and Brian Redhead on Radio 4 news. Now I wake up to Simon Lederman on 3cr, Stuart Linnell on Northampton or Phil Gayle/Louisa Hannan on Oxford.

Ian H. I wake up to someone speaking French;-)

Marc H. Blimey what station is that Ian?

Ian H. RTL

Marc H. Ahh I see you're in Franceshire!

Pina R. That RTL man is bi-lingual....he speaks Italian here!!

Chris G. Quadlingual, he speaks Dutch and German too. Clever fella.

Ruth E. I now love Radio 2. Miss Terry in the morning though!

Ian H. You know us Europeans are worth it Piña :-)

Pina R. In my youth I always used to listen to Radio 1 in the mornings before going to work. Dom wrote in to Radio 1 and had a song dedicated to me for my 18th....(in the days when he was trying impress! me)......unfortunately I didn't hear the dedication.. My mates told me about it......!!

Hayley D. Radio one, Steve right in the afternoon and Dave Lee Travis. And listening to the Dear John letters.

Hayley D. I also love radio two now.

Pat C. Anyone remember Radio Luxembourg, my hand used to go out automatically to tune in its wandering signal on my Philco radio. The radio bought in 1961 in Aylesbury for £2.7s.6d. out of my first salary from TSB, take home approx £3.19s.0. per week.

Chris G. Yep Pat I was a regular Luxembourg overnight listener in my teens.

Len E. 208 Radio Luxembourg...listening to it under the bed clothes at night. Radio being confiscated for getting caught.

Hayley D. Forgot about radio Luxemburg.

Ron B. Keynsham, That's K-E-Y-N-S-H-A-M. Bristol. Good old Horace Batchelor.

Ian H. 208 metres Medium Wave...............spelt K.E.Y.N.S.H.A.M
Keynsham near Bristol ;-)Ha

Len E. Ron, Ian, can either of you explain the relevance of
K.E.Y.N.S.H.A.M. please? thanks

Ron B. It was where you sent your football pools to Len. Horace
Batchelor ran it I think. from Keynsham near Bristol. I think this is
right, but it was a long time ago

Ron B. Batchelor sponsored programmes on Radio Luxembourg
to promote his "famous Infra-Draw Method", a system supposed
to increase chances of winning large sums on the football pools.
Before the National Lottery started in 1994, the "Pools" was the
only way to win large sums for a small stake. Listeners were asked
to submit their stakes to Batchelor, who then determined how the
stake was placed. He was paid only if the bet won, which also
meant he received a lot of free stakes. Infra-draw was thus not
dependent on his predictive talent for its financial success.
Thanks Wikipedia.

Len E. Remember the Littlewoods pools rep calling on a
Thursday evening for the coupon and money. Then having to
write down the football results printed in the Saturday paper for
my dad.

Jane B. I remember my Dad every Saturday at 4:45 kneeling in
front of the TV with the paper and marking down the Footie
Results - and shushing me if I made a noise - not that we ever won
mind you !!!!

Nick C. Ah ! Sports Report......dee dum dee dum dee duddly dum,
dee dum de dum dee da.....or something like that ! Lmao

Ian H. Jane B.your comment made me smile. One day my dad
won £50 on Littlewoods and I thought he was going to climb the
wall. All those X's 1's and 2's :-)

Nick C. D E C C A .....decca decca Decca.............The Jack
Jackson Show...miaouw !

Steve B......listening to all those chaps on Radio Caroline, who
became legit overnight in 1967 when the Government finally
admitted defeat by establishing Radio 1. Suddenly it wasn't as
much fun listening to them anymore (as you no longer had to
listen on a tyranny radio under the bedclothes!)

119

Cinema Days (and Nights)

P 21: Palace Cinema on the Stratford Road

Jill G. Who remembers their first ever film they went to see at the cinema? Apparently mine was when I was 3 yrs old. Mum and Dad took me to the Odeon in Willesden to see Snow White and half way into the film I had finished my sweet treats and was ready to go home I kicked up such a stink they had to take me home. Of course I don't remember this :). We came to Bradwell when I was 4 and I think I was about six when I went to see Bambi in Wolverton.

Len E. My first film I recall is the Sound of Music but saw that in Leeds when it came out, however I must have been to the cinema before that since I lived opposite the one in Church St

Chris G. Can remember going to see a re-run of the 1966 World Cup Final with my Dad at Wolverton Empire a few week after it had happened because it was in colour. I think I promptly fell asleep.

Jane B. "Mary Poppins" in Scunthorpe when I was 4 - the girl across the road took me - can't really remember much except I wanted my Mum!!!

Len E. My daughter and I were watching Mary Poppins on DVD a couple of days ago and It struck me how cleverly the script and the songs were written back in those days.

Brian E. My first and only visit to the cinema was with my father to see Cliff Richard & the Shadows in Summer Holiday. I think I was about 10 or 11. I checked this film out when it appeared on Channel Four a year or so ago, and it was even more awful than I remembered at the time. After this, I was not to visit the cinema gain for years. In fact, I believe then 2nd time was to see Soldier Blue at Bletchley. My main memory of that evening at the Empire was the Billinghams fish 'n chips afterwards!

Theresa W. Went to see Grease with my mum and one of her friends.

Julia B. Help!

June L. I doubt if any of you have even heard of mine let alone seen it (I do hope some one has.) a good old British black & white film, *It Always Rains On Sunday*. I went to see it at Romford with my mum when I was a teenager. Googie Withers was starring in the film. She was a very big Star. Brilliant.

Julie L. *Grease* in Northampton cinema.

Faye L. *Lion King* in 1994! x

John R. *Jurassic Park* October 1993 is the first one I can remember.

Faye L. I do like the old black and white films from the 30's and 40's but rarely see them on TV anymore. x

David E. *King Kong* at the empire, also remember Eleanor Rigby by the Beatles being played at the interval don't know what yr though.

Sarah K. Probably *Born Free* at Wolverton - I remember going to Bletchley to see Bambi with Jane Bailey and a few others including my sister Rachel Daville - we wouldn't let our kids go to the pictures on their own now.

Constance O. *Live and Let Die* with my Mum in Northampton.

121

Len E. Blimey David yes! an interval halfway through the film to buy your choc ices and Kiaora orange juice.

Len E. ... and the old style film classifications, e.g. X rated

Janice M. *Bed Knobs and Broom Sticks.*

Chris G. Talking of Bedknobs and Broomsticks, anyone remember David Tomlinson bringing his kids up to Wolverton pool a few times in that big back Rolls Royce or Bentley? Lived out Mursley way I think?

David E. Yes Chris I remember David Tomlinson bringing his son up once couldn't believe my eyes when his son stood at the side of the pool and peed in it unbelievable!!

Linda K. Never saw him at the pool Chris but he was a regular at the Point Cinema when I worked there in the 80s. A fact that I bring up every time the kids watch that film!

Alan Cr. I think it was *Dr Who* at the Empire in Wolverton

Sarah D. I kept asking and pestering my dad to take me to see Grease. he kept taking the micky and showing me a pot of grease from the kitchen, until he eventually gave in and took me to Electra (NP). I think that's what the cinema was called.

Sarah D. Ooh, no. Actually it was the *The Sword in the Stone* - the cartoon!

Jane D. I remember going to see *Swiss Family Robinson*. The film came out in the 60's but the cinema must have been re-showing it in the late 70's too.

Doug M. I only went once and that was to watch a very early James Bond film. The one with the divers in I think.

Steve A. In a different town this would have been cherished and turned into an arthouse cinema. Unfortunately I think it's too late. At least the buildings are still standing. Anyone know what it's like inside now? Is the balcony still there?

Jane B. I saw *Born Free* there and cried my eyes out so my Mum and Dad had to bring me home early !!!!

Donna S. Is this on Church Street? If so I saw *Snow White* there. We have an old movie theater in our town, one room. Just got new seats in, only open on Fri, Sat, Sun.... $6.00 each if you go on Fri or Sat... $3.00 each if you go on Sunday.

Donna S. Jane, I still cry when I watch *Born Free...*

P 22: The Empire Cinema in the 1930s. The Post Office is being built next door.

Maurice H. That's were I saw *Bambi*. And *Flash Gordon* on a Saturday Morning.

Jill G. I remember *Bambi* in there.

John R. I saw Help there. I also remember seeing a movie with the Dave Clark 5, but haven't a clue what it was called.

Margaret C. I think it was called, *Catch us if you can...*

Ron B. Played today on Radio 2.

John R. Now that you say that, I can hear the song in my head. Probably going to be there all day!

Jackie N. The Empire is part of Wolverton Mosque.......

David E. I remember watching *King Kong* there followed by *Sword in the Stone* a Walt Disney cartoon. My mum was a cleaner there so got cheap tickets.

Trevor I. Didn't the Empire then become the Post Office? I vaguely remember working out of there as a temp mail deliverer at Xmas- got a red bike, bad brakes and a route down the hill to Haversham.

John R. I have the same recollection about the Empire - can't vouch for the bicycling.

Donna S. I thought the Empire was beside the post office.... my dad worked at post office.

Trevor I. Maybe that was it. Then my other recollection was that the PO became a rug store at some point?? Or am I really losing it?

Donna S. Don't know Trevor, as I left England for Canada in 76. It was still there then. Thought someone mentioned it's a mosque now. I always remember the smell of post office. Dad would take us there once in a while and we would play in the big wicker baskets... well ok, my brothers would.

Trevor I. I left the UK in 76 also - so we are talking before that?

Donna S. Someone posted a photo a little while back. It clearly shows the empire beside the post office..

Trevor I. OK thanks for helping the failing memory:)

Donna S. That's ironic Trevor. I left so long ago I can't remember much and I helped you! Must be something good in this coffee I'm drinking.

Chris G. Building still there, cinema shut 1960/70s, last film *Carry On Screaming* if anybody can look up date.

Pamela J. I remember taking my brother to see *Davy Crockett.* OHHHHHHH memories

Kim P. Carry on Screaming was 1966 I believe. Mo Dackombe was one of the usherettes, she was there for years, I'm sure I remember her telling me she was there right up until t he last night. It was next to the PO, was used as the sorting office for a long time in the 1970's and I think into the 80's tho' it looked empty from the outside.

Trevor I. So part of the PO was in the cinema after it closed?

Chris G. Yep for a while.

Trevor I. Thanks Chris, I thought that's where I got on me bike:) for my deliveries.

Margaret C. Brings back Sat morning memories. Thats when I could get round my Uncle Pearce. He would treat me..

Ian S. It look's magnificent in this picture.

Geoff L. Is that the empire cinema? If so remember 9d matinee tickets on sat morns to watch *Tarzan.*

Margaret C. I thought it was the Palace, but so many years ago i may be getting mixed up. It's one of them any way and went to both.

June L. I wish the picture houses were still here.

June L. One of the last pictures I saw in the Palace was *Half a Sixpence*, Tommy Steele & in the Scala S.S. was Someone Up There Likes Me, Paul Newman. Later in life Pete went to work for Paul Newman in America.

Ian H. Mr. Edwards was the manager at the Palace, he just couldn't control us when *Rock Around The Clock* came, we were "rocking" in the aisles!!

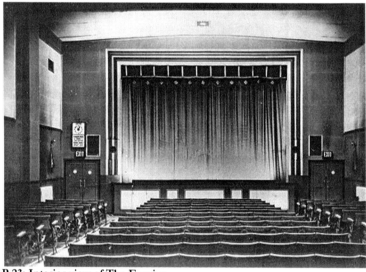

P 23: Interior view of The Empire

Chris G. Carry on Screaming was the last ever film shown I think?

Bryan D. Yes I remember *Rock around the Clock* at the Palace also and the fact that the cinema was crammed. Looking back it's hard to imagine that it was all so revolutionary, that four or five middle aged roadies could change music forever. Prior to that we were served such hits as "How much is that doggie in the window?"

Sheila Se. Last film I saw was Help - The Beatles.

Gill B. Remember going to see *Rock around the Clock* at The Palace and seeing Sheila Alderman and Eva Oldham jiving in the aisles.

Ian H. Is that Eva the "tall" lass from Bradwell a friend of Maureen Dilley at the time?

125

Gill B. Yes Ian Eva did come from Bradwell and lived in the "Corner Pin" area, and as you say she was a "tall" lass.

Palace Nights

Elaine Mn. Does anyone remember going to the Palace dance hall in the mid 60s - wonderful place and all the famous groups too?

Jackie A. Oh yes met lots of stars there.

Nick C. Arrived there every week, after playing rugby for Olney. Met my ex there too! Brenda Lee stopped her car outside the Western and asked 'can you show me the way to the Palace, please?'...great nights were had there. Then they changed it to a bingo hall!

June L. It was a cinema when I used it. I saw Tommy Steele in Half a Sixpence there or was it called Singing the Blues?

Pam F. Half a Sixpence, I saw it there as well.

Pam F. Elaine Mary Martin hopes you don't mind me asking, do you have a sister Marilyn? If so we were in the same class at school in Wolverton.

Jennifer T. I was going to ask the same thing Pam.

Hazel S. Saw the film Rock Around the Clock with Bill Hayley and his Comets. Dancing in the aisles - good fun had by all.

Brian E. The only visit I made was to see Cliff & The Shadows in Summer Holiday! A particularly awful film!

Ruth E. I was a regular there in the 60s had pics and autographs from Small Faces. Four Pennies. Wayne Fontana Pretty Things, Troggs, also saw Long John Baldry, Brenda Lee met my one ex husband there on the Monday night local live groups night 3/6d. to go in I think?

Lin G. My Nan used to love her bingo there with her friend May.

Gareth G. Remember winning a raffle after the Wednesday night disco they used to have, and getting to meet Wayne Fontana and the Mindbenders and being presented with a signed album. Only band I went to see, think it must have been about 1967 as I don't think I had left school. Both my brothers had seen quite a few bands there though, the Honeycombs is one I remember. As I remember it closed as a cinema in around 1962/3 and we were left only with the Empire. So when you come to think about it some quite famous bands appeared in that little fleapit in a one horse town.

Deborah G. Lin, My Nan, May Williams, was a big Zetters/bingo lady - could she have been your Nan's friend May?

Elaine H. The Four Pennies played there.

Nick C. Loads of top acts played there....then were whisked off to the California, in Dunstable for later turn ....However, I think best act I ever saw there was the local boys - The Barron Knights!

Lynnette M. Wow I didn't realize all these famous faces ad played there I only remember it as a cinema n a bingo hall.

Nick C. Lynnette Mallows......you youngsters don't always get the best stuff!

Kathleen A. We had some good nights there Lulu, Brenda Lee.

Lin G. Hi Deborah Green, my Nan was Rose Millar and May was her good friend, don't know May's other name, last time I saw May was on a bus to Northampton.

Ron B. Saw the Four Pennies there.

Ruth E. Think I was behind you that night Ron.

Nick C. It was reasonable price to get in too!

Geoffrey W. I remember playing there in a group called The Shames. I think Gene Vincent was on the same bill, although he was well past his sell-by date.

Janet S. It was 2/6 on a Monday, the Walker Bros played there I think. Lulu also played there she was going on to the Cali in Luton but they wouldn't let her as she had jeans on with holes in the legs so she went in the Crawford for a drink with a bouncer.

Marc H. I had the pleasure of meeting David Sutch a couple of times over the years - a true showman, loved his stage acts.

Ron B. Met him back stage at Wilton Hall one night. Nice guy!

Elaine M. It was a great place for all the groups - Small Faces/Sonny and Cher/ Four Pennies/Brenda Lee/Dozy Beaky Mick and Titch and loads more, have wonderful memories.

Geoffrey W. Sadly, I remember watching 'The Blackboard Jungle' film at the Palace, which kicked off a lot of people's interest in Rock and Roll. In its late form I played there. That was after I played with Nicky Malone in the Fenders and afterwards with the Shames. We then travelled all over the UK backing the popular groups of the day. I started playing guitar while I was in the youth club and there, met some young lads from Leighton Buzzard and played often with them. They became the Barron Knights. Someone mentioned Screaming Lord Sutch, but no-one mentioned his pianist Freddie Fingers Lee (see him on YouTube), an amazing character.

June L. I remember the name Nicky Malone.

Pam F. Nicky was Molly Hagan's brother, sadly now passed away.

Park Memories

Gary Cr. Does anyone remember the old clubhouse at the park before they built the one at the top of the pitch? It was an old railway carriage sited against the wall at the top right hand side of the park, the bottom end had a small bar and at the top end had the tea/coffee and pop, there were some HUGE rat holes in the bottom of it.

Lorraine B. I have many happy memories of Saturday afternoons at Wolverton Park with my sister and my Dad (Colin Willett, who was Press Reporter for Wolverton Town in the late sixties and seventies). I can remember helping Doris and Mary Atterbury and Mary's Mum Thelma serve teas from the enormous urn and going in there for a warm. It was nearly always a really cold day!!

Chris G. Yep remember it well, they shifted the bar down one end towards the end of its life because the floor was rotten at the other. After training one night Fergie wandered, pint in hand, up the condemned end and promptly went through the floor. Typical Ferg, didn't spill a drop.

Jane B. Is that where we used to go after the Annual Fireworks Display ? I remember having a Hot Dog and polystyrene cup of Tomato Soup in there - it was a bit of a squeeze with most of Wolvey in there at the same time !!!!

Pat F. I remember that too the Tomato soup tasted great after the freezing outing !!

Andrew L. Ancient B&W TV at the opposite end from the bar showing football results on the BBC Video printer (Grandstand).

P 24: Part of a Football Crowd at a Saturday Afternoon game.

Gary Cr. Colin was a good friend of my folks Lorraine.

Lorraine B. He was Gary, your Mum would often come round to our house on an evening to rehearse for a play when her and dad were in St. George's Players amateur drama group. :o) I also worked with her at Greenleys Middle School, she's a lovely lady!! :o)

Gary C. Didn't he have a red setter called Roo or was that someone else.

Lorraine B. Yeah, that was us, she was as mad as a hatter!! :o)

Gary Cr. I remember helping mum serve hotdogs out of the back of an old lorry with sun blessed bread on the side of it, it was put next to the other old railway carriage they collected the newspapers in.

Angie A. Our dog Rhu used to steal all of my son Adam's Lego and chew it up behind the sofa bless her - NOT.

Brian E. Oh, Lego! I thought you said leg at first!

Paul S. Yes, sure do Gary. Its amazing how you forget things though. I seem to recollect it may have had a drop down counter that opened outwards of course. dad used to take us down there in

129

the twin pram and I have many memories of watching the Wolves with Billy Atterbury for example and then later Ian Capel. I used to love the dam busters march which the teams used to walk out to I think it was.

Nick C. I remember watching the Wolves the day Billy Atterbury had his leg broken..........the crack echoed all around the park....I'll never forget that !

Paul S. Yes, I remember that too. What about Wolverton Works sports days. They were fun but also tinged with danger as we watched cyclists go over the top down the bottom end.

Steve P. Lorraine, remember your Dad Colin when I used to play cricket for Wolverton. While I was an apprentice for almost 4 years every time the works cricket competition was being organised Colin would come to see me wherever I was "working" & sign me up with a bribe of a cup of coffee! Seem to remember all the preliminary games being played at Radcliffe School then the semis & final at Wolvertons ground at Osbourne St. I only packed up playing last year after 36 seasons

Lorraine B. That sounds like him Steve, those works cricket competitions were great fun. I played in the ladies team one year. :0) I remember watching the semis and finals at the cricket club. Good times!!

Steve P. Yes definitely Lorraine, although when I batted with your Dad he couldn't take a quick single that I wanted to, he was a steady "old head" Got valuable runs in the last few over's though

Kazza B. I remember the old clubhouse....... I remember the ceiling was covered with hundreds of beer mats...... and it was always freezing cold in there!!! Happy days though!! xxx My dad (Dave Rome) used to work behind the bar. xxx

Springtime

Ian H. Springtime memories. Sunny afternoons in Linford Wood and children with armfuls of bluebells.

Sheila S. You are not allowed to pick them now Ian.

Andrew L. Picking wild bluebells is OK, as long as it is for your own use.

Brian E. There used to be a tree stump there, carved into a troll head, till some idiots kindly burnt it.

Ruth E. I used to go to Whittlebury and walk from Puxley and back laden down with bluebells

Lesley W. Just back from a walk round Lodge Lake. The swan on her nest a very pleasing sight.

Ian H. Not forgetting the rhododendrons Ruth therein the hedgerows.

Ian H. I hope they still pick a few for their mums.

Elaine S. I am sure it is illegal to pick wild flowers in MK. Brian there are lots of carvings in Linford Wood now. Paul and I met the carver one day. An old boy who loved carving and asked whoever it is who owns the Wood if he could work there.

Andrew L. Nobody is going to be hung for picking wild flowers, but it's generally illegal to pick them to sell on, and also illegal to uproot them, or dig up bulbs. Any other house rules are down to the land owner but everyone is OK with kids plucking a few. But really, bluebells are best enjoyed where they grow. They will wilt quickly in water, so best to leave them.

Elaine S. Glad we sorted that one. I needed the bit about uprooting as I wanted some primroses. Best leave them alone I think.

Under the arches

Pat B. Has Summer arrived?

Ron B. Nice pic Pat

June L. What a lovely site.

Chris G. Blimey Pat, you almost caught me, just walked over that wooden bridge you took this from an hour or so ago.

Bryan D. Idyllic.

Pat B. That's not you skinny dipping near the swans is it?.

Ron B. Didn't know you had your camera Pat lol

Chris G. Might be of interest to you Bryan, you can't see it but on the left of that picture an old stone bridge is being revealed by bank erosion, looking from the air you can clearly see a track leading towards it from Manor Farm direction.

131

P 25: The Viaduct over the River Ouse

Bryan D. I've just taken a look at the Google Earth view. It might have been the old river bridge. The Haversham Road has been moved a few times. Prior to 1837 it might have branched off the Old Wolverton Rd. from where Colts Holm is. But when they built the railway and the viaduct they moved the road to the east of the track and diverted the course of the river. The Haversham road turn off was moved again in 1881 when the loop line was built. Anyway Wolverton is looking very scenic today.

Darren S. I knew it as the seven arches over the Ouse river, I used to fish there as a kid

John R. I wonder how it got named the 7 arches as they is only 6 big arches and many smaller ones there

Maurice H. I nearly drowned by there when I was about 7 or 8. Paddling I must have stepped into a deep pothole or something and disappeared. My Dad pulled me out and did the CPR thing. So I survived, to the chagrin of some people.

132

Swimming Pool Opening

WOLVERTON
SWIMMING
POOL

OFFICIAL OPENING

SATURDAY, 1st AUGUST, 1964

P 26: Opening Day Brochure.

Steve A. Fantastic!! Never seen this before....... look you can see the works chimney puffing away in the distance.

Jane B. What a fabbo pic - didn't it look all nice and clean - pity they had to do away with it - had some happy (and not so happy) memories there !!!

Ian B. In the days before health and safety went mad and you could do all sorts of mad things off the 3 meter board and the spring board.

Andy C. That's a great memory - my uncle (Reg Pateman) was on the committee that organised the construction of the pool.

Pat F. I remember going to swimming lessons there and it was freezing and mum had to take a flask of hot drink to warm me up!!!

Nahida K. Lot of memories in this pool. Used to go swimming also have Radcliffe school House competitions. (lots of happy memories) there.!!!!!!!!!!!

Brian E. I never liked going to The Pool, but, then again. I can't swim!

June L. When I lived in Green Lane early 1960's they use to come & knock on our door every week for a small payment towards the new Swimming board to be built.

Chris G. We used to give them a bucket of water each week when they knocked saying they were collecting for a swimming pool.

133

Donna S. lmao

Pam B. My mum went round for weeks collecting money for the pool.

Elizabeth M. They collected in New Bradwell as well and my parents contributed weekly to the fund for swimming pool.

June L. I can't swim either Brian. I'm frightened of water. When I was at school we were taken in a group to Romford swimming baths to learn his to swim. All was going well until I went with some girlfriends. One Saturday morning some boys grabbed hold of me and threw me in the deep end, which terrified me, so I wouldn't go again. In later years Pete tried to teach me in France when we were there with the Race team but I was still frightened.

Brian E. It's not there now, but Moon Street school had it's own outdoor UNHEATED pool! Mr Cockerill built the Swiss Chalet style changing room adjacent. Also gone now! In the Summer we had PE lessons there. Tom Winnett was the PE teacher, but he never came close to teaching me to swim.

Susan B. Lovely memories of the pool, going there everyday in the summer holidays, rain or shine, now I hardly go swimming, must make more effort and start going with the grandchildren. and JERONIMO...................

Sheila Se. My Dad was on the New Bradwell committee. Did lots of other fund raising including climbing up a lit bonfire to put the guy on top.

Steve Tw. It was fantastic spent hours and hours up there, even used to pick the litter up to get free entry the next day.

Terry L. Yeah I remember that now x

Andrew D. Who used to run the pool?

Chris G. Mr Walsh?

Helen P. My dad was on the gang that built the pool. I have a couple of photos of him standing in it before it was filled!

Andrew D. That's the man!

Steve Tw. and his son Ian I think.

Chris G. Yep and Mrs Walsh too, a real family concern.

Andrew D. The good old days.

Stephen M. Won't look like that now.

Susan B. Did they have a daughter as well?

Marc H. Good place to learn to swim along with the Mounts pool in Northampton.

Jackie N. My Mum worked a few summers at the pool as cashier. I also remember the collection that went on for a long time before. I think someone came round weekly and Dad paid about half a crown a time to fund the building of the pool........

Becca H. Pamela Pointer's mum (Marina Drive) also worked there as a cashier at the entrance for quite a while. You could also get a hot Oxo or Bovril drink in the cafe. The Walsh's originally came from Wokingham. Ian Walsh was a tallish skinny lad and he went out with a dark haired girl from Sandra from Bradwell for quite a while. I think she was a either a twin or had a sister of a very close age who MAY have been called Lorraine. I seem to remember the Walsh's lived in a house opposite the tennis courts/pineapple.

Sheila Se. Later the Walsh's had the shop down corner pin in New Bradwell.

Toni B. Went there most days in 1964 rain or shine loved it.

Summer days

Gary C. I have nicked this from a mates FB photo's, Wolverton Pool early 80's when we had sunshine in the summer time!!!!!!!

Julie W. So many happy memories xx

Becca H. Agree with Julie's comments above - but ......eewww! Budgie Smugglers.....one of the worst items of 80's fashion must haves for the boys! lol x

Ron B. I had some speedo trunks. had to throw them away when the 's' fell off. lol

Steve P. Steve Watts front left?

Richie B. Woof "!

Steve P. Possibly Kirk Davies from 'Bradall centre in maroon trunks?

Becca H. Was Kirk Shelly's brother?

Ian S. Yes thats right Becca.

Becca H. Thanks Ian. Had some good times and laughs with Shelly early 70's! x

Ian S. I still see her about now and then. Kirk is always good fun as well.

P 27: Wolverton Swimming Pool in the 1980s.

Becca H. She was the year below us at school but we all used to hang out together, as we all did in those days in either Wolv, Braddle, Stony, Newport or the villages - wherever we decided to be. Really nice now to think back to how we all went miles in our groups to have fun and experience our youth!
Steve P. Spiz, remember having a beer in The County at New Bradwell on a Friday afternoon, must be early 90s as my eldest wasn't long born. Kirk came in & he had a baby with a girl in Cornwall. Bob Jolley (Dex's brother) came in & had a Rover 3.5. About teatime Kirk decided he wanted to see his boy & Bob agreed to drive down there. We got to Perranporth before 10 & still had a good night. Kirk's ex wasn't too impressed but she put us up & had a great weekend leaving Sunday teatime. Kirk still owes me £20 from that weekend!
Becca H. Fab story Steve !

Steve P. I definitely had a twinge of conscience as bought a 12 to 18 month outfit for my boy on Saturday morning, before the pub opened! Not big or clever but good fun at the time.

Gary C. Yes it's Steve Watts and Dean Gunthorpe behind him.

Ian S. Yes that'd be Kirk. Mad as a box of frogs.

Steve P. Think Kirk's had a lazier summer than Steve judging by the comparison of tans. lol

Helen P. I think it's Leslie Emery, not Kirk.

Ian S. Ha ha you should see it now.

Ian S. Helen I thought may be David, Les's brother.

Ian S. Nope you are right Helen, Leslie Emery.

Steve P. Just enlarged the picture as suppose I should do, agree now Spiz. Their elder brother Paul, remember him?

Chris G. I'm not sure it's anyone mentioned before going on the ages of the other lads, Steve Watts will know? That may be Clive Smith in the blue and Jez Reilly with his back to us.

Chris G. Just had a look on Steve's page. There's a group shot, its someone called 'Little' Dave, not anyone mentioned above, and its not Jez Reilly its Tyrone Mccormack. It is Clive Smith though.

Roy G. Guys, I know it's been over 30 years since I left Wolverton and not sure what's been going on but those of you I knew back then would have been looking at the girl in the background not the guys in speedo's !! Is it GIllian Turnbull by the way ?

Chris G. Pauline Geddes, now Valentine (married to Dean) apparently.

Terry L. Looks like Paul Emery and Spike to me..

Len E. Chris you mention Dean Valentine, do you know what became of his elder sister Madeline?

Becca H. Were they related to Jacqui Valentine?

Len E. Not sure But their father was Terry. a keen fisherman iirc

Becca H. Jacqui (or Jackie) would be 54/55 now. She lived in Stony when I knew her at school but often used to come and lark about with us in the Top Rec on summer evenings. Pretty girl with very dark hair and olive-ish skin.

Deborah C. Such a great place it was!

Tracy S. Would that be the Terry Valentine that drinks in the White Horse and the Conservative Club?

Ron B. That's right Tracy. Jackie Valentine was Bob Valentine's sister I believe. Lived in Clarence road. Bob lives in MK still.
Tracy S. Ah thought so. If we're out in Stony and we bump in to him he always has a joke to tell.
Ron B. Yea, and not always a good one, lol
Jackie A. Just spoke to Dave Emery and he says its not either of his brothers.
David E. Yes sorry guys it's not me or Les. He was living in Bedford when this photo was taken. Nnice to know people are thinking of you though. lol.

The New Pool

Chris G. It's getting bigger...
Phillip W. It's going up quick.

P 28: The New Swimming Pool under construction 2012.

Ron B. It's getting bigger. It's going up quick. Must add these to my book on innuendo. Due out as soon as Lent is over. lol

138

John R. On the plus side, it looks like the grass is doing well and the bushes are starting to bud and flower.

Alan Cr. It's a great concept, I ran past there the other day and it will be a great improvement on the old pool which sat there doing bugger all for probably 8 months of the year. If you fancied a swim in December you had no choice but to visit Stantonbury or Bletchley. But I'm probably in a minority of one.....

Dave M. As long as the kids are not priced out Alan, some of the ones up here charge £5 for an hour session.

Brian E. It looks a bit draughty to me? The wind will whistle through it. I would not fancy swimming in December in that?

Andrew L. I would have had the old Works Chimney moved to here, canted it over about 10 degrees and used it as a giant water slide.

Pat C. Or even the leaning tower of Wolverton, pull in tourists.

Mike W. Like that it will be no different to the old pool?

Faye L. Its too big and ugly, boohoo x

Underage drinking

Ruth E. Seeing as it's Friday. Which pub served you your first alcoholic drink legally or illegally? Mine was the North Western at 17 yrs old along with my then future husband Chris Berry....

Andrew L. I used to buy from the Off License on the Stratford Road, near the chippy. I could get served in there. Bought Carlsberg Special Brew and wished I hadn't. The first pub that served me was the Galleon, with my winter coat zipped up so they couldn't see my Radcliffe uniform.

Lesley W. The Plough at Stony Stratford....aged 14

Steve A. Crauford I think, would have been 15 ish 1979.

Jennifer T. The Engineers aged 15. 1959/60

Terry L. Think it was Tony Stone at the Galleon !

Julie W. Wolverton Top Club I think xx

Ian H. Foresters Stony 1957

Chris G. Engineers 15yrs old

Terry L. But before that it was Party 7 supplied by the Holman's at Peter Levitt's bar Oxford street Wolverton at about 13 years old. Did anyone else have a bar in their living room in the 70's ????

Ian H. Bar..............we never had a wardrobe let alone a bar!!

Jennifer T. Ian you are telling Porkies I was in your house many a time.

Jane B. The Greyhound at Haversham when I was 14 !! Mind you, the lad I was with at the time was a regular there and he was 20 - so a much older man !!!!

Marc H. I was using the Royal Oak in Silverstone when I moved there for a while able to buy Watney Special or Manns Brown ale. Got change out of a pound.

Deborah B. I was a good girl didn't drink till later on. Ha Ha. x

Becca H. Galleon - 15 -yrs. but looked about 13 yrs.

Chris G. I'm telling Mum!

Becca H. Well you won't cos I covered for you when you did it at 16 - the night that Bing died - and that bloke got buried alive in the Galleon garden lol !

Chris G. Paul Brown had a fight with someone, his excuse in the aftermath was that he was upset that Bing Crosby had died, typical off the wall Brownie.

Becca H. Remember it well. Where is Paul Brown

Chris G. No idea, not heard of him in years, anybody?

Alan Cr. The Vic in the back room aged about 16 Light and Bitter with John Parker and Mark Sherwood I think...

Gareth G. Galleon at 15 Friday dinner after first pay packet. Couldn't get served in any pub or club in Wolverton Bradwell or Stony as all the landlords new my Mum and Dad.

Becca H. Perils of the 'trade' Gareth G. - I remember being about 16 and getting a tad merry with Anita at your house on Port and Lemon.

John Mc. Queen Vic 15 yrs old.

Julia B. The County Arms, Bradwell , aged 13/14ish

Diane R. North Western, about 15, even though I never reached above 4ft 11 I was never ever asked my age.

Becca H. Diane Richards - thanks for the comical pic you just planted in my mind!

John R. I started my downward spiral at the North Western via the Top Club where my Dad managed to get me a membership card when I was 16. I think this was a path that a number of us followed. Thanks to Marnie and George for setting me up with a foundation of drinking Charlie Wells light and bitter - I can now pretty much handle any beer you want to throw my way - and I appreciate it!

Julia B. There was a rhyme....."Charlie Wells clears your bowels, we don't drink nothing else, lalalalalalala" :)

Bryan D. Royal Oak on Horsefair Green, Stony Stratford.

Julie K. Stony Working Man's Club.

Pina R. Crauford, 14yrs

Ian B. My first would have been cider from the Green Lane/Oxford Street offy. The pub would have been the Vic in the skittle room and would have been a brown ale would have been 16 or 17.

Gary C. Galleon 17

Jacqueline G. Same as you Gary - The Galleon aged 17 with Neil Mac, Alan Neal, Andrew Parker and Cathy

Jackie S. Been trying to recall and the only one I can remember is the Plough in Stony @ 15.

Billy L. Top club, 17.

Karen W. Galleon 15/16. There were loads of us that used to go in there - mostly under age!!

Mark B. Starting Gate 14

Gary Cr. The Starting Gate. Bloody Hell! There's a blast from the past, used to be a it of a biker hang out, had some awesome bands on.

Deborah C. Probably the Cannon, Newport

Jacqueline G. Didn't Marillion play the Starting Gate?

Mark B. The Slade 14

Sheila H. The Pilgrims Bottle, Linford, 15

Andrew L. Pilgrims Bottle! I can remember walking home from there and puking most of the way.

Mike W. Galleon.

Vicky L. Having an older brother :) I was grassed up & sent packing from all Wolverton pubs at 16!!! So it was outside the air vents at Agora 4 sharing cider !! Classy!!! Ist drink was in the Vic at 17 !!!

Sheila H. I have just had a flashback to Austin's Nightclub in CMK. What happened to it?

Jacqueline G. OMG I remember AUSTINS too......the shame

Vicki L. Loved Austin's & Zumer Beach!!!

Jacqueline G. Was Austin's opened in same place as Starting Gate when it closed? I don't know what happened after that.

Deborah C. On 2nd thoughts - Stantonbury Disco - rum and black ..... probably whilst dancing to I will Survive!!! (and far far too young).

Pina R. That brings back memories....Stantonbury disco....I used to drink rum & black there too, lol

Jacqueline G. I loved the RUGBY club at Greenleys...who was the DJ?

Steve A. Yes the Saturday night blood-bath.

Jacqueline G. I remember the running chases with other 'clans' who would come over to give us a good beating so we ran at them and they ran all the way home hahahhahaha,

Wendy C. Royal engineers 1975...

Mark B. I was 9yrs old Living in Fullers Slade 1yr From Australia.

John B. Queen Vic 16 with my dad Dennis.

Susan H. North Western - I was 15 and was drinking vodka and lime which was THE drink at the time.

Helen P. Cherry B and cider at the Crauford, Bacardi and coke at the rugby club discos, forgot about Hovis!!! Used to pop in the Vic and the Western if I couldn't get served anywhere else! First drink has to be cider from the offy, drunk in the back alleys on the way to youth club.

Chris G. Hovie Brown, still bump into him every couple of years in Northampton, looks no different from back in the day. Remember Kenny Brown and Bilko Marshall on the door too?

Steve A. Chris don't know if it's my memory playing tricks on me but the music he played was pretty good and a bit off the beaten track for a local disco, who were the two girls that dressed and danced like the two in the Human league, think they may have been from Stratford.

Chris G. How old Steve?

142

Steve A. I'd have said your age or mine. Always together and anywhere there was a disco pretty much.

Ian S. Navigation half of starlight

Chris G. Spike I can remember that in Starlight shandy the lemonade used to be the strongest component. Did you used to go and see the bands in the Navvy garden around that era?

Mike W. Got barred from Galleon for celebrating a friend's 18th birthday in there, well part of a pub crawl actually. Sounds harsh but we had all been going there as a group for years, she was the youngest!

Pete B. Navigation,16 on my fizzy ,

Chris G. I'm quite surprised that a thread about drinking is the most popular.

Ruth E. Well what a surprise ! I did start the thread on Friday looks like it will run on for a bit xxx

Terry L. I can tell you where my last drink was! 4 pints of the Black stuff in the New Inn, with Eggy, Steve Hayfield, my lad Mick, Bob Gascoigne, and Egg's lad Tom. Love the tattooed ladies in there. Drove past two tattoo parlours in Braddle last night and both were still open, nearly popped in for one but the Mrs wouldn't let me.

Top Club Remembered

Becca H. A lovely old little Wolverton memento from our late dad's 'clubbing days'!

Vicki L. My Dad still has his & still goes there!!!

Marc H. Used it for two years when I lived across the road from it although I was Hanslope club member.

I use to chat with your mum and dad in there Vicki

Ian H. Becca with your permission (assumée) I would love to add a few of my many memories of the "Top Club" here goes. Firstly the building and the rules in the 40's when I first went there with my parents. As you go in through the heavy double swinging glass doors the first room on the left was the Library (my father was the librarian for many years) it later changed to the Cocktail Lounge!! As you walked towards the bar the room on the right was the skittle room with two skittle tables, and a dartboard, through the swinging door to the bar (I can still see my Dad coming thro' there with his trilby hat.) On the left of the bar as you go in another entry opened into the snooker room with 3 tables, the first one was allegedly the truest. Up stairs the concert room was on the left (what nights were enjoyed there with the music and the bingo!) On the other side of the upstairs bar(complete with dumb waiter) was the Wicker Room (because the chairs were made of Wicker.

P 29: Club Centenary mementos

Women were only allowed upstairs and children had to leave by 10 o'clock from upstairs only at the week-ends. Visitors had to be signed in by the doorman (at the entry in a little room.)In the fifties the Tic Tac Toe machines were installed, if you were lucky enough to win, all the money in the machine came crashing through a hole in the front and had to be counted by a committee member (Bert Buckingham usually!!) Mr Fred Attlebury was the chairman wonderful man, Johnny Lucas looked after the snooker tables (he told me of his time in WW1!!) Mr Turner used to re-tip billiard cues (billiards was also popular on the tables). He lived down Jersey Rd. Geoff Labrum may recall him. In August time they covered the tables and held the annual Garden & Flower Show (Mr Wood from Eton Crescent won most of the prizes, the father of Kathleen Wood who married John Smith from Glos Rd/Mar Dr.) After the show all the exhibits were auctioned off so the ladies at least once a year got a bouquet from their hubbies. I'm sure you are bored by now but I'll maybe add more later. Thanks for the permission:) :)

Geoff L. Mr Turner son Fred was at school with me also a mate.

Becca H. Ian H. Nous vous remercions de vos souvenirs, Ian et vous sont bienvenus à ajouter quelque chose à mes histoires à tout moment.

Gill B. I also have fond memories of the "Top Club". We lived in Peel Rd, and my Dad Albert "Geordie" Robinson was barman/cellar man at the club during the sixties. In fact in my last year at the Grammar school I also worked behind the bar for a few months. Friday night was men's bingo night upstairs but at half time they would come down to the bar. It was usually three deep, everyone wanting to be served quickly before going back upstairs for the second half of the bingo.

Gareth G. Hi Gill. I remember your dad (Robbie) fondly, my Dad was steward at the club from 1960 to1973. I remember spending time at your house as a kid with Mick and Judith in the sixties.

Ian H. Becca, c'est très gentil de votre part. Merci bien. The first ladies I can recall regularly being in the bar, after the rules changed, were Mrs Faulkener & Mrs Lucas, Johnny's wife (see part about billiard tables earlier on), both aged widows with their bottles of Mackeson, also Iris? Rainbow Jack's wife and mother of Jackie from up Windsor St.

Becca H. I remember the Rainbow family! Also remember as a child, the strict 'gender' rules of who could go where and when! I also remember a regular band who seemed to sing a song everyone liked - over and over again. The name of the song is coming to me. .... More later on that one. I had some black patent lace up shoes that I was only allowed to wear when we went to the top club (oh - and I think at a push, the works Christmas party! Our dad called them my "light evening shoes" which was quite alien and weird a term to discuss with a kid! My bro Chris and I have often had a chuckle about this.

145

Ian H. Becca do you remember those odd seats/ benches in the "Concert Room" with metal holders at the back to put your drinks in!!

Becca H. Yes Ian H. - and as a kid seeming to spend quite a bit of time hanging out with other kids (for as long as you could get away with, without getting dragged or sent back to your parents) in the area outside the concert room doors! I would have been 12 or 13 when the song I memtioned earlier was repeatedly sung. "Blame it on the Pony Express!" and HI HO SILVER LINING! (a song written for Dad dancing if ever there was. I now feel REALLY bad that a few of you will be plagued by these tunes dancing round your heads for hours now!!! hahaha x

Ian H. I remember Alan Leeson with his group "covering" the Stones. Wonder if Al has found "Satisfaction"?

Hayley D. Ian if you mean Jackie Nash her mum name is Sylvia, they used to lived next door to me, I remember those songs. what memories.

Ian H. Don't think so? Jackie was slightly deaf and her mum's name was def. Iris/Irene Wotton before she married Jack Rainbow.:)

Hayley D. Sorry definitely not the same Jackie. I'm probably a bit to young to remember who your are talking about as I was born in 1971, lived in Windsor st for 23 years, my mum and dad will know exactly who you are talking about.

Gill B. Hi Gary, yes I remember you. You were the younger brother. Your Mum & Dad, Nancy and Ivor. In fact when I worked at The Post Office Training College Dawn and Marilyn were also working there. Judith still lives in Peel Rd., she moved in with Mum after her divorce though sadly Mum died in 2003. Lots of happy memories .

Sheila H. Would like to thank Becca H. as I now cannot get Chirpy chirpy cheep cheep out of my head...."last night I heard my momma singing a song...." Arghhhhhhhhhhhhh!!!!!!!!

Ian H. Hayley, thanks a bunch for reminding me I'm really old!!!

Becca H. I am sitting here with my single malt, wood burner roaring, keeping out the Yorkshire cold .... and trying to feel as sorry..... as I POSSIBLY can for Sheila in her current predicament. Its not working yet Sheila .... but I'll keep trying (snigger snigger) x

Ian H. You're probably having a Mac Do in Leeds somewhere after spending too much money in Tesco:)

Sheila H. It's ok Becca I am moving on to "Baby's first Christmas" by Connie Francis. lol

Becca H. Top that off with a shot of Patsy Cline's "Crazy" Sheila Higginbotham - and you got your self a cracking' evening' going' on there hahaha.

Sheila H. Throw in a bit of My Ding a Ling for good measure!!!

Julia B. "Last night I heard my momma singing a song"....oh hell!

HayleyD. Sorry Ian your only as old as you feel inside lol.

Becca H. Well Sheila & Julia - I can't sit here by the fire too long as I'll get "Needles and Pins ah" So I'll pop and put my milk bottles out for "Ernie" and shut up for a while - cos after all "Silence is Golden" x x

Julia B. No no no no.....torture....x

Sheila H. You "Sad sweet Dreamer" Becca. Oh "Mama we're all crazy now" x x

Becca H. ....tra la la ..."its just one of these things you put down to experience ....tra lala Anyways Sheila - all this typing has turned me a "Whiter Shade of Pale" (and I don't mean WATNEYS) X

Sheila H. Sounds like you have "Night Fever" !!! Really scraping the barrel now!!!

Becca H. Yes and I hope its not the 'bitter barrel Sheila! Off to lie down now so got to put the "Blanket on the Ground" x

Julia B. This is awful, I'm just going to have to "walk away Rene" xx

Becca H. Gareth G. - I remember you and all your family - and your mum and dad Nan and Ivor. Also recently found a couple of old black and white pics of that 'teal blue' mini you and I bought!

Gareth G. -which was 38 years ago!!

Sheila H. Any relation to David Griffiths who married Nina?

Becca H. Oh Julia B. dear - Let me know if you need a "Bridge over Troubled Water - and I'll send round Lily the Pink x

Julia B. ENOUGH ;))))) X

Becca H. O.K .... so I'll STOP! (in the name of love!) ha-ha

Billy L. The Jackie you were speaking of earlier was Jackie Rainbow. Married a chap early 70's named Flynn had 2 kids, then

147

married Mick Duff lived on Greenleys. I think she now lives on one of the estates "up the city" parents Iris and Jack, lovely couple.

Becca H. Ian - we aren't all flat caps and whippets up here you know! However (and my brother Chris can verify this) I have in recent years, taken a very strong liking for Mackeson - which older ladies and 'nursing mothers' used to drink in the top club. If it wasn't Mackeson it was another brand of Milk Stout!

Jackie S. Becca, I love a Mackeson shandy.

Becca H. All the classy girls of today like Macky Jackie! We are so retro - and so now love x

Becca H. Off to bed - late turn tomorrow so no new year drink 4 me at the TOP CLUB or anywhere else! Nite all x

Colin T. Night God bless, sending ya Love Hugs & kisses xxxx

Chris G. My only Top Club memories were the Hubbley-Bubbley bubbles went up your nose, Unit6 seemed to play every other week and the sign by the stage that stated 'Bands are reminded that the playing of March of the Mods is prohibited in this establishment'

Gareth G. Hi Becca, yep remember it well just before we moved to Nottingham in 1974. How's things?

Becca H. Hi Gareth! Things are good with me. Have lived in Yorkshire since the mid 80's. See you are still in Arnold. You look really well in your pic - and obviously did OK for yourself judging by the lovely looking lady in your pic! ... Got loads of fond memories of your family. (even though it did drive your dad Ivor mad having a mad teenage girl in the house for the time I lived with your family!) To this day I never let my potatoes over boil as I can still hear your mum Nan's voice asking me if I was making potato soup! Will post one of the pics of our wee car later this evening. Do you still have your fab vinyl record collection? Nice to touch base with you again.

Billy L. The top club was the place to be on a Friday night ...... Your memories of the discos.

Julie W. Kevin and his air guitar xx

Pina R. Sounds 2000 disco........

Susan K. Yes, Kevin, Rocking all over the world! GREAT!

John S. Do you remember the NGMT DISCO ?

Helen P. Me, Cheryl Roberts, Jane Tipping, and Jive Talking by the Bee Gees!

148

Donnah O. Me and Susan and blue Monday by new order
Susan K. "The Wanderer" and "Run around Sue"
Stephen G. Lots of good soul music from the 70's. Good times.
Andrew L. Rendezvous
Hayley D. Definitely great memories. Rocking all over the world, prince charming and goodies two shoes.
Hayley D. The time warp and spirit in the sky.
Peter L. Haven't seen Kevin up club for some time, some body told me Kevin and his guitar had gone on tour.
Toni B. mmm night out up there for less than a tenner. lol

P 30: Working Men's Club on Western Road. The "Top Club."

Ian H. A tenner Toni Brown!!!! In my day it was ten bob and that included the bingo:-
Toni B. LOL possibly was a LOT less than a tenner! Got to try and make out I'm younger than my years.
Theresa W. As a kid, used to have a drink at the top club - something and blackcurrant, can anyone tell me what the other drink was (non alcoholic of course LOL)
Toni B. Teresa-- was it lemonade use to drink that too.

149

Theresa W. Thanks Toni - I used to love that drink

Theresa W. Toni - brought some blackcurrant and some lemonade yesterday; lovely - took me right back to being a kid :0)

Toni B. Teresa---- glad you still liked it -I also liked lime and lemonade done the same way, really nice if its hot.

Dean W. God I remember going up the top club for the disco with my little sis on the Friday nights and as I got older used to go up there for the cheap drink.

Ian H. Bingo was 2/6d a pint about 1/3d so if you went steady on the ale you still had some change for the Tic Tac Toe machine and/or a game of brag :-)

Toni B. Worked there in the late 60's early 70's --all them bloody 1/3d adding up why wasn't it round numbers.

Toni B. All the older blokes many had their own glass jugs--get it wrong and you'd get a bollocking some miserable sods too.

Ian H. Was Nita still there then and Reuben Smith! Not forgetting Jennifer of course:-)

Toni B. hmmm don't know, my memory isn't what it used to be.

Ian H. ....and you took your beer back if it was a bit "iffy" and got it changed. Did you know that Bert Buckingham could down a pint without swallowing, like a drain that bloke, great chap though' remember he stood outside the club when my father's hearse left my late sister's (MARY Cox) house in Western Rd. Respected that I did.

Toni B. Also if you didn't fill their pints up enough back they came-don't know if it was the club or rugby club 1 bloke after a few would want to drink the slope trays empty YUK !! but he got pissed for nowt.

Richie B. Used to get asked to leave because we wore string vests and had spiked colour hair l

Jennifer T. Ian it was Nina not Nita, but then you are getting on now. xx

Toni B. Remember Nina-but that was after I worked there.

Richie B. Nina Griffiths.

Jennifer T. Yes that's right, Stan & Joan were the stewards when I worked there, then Les & Bet

Theresa W. Toni - brought some blackcurrant and some lemonade yesterday; lovely - took me right back to being a kid :0)

Toni B. Theresa---- glad you still liked it -I also liked lime and lemonade done the same way, really nice if its hot

Ivor S. Foxtrot, tangos and waltz's in my day with Mum and Dad doing the dancing.

Toni B. Ha ha !! Ivor I can hear the music.

Pat B. The Top Club is still thriving if anyone wants to pay a visit. Still has live music in the bar every weekend but drinks are a bit dearer than the prices mentioned above.

Ian H. Thieving bar stewards Pat :-)

Those were the days

Ian H. Those were the days when.......... the dustman came to the back of your house to collect the bin, then bring it back.

Sheila B. And my mum always gave them a glass of sherry at Xmas to guarantee they never dropped her bin!

Pat C. Last Friday saw dustman hurl two bins 10 - 12 feet into a driveway in town. Last two years I bag in the bins and take bags to local centre costs 1/4 of the price.

Ian H. And young lads had combs in their pockets (Cookie Cookie lend me your comb).

Ian H. .and public telephones had "A" and "B" buttons which you had to push to get the coins to work to be connected!!

Hazel S. Children went into the phone boxes to press button 'B' in case somebody had left some money there.

Ian B. You got two packets of chewing gum every fourth turn of the knob. In the chewing gum machine.

Ian H......when cigarette lighters had to have their wool wadding refilled with fuel, remember those rubbery yellowish oblong tubes that you pierced with a pin then squeezed gently into the Ronson:-) (a euphoric smell)

Pat C. Ian they are doing that with super glue these days. Plus there is an elderly gent still goes round Tralee pushing the buttons in what telephone boxes are left.

Ian H. .... When children thought McDonalds was a farmer (He Hi He Hi Ho)

Hazel S. Visiting Inverness many years ago saw a roadside advert announcing 'McDonalds are coming here'. Someone had scrawled underneath 'We've been here for years'.

Ian H. ....Names on letters had *Esq* as a suffix. (To men of course)

Nick C. I lived in Great Linford in the 60s...we still had a Squire!

Ian H. Trousers were fastened(flies) by buttons, not zips ;-)

Kim P. When the milkman came round so early you had to set the alarm clock to get to it before the blue tits. Is there still a milk man in Wolverton? We don't have them here. I also miss seeing letters addresses to couples as "Mr. & Mrs. Fred Bloggs" but apparently that's considered sexist now.

June L. Remember braces as well as belts & granddad collar on men's shirts, I love that look. When my dad use to give me a letter to put in the red pillar box for him I remember he a always put Esq. after the name.

Ian H. Bought a pair of braces (very chic though') a couple of years ago. Help no end when you have a bit of a beer belly June :-)

Pat C. Is someone suggesting people on this post need braces?

Brian E. When milk had gone off slightly, and there were always bits in your tea, no matter how many times you scooped one out.

Ron B. Used to love 'twanging' my dads braces and running off. Never did catch me though.

Kim P. Skin on your coffee or hot chocolate.

Brian E. An American woman was telling me once how she wanted to twang the suspenders worn by an Amish man. Whilst my mind boggled at this thought, I remembered that in the USA they call braces suspenders.

Ian H. ....when a "hundred poles " was someone's allotment size not immigrants.

Hazel S. When the Heath Robinson influence was seen, particularly in Wolverton Allotments.

Ian H. Ah!! When rhubarb was forced in old rusty upside down buckets!

June L. I've brought my rhubarb on with a large plastic bucket.

Kim P. My Dad used to smoke a pipe when I was little. I was just thinking the other day you never see people smoking pipes any more.

June L. My Dad did too, I always liked the smell of pipe smoke.

Ron B. My dad smoked a pipe to, always said "you can't beat a rough shag"

Ian H... ..and page 3 was just a page between 2 and 4 :-)

Jennifer T. And they were metal bins

Ron B. The lids made Brilliant shields

Ian H........pole dancing is what innocent children did in the month of May.

Ian H. Burt Lancaster or Tony Curtis Ron ;-)

Ron B. Burt, every time Ian.

Ian H. I was more the Peter Ustinov type.................terribly misunderstood:-)

Ian H. Still am come to that!!!!!!!!

Pat B. Suspenders and seamed stockings... Making sure the seam was up the back of your leg and not creeping round the side.

Ron B. Easy Pat, There are people on here with high enough blood pressure.

Ron B. I get the same reaction Ian.

Pat C. I always took pride in my straight seams, or was it creases?

Pat B. Just keep taking the tablets Ron.

June L. I dressed as a Teddy Girl when I was 16, the time of Bill Haley. I had a grey Herringbone costume with a black velvet collar & cuffs, my stockings were shire black with seam at the back & embroider butterflies at the side of each leg, I wore a pony tail then as it was the done thing as my boyfriends were as they use to call them Teddy Boys, Happy Days.

Pat C. The Teds had a spate of wearing the Luminous Green socks went well with the winkle pickers, fancy jacket and of course the DA.

Ron B. Some had one green and one red one Pat.

Brian E. We may have to inform the young ones what a DA is!

Brian E. Duck's arse!

Ron B. Brian, Vidal Sassoon created the DA, sadly died yesterday.

Pat C. I knew someone would have to explain the DA!

June L. They wore thick crepe sole shoes in my day, the winkle pickers came later, I didn't like them, I never saw Teddy boys wearing them. They did have a DA (ducks arse) I also had a DA at one time, I have a photo of me somewhere, I think Terry's got it.

153

Ian H. The Mohican came a bit later.............for some!!!! Arthur from Braddle for one!

June L. It was also called The Tony Curtis, I loved the front bit they pulled over onto their forehead.

Pat C. I remember the winkle pickers in the late 50s June.

June L. Yes Pat I definitely remember having a pair of Winkle pickers then. I was 18 yrs old had only just moved to Wolverton & Sylvia Bull took me in the Plough where I met Pete for the 1st time. The last bus at 10pm had gone so Pete walked me home & I was wearing brown leather 6inch stiletto Winkle Picker Shoes, by the time we got to Wolverton I was walking like Dick Emery. That's why I don't like them.

Ian H. June did you come thro' the "Happy Morn" or keep to the main road;-)

June L. I know we had a down pour of rain & my dad lent Pete one of his jackets to wear walking back to Stony in the rain, & we also remember the date 29th June.

Ron B. If I tried to do that now June, my arse would be between my shoulder blades. *Do you like my shoes? They're crepe. Oh they are not that bad.*

June L. Have you got any Blue Suede Shoes Ron? Would go nice with your DA shoulder blades.

Ian H. ....when potatoes were weighed on scales with those heavy dull metal weights, especially in the market hall!!

Ian B. You had to be able to do calculations in base 12 to make sure you weren't being overcharged by the stallholder.

Ian H..............and Geoffrey (Goff) told the health visitor that the nicotine stains on his fingers was due to rust!!!!!!

Geoffrey W. Those were the days when we could afford to smoke. Now it only stretches to a pint on Monday night after practice with the Mevagissey Male Choir.

. . . when we were young and stupid

Len E. What was the dumbest thing you did when you were younger? Mine was trying to push back into place a brake block on my bike whilst riding it

Richie B. Ooh where to start lol ... I did put my automatic BMW into drive whilst leaning through the window when topping up the gear box oil and proceed up Stony High St with my legs out the window until I managed to slam it into park ...much to the amusement of passers by ...nearly hit some parked cars and bruised some ribs in the process!

Jane B. When I was 7 I rode my bike whilst wearing flip flops (against my Mums advice) - and promptly ran into a brick wall - tearing all the skin off the ends of my toes!!!! (Did a similar thing aged 3 when I was pushing a baby walker down a slope in Scunthorpe - dragged me along and ended up with no tips on my toes - thought I'd have learnt my lesson, but hey ho, such is life!!!!!!

Ian S. The canal was iced over. Unhappy with this proceeded to jump up and down on the ice to no avail. Undeterred I proceeded to get a log and jump in unison with the log banging on the ice. Yes you have guessed the rest. (What a twat!)

Steve A. Squaring up to a bloke called Steve Mcfarland (I think that's the correct spelling) when I was about 12. He was built like a brick out house, I wasn't. I got the first punch in but after that it was all downhill.

Dave M. Agreeing to absail down the Radcliffe tower block, really stupid considering I suffer from vertigo! Wasn't helped when half way down one of the cleaners shoved a mop through the window to shake the dust off and hit me square in the face.

Jane B. Steve, I remember Steve McFarland - lived on Greenleys - huge for his age - about as wide as he was tall - black curly hair. He used to hang around with my cousins Jo & Tish - haven't seen him for years.

John R. Testing a stapler to see if it worked by holding a piece of paper up to the business end and the pushing. Managed to staple the paper through my finger and finger nail. Hurt like hell and I had to have the staple pulled out with pliers, which hurt a lot more.

Steve A. That's him Jane. Wasn't just my imagination then. I remember looking up at him and having to punch skywards to connect with his chin.

Pat C. Heading into Cornwall from Bucks for our holiday when I was very young 1949/50 grinding up steep hill in first gear. I was in front, stood up to see out put my hand under dashboard to get grip but pulled some wires out instead, car stops on hill, narrow road, holiday traffic. Took Dad about two hours to repair. I was popular!

Lynette M. I remember someone absailing down the Radcliffe tower block. I thought at the time that's a dumb thing to do LOL.

John Rd. Dunno... I think accidently burning down my mum's house was the dumbest but I've done too much dumb shit and still continue to do more dumb shit as I get older

Ron B. Had a Vauxhall 101 in the early 70s. My pride and joy. Stopped outside a shop in Wolverton to get a paper. Left my lit cigarette in ashtray, which had some toffee papers in. When I returned flames were licking up melting all the knobs on the radio. Idiot!

Terry L. After being round Ian Lawson's house decided to go home for tea, I decided to see how far I could get riding my bike with my eyes closed, I started my experiment at the end of Marina Drive and managed about 30 yards before I hit a parked car in Stacey Avenue, OUCH ! Doh !

Becca H. Our Dad once brought home some huge plastic concentrated orange juice containers. Very heavy and full. Chris would have been about 2 at the time. Anyway Mum said me and Tricia Old who lived opposite us at the time, could fill the paddling pool as long as we kept an eye on Chris. For some stupid reraon I decided whilst filling it with saucepan after saucepan of water that it would be fun if we also had orange in it, then we could sit in pool and drink at the same time. (I was only 7).

Ian S. It's the future Becca.

Becca H. Guess who got sent to bed without any tea for risking getting her baby brother stung by wasps and bees??? He didn't get stung by the way ..... but by the severity of the telling off I got you'd have thought the little fella had lost a limb! He was very happy and chuckling throughout the whole 'incident'

Dave M. Surprised Ian didn't lift the car out of the way for you Tel.

June L. When I was about 3 yrs old I thought I could pick my younger cousin David up while we were playing in the garden, I dropped him on his head.

Kim P. Mine's bike related too, I tried to adjust the saddle while I was riding it, the saddle came loose and flipped up and hit me in a rather painful spot - could have been worse.

Janet S. Cutting my sister's hair. My Dad had to sort it out and she ended up with it above her ears. Sorry got no photos to show you.

Jill G. I was about 8 and the start of the summer hols, I had a pair of them roller skates on that you slipped over your shoes and a strap round the ankles i tripped over a raised pavement and fractured both ankles so 6 weeks of crawling on hands and knees

Chris G. I fought the law, and the law won!

Steve C. Squaring up to Bilko. Did not win. Black-eye was very colourful two days later.

Kim P. John Reed. Did you actually burn the whole house down?

John Rd. Pretty much Kim. Was a couple days after Xmas 1998. was home alone and mucking around with matches. Inside the house was gutted pretty much

Andrew L. I did the indoor fire thing often :) worst damage was a shattered ashtray and melted rubbish bin. I remember squirting lighter fuel onto a fire in the bin and seeing the whole stream alight. Don't know how I got away with it ....

Steve P. I must have been about 12 & decided to tie a crow scarer to the frame, underneath the seat, of my pushbike. I lit it & pedalled off, it exploded with a large bang, no injuries but the frame cracked & separated & could no longer tighten saddle. Expensive experiment!

Chris G. Falling off the roof at the Swing Rec, managed to snap both bones in my wrist and shattered my elbow, spent a year in plaster and had to have several ops to have it plated etc. Still got the scars to this day. Happy days...

Becca H. Remember it well!

David E. Talking of fires I remember sitting in Derek Morgan's back garden with my my brother Les. Derek was having a crafty fag and he decided to start a small bonfire before we knew it the whole garden was ablaze, he was running back and forth across the green like a headless chicken. Someone called the fire brigade and when the fire was out we went to view the damage and found a roasted hedgehog, poor thing.

Lynette M. Playing kiss chase with Derek Morgan at Wolverton infants. That was pretty dumb. Oh no actually was pretty damn nice. LOL.

Richie B. Wetting myself laughing at Terry on his bike ....My mum left me on my own when she popped to the shop and I sat on the kitchen work top blowing at the pilot light on the water heater ....in those days they were very basic. Any how, the boiler light went out ..took me about 20 mins to find some matches climbing on the counter and struck a match lol and got blown to the floor losing most of my eye brows and fringe lol ...Never went near it again!

Helen P. When my brother Bill Lisle was younger he decided to whack his space hopper with our mum's frying pan.....rebounded hitting him in the mush and knocked his front teeth out! HAHAHAHAH!

Deborah B. David yes I remember the fire engines!!!! Was Colin Hayle not in it with my brother as well?

David E. I think Colin arrived on the scene when the fire engine turned up Deborah, there was quite a big crowd outside your house as I recall.

5 Notes from daily life

Unusual eating habits.

Ian H. One day of the year we ALWAYS had fish, Good Friday. My friend Trevor's family always had their Yorkshire pudding first on a Sunday on it's own or with a syrup; think this may have been a frugal way to reduce meat consumption ,i.e. you weren't as hungry if you "noshed" on YP first, any more?

Andy C. Last season I went to see Northampton Saints at Leeds Carnegie and was amazed at the amount of locals filling their faces with Yorkshire Pud and sweet fillings - very odd!

Julia B. Mother Bennett made "Yorkshire pudding with currents in" every week as an afters. We ate it with Golden Syrup on, yum...

Julia B. An ex boyfriend's family came from Yorkshire. They always had the Yorkie with gravy first; it made the Yorkie a bit more important and appreciated it more. And we always had fish on a Friday, all year round. That is a tradition with roots in religion, but I can't think why!

Julia K. Something to do with Good Friday and Jesus feeding the masses with bread and fish, me thinks. We always used to have fish on Fridays. Yorkshire pud with beef on a Sunday if mum could afford beef and any pudding left would be eaten later on cold with jam spread on it and it was yummy. Tripe and onions on freezing cold winter nights to keep us warm, yummy.

Julia B. Oh yes Julie, forgotten the jam on Yorkie pud!

Angie A. My Dad always said grace when we all sat down for Sunday lunch and we always went to church. My sister and I and Sunday School then home for lunch and family favourites on the radio.

Mike L. Fish on Friday. The old Wolverton market was always on a Friday and there was a very good fishmonger. Friday's main meal was invariably based on what my mother could afford. Remember; shrimps, prawns in batter, plaice, skate - all depended on how much was left in the household kitty.

John R. I just remember the strange stuff - banana sandwiches, chip butties, and Saturday afternoon tea - which my dad made and could be any combination of stuff he liked - all healthy food like bacon, mushrooms, black pudding, and faggots - typically fries up together.

Julia B. Mr Robinson, none of the above is "strange"...it's wonderful, especially the chip butties plenty of tomato sauce. Yum yum

John R. I agree - I used to like salad cream on my chip butties - but you have to admit the whole idea of a chip buttie is strange, especially if you try to explain it to someone.

Julia B. John, did you know they were going to stop making salad cream a couple of years ago, there was public uproar so they carried on. Funny really, I guess people only wanted it again, when they were reminded of it's existence!

John R. I think we can even buy it at an "Irish" food shop in Cleveland - You'll notice there are never any English food shops. I've seen British, Scottish, and Irish but never English, with the exception of "Ye Olde English Tea Shoppe" -

Home made wine

Bryan D. Any home made wine stories out there? Aunt Edna getting tiddly on a glass of elderflower wine. Cousin Eric crawling home after believing that Potato wine was no stronger than tea?

Celia R. Made some my self - potato and elderberry and made beer.

Ian H. Trevor Hobson, on behalf of his mother, tapped sap from willow trees as a basis for wine. I have done blackberry and rose-hip. Now I have a more refined taste, given my location.

Ruth E. When we cycled from Puxley to Deanshanger aged 11 my Aunty Clara gave us a small glass of home made wine to warm us. No one told us it was probably 80% proof.

Ian H. The bloke over the way from me invited us over for his daughter's birth. His wife is from the Cameroons and he had this big bottle of pure alcohol which he had put all these exotic fruits in to add a touch of the dark continent. We drank it!! Biggest hangover since I left Plessey in 1960.

Sharon S. My demi-john of home made red exploded in my mum's airing cupboard many years ago. I wasn't popular.

June L. Not wine I'm afraid but I have a story on Beer. All my family from Wolveton went to my Cousin's Birthday party in Essex. Terry was about 6yrs old. One the way home after a Good Old Knees up & plenty of Booze (except for the driver of course who was my husband Pete). My brother Peter sat in the back of our car with Terry sat on his lap both asleep. Suddenly I heard Terry crying " Mum I've been sick" & clutching the top of his head. BUT it wasn't Terry who had been sick it was Brother Pete straight on top of poor old Terry's Head. No wonder Terry's hair went curly after that Ha-Ha!

Jill G. My Nan used to make homemade wines. Quite funny really as she never drank. I can remember helping with the preps sometimes as a kid the cellar was full of all sorts of wine but my fav was her banana wine. It was like a liqueur very yummy. Also I got hammered once on a friend's rice wine. Oh dear, never again! I was intoxicated for a week.

Richie B. I remember having pochine not sure of the spelling 100 % proof round my Irish mates house only had half a small glass and he'd diluted it I staggered home sick as a dog

Barbara L. Ginger beer made by neighbour, Whenam family, smells like sick and burns your throat, but strangely addictive.

Penny G. My aunt who lived in Stony always had a stash of parsnip wine in her cellar, also wheat & potato. The smell was unbelievable when you went down there. It still remains in my memory.

Jill G. What's pochine?

Penny G. Pot-chine Jill is Irish moonshine will burn the back of your throat off.

Pat C. Poitin is the real stuff

Richie B. It was shocking whatever the spelling and yes it did ruin my throat. x

Ian H. That sounds a little French Pat.

Pat C. That's the correct Irish spelling Ian, I can remember as a young fella my Dad bringing it back from his hometown in Bantry,

Co Cork every holiday to Bucks in Schweppes bottles to fool the customs!

Ian H. I've had a Google at it Pat looks like a mighty fine drop. The "paysans" in these parts make a distilled hooch (very illegal) from one of the marsh plants, the name escapes me. I did have a swig from a secreted bottle of it at a do and it was very fiery............time for a drink I think, bottoms up!!

Bryan D. Absinthe?

Ian H. No not Absinthe Bryan, although' that is another mind boggler, this one is local to the Charente marshes I was told.

Bryan D. In that case you won't be able to say "Absinthe makes the heart grow fonder."

Ian H. The only time I'm Absinthe is at Lent.

Ian H. As an aside, again, when I first moved to St. Sulpice in 1999 I was out walking with my dog and I came across a mobile distillery which was parked up near to the local cemetery. The local farmers who grew grapes brought there wine there to be distilled into brandy. The "business" was passed down through families and was strictly licensed, the boiler was fed with wood provided by the farmers. It was a treat to behold this old tradition which sadly has since been banned and no licences have been issued. I wouldn't mind betting though that it's going on still somewhere - well I hope so!!

Stephen C. Not wine, but the Clarridge Brewery tried brown ale. Spilt some on the coffee table and stripped the varnish away. Pete Clarke drank about 3 bottles and was not seen for a couple of days. The rest of the bottles exploded in the cellar. End of Clarridge Brewers.

David Wn. Most stories with references to "stronger than whisky and 100% proof" as the reasons for the adverse effects of drinking home made wine are all sadly untrue. Even the most alcohol tolerant yeasts can only yield around 13% alcohol. The major causes of its devastating effects were "drinking too much, too quickly" but more seriously the fermentation of starch and grain liquors unfortunately resulted in the formation of traces of methanol- quite toxic!

Maurice H. We always used to make wine at home. Then one night, having put about a dozen bottles and a very large carboy behind the wardrobe to brew and mature, around midnight when we were all asleep, pop, pop, Boom the whole lot exploded and soaked everything in sight, it was like the Victoria Falls. Needless to say, more care was taken next time to store it.

Kim P. My Dad made his own wine and beer in the cellar at Victoria Street. The wine was usually elderberry, I remember helping pick, sort and crush the berries. Took forever and our hands were stained for weeks. Very dry, bitter wine. He made dandelion wine too which was slightly sweeter. One year he got ambitious and tried to make a champagne type wine. Turned out he wasn't really that good at home carbonation, I forget if it was 12 or 24 bottles but the whole lot went off bang one night when everyone was asleep, sounded like the house was coming down around us.

Barbara L. Rum and Black made me ill on ferry to France, used to have scrumpy cider, sweet but deadly

Maria M. My Dad made and makes his homemade wine. Don't know what it tastes like... don't touch the stuff.

Pop

Kazza B. Who remembers the Alpine pop man doing the rounds....... OMG I remember the wonderful flavours that were so new to us then!! Pineapple..... who'd of thought it? Pop was a rarity in those days, unless it was Dayla pop from the offy or the working men's clubs. Dayla golden lemonade!!! and of course taking the Dayla bottle back to the off license to get the deposit back for penny sweets!!!

Jennifer T. We used to have the Corona man come round; us 3 kids could choose a flavour each, mine was cream soda

Terry L. Hubbly Bubbly ! Strike cola ! For some strange reason Red Corona was called Clarona Corona, that was my fave...

Kazza B. We used to have a bread van come round too and we used to buy a dozen penny rolls. For years I used to think he couldn't count cos we always got 13!

Becca H. Bakers dozen.

Len E. Yeah, the Corona man!! Dandelion and Burdock, takes me back all those years when I drink it now.:)

163

Angie A. I remember the Corona Man used to call when we were at my nannies in Bradwell. I loved the green one. And when we went to the footy at Wolverton Park we used to have a bottle of Cherry pop and a packet of Smiths crisps with a little twist of salt inside to shake on ourselves. Happy days :))))

Heather W. I remember Hubbly Bubbly. We used to go down to the working man club and my Dad used to buy it for me on the walk down everyone who passed you in the street would say good evening they were the days when people were polite

I remember looking around for empty pop bottles so we could get some money to buy sweets

Toni B. Ginger beer (whole new meaning now)

June L. My Dad use to get the Cream Soda & put a scoop of ice cream in the glass for us, it was lovely as it melted into the Fizz

Heather W. Ice cream soda we get different flavours down on beach

Kim P. What flavour was the green corona? I liked that one, also cream soda, dandelion and burdock and pineapple. I liked all the weird ones

Pat C. Nothing like the Dando and Burdock, further north Tizer the Appetiser

Kim P. This has reminded me I have a small bottle of (very expensive!) Irn-Bru in my fridge... Oh yeah! And you got 2p back on the bottles! I forgot about that.

Barbara L. Cherry yum, real fizzy

Pat C. When I came over to Ireland in 1964 I had a shock, my pint of shandy had a red head, instead of white lemonade the national pop was Nash's Red, also missed ready salted crisps, cottage loaves and pork pies.

Danny K. Ah Pat tayto crisps and lemon soda or cidona yum yum.

Janice M. Yes Dayla golden lemonade was great and shandy here is pretty non-existent as we use ginger ale or sprite in as we don't have fizzy lemonade here!

Milk

June.L. Who knows what this is?

Margaret C. You already took the cream off the top. ha!
Marc H. Is that condensed stuff mind you it would not pour out very easily? Or is it goat's milk
Donna. S. It's milk, didn't goat's milk come in taller skinnier bottle... my Gran drank it in her tea.... personally didn't like the taste, found out later it's because cows milk was too hard on my stomach when a baby and my Mum gave me goats milk...
Brian E. I used to have to take my own container to buy goats' milk.
Ron B. Milk of magnesia?
Chris G. Llama milk from down the road
Ron B. Someone been expressing????

Jill G. Oh God Ron that's not right ha-ha.
Terry L. Ron you are a bad man!
Ian B. The sterilised milk came in the taller thinner bottles I seem to think they had a top that needed a bottle opener to remove; the milk was a cream colour and mum made the best rice puddings using it.
Jill G. You can still get it from the co-op Ian they sell it in the Newport.
June L. I just saved my Dairy Crest bottle from when I had it delivered in the days I put my milk checks out. I put Cow's milk in out of my Super market plastic bottle, like it better.
Chris G. Milk checks and bread tokens, how many years since they've gone? You still see the odd Wolverton one pop up on E Bay.
Ian S. I have one of these milk cheques from Wolverton co-op its oval and made of brass dug up in Castlethorpe.
Jill G. I have some orange round plastic ones somewhere
Ian. B. Leaving the empty milk bottles and checks on the door step, in the winter the tops would be forced off as the milk froze and in summer the blue tits would peck the tops to get at the cream.
June. L. When they put the price of milk up, they changed the colour of the checks from orange to lemon.

Chores

Julie W. Who used to do chores as kids, before or after school?
Barbara L. Yes only had a boiler and mangle too.
Elvia W. I used to. My mum died when I was ten so I helped my Dad. Bless, now they're both together.
Len E. A mountain of spuds were left for me to peel when I got home from school.
Jennifer T. My brother and I had our daily tasks before and after school, mum washed up we dried up, I hated to dry the cutlery, still do 60 odd years later.
David E. I used to cook the dinner for Mum and Dad coming home from work when my Sis left home, thanks for those cookery lessons June Scott.

166

Tracy S. We all had to help with the dishes every night after dinner.

Brian E. Chopping the logs into sticks, filling the coal scuttle, scattering the ashes in the morning. Occasionally, getting the paraffin can filled. 2/3d a gallon.

Ron B. Climbing up the chimney to sweep it lol

Ian H. Those paraffin cans were something else, remember the little spouts for pouring with the screw caps:-)

Constance O. We had chores, dusting, cleaning and washing dishes.

Ruth E. I was just called "Cinders". My Mum was always very poorly so I learnt about housework young and fast. Did not do me any harm I suspect.

Ian H. We just pushed the dust under the mat, a v. small mat. :-)

Pat C. Wiping up, washing car, digging allotment.

June L. I did the washing up & Bruv Pete had to wipe up.

Kim P. I don't remember being made to do chores as such but I did my own laundry and cooking once I got to around 15 because I went vegetarian and developed a fondness for special-care fabrics like Lurex :) and of course I was expected to do things like keep my room clean and pick up after myself but I think most of us did things like that anyway.

Jill G. Always keeping the teapot topped up and helping mum clean the bedrooms on Sunday mornings.

Togetherness

Ian H. Whilst finishing my meal with a fine glass of Bordeaux I have been musing. It is clear to me that my generation and the one that immediately followed it had an extraordinarily strong feeling of community, you only have to look at the copious examples on this remarkable site. I have spoken to my French wife about this and she assures me her life wasn't like mine (ours). Now that could be due to her upbringing which was much more reserved than mine, her being feminine, and catholic. However I think it is more than that, I look around where I live now and whilst I know my neighbours and our church's congregation I don't have the same "knowledge" of my fellow St Sulpiciens as I did of Wolvertonians,

167

and I suspect back in the UK it is much the same for you folks. It may be because of "rose tinted glasses way" the way we see the corner shops or the nostalgia surrounding our grotty houses and the carefree playing of children............but I think and hope it's more, is it because we lived in a time when respect and mutual respect prevailed, when communication was more by mouth than Microsoft?. If the politicians of today could tap into something like we had then, then Wolverton and St Sulpice would be better for it. ....and by the way Wolverton was, is and shall be Bucks!!.

Geoff L. Very well put Ian

Julie M. I watch this site and read this site I grew up in Wolverton went to the schools from nursery to Radcliffe my children went to Radcliffe also and I can walk though Wolverton at many times of the day and even though I know many people still here never meet any body to talk to why is that?

Ian H. Probably the same wherever you live in the UK(France Tip of the day :I go out of my way to smile and talk to people and surprise it works for me ,but people don't do it to me!

Julie M. Lived in Spain for a while been back a couple of years but there no matter what time of day always some body to speak to Spanish as well as English.

Mason M. Ian my sister lives in La Cocherie in Normandy just a small village of about 18 houses the nearest town village is Sourdeva They have been there over 7 yrs now And when they moved there it was like going back 40 yrs to the old Wolverton Where everyone said hello and you had a community not like bad old MK.

Terry L. I live in a village just outside MK , and all of the older community (70's+) will always speak and are generally lovely, the 50 some things who have lived here 10 to 15 years are all so far up there own arses it's a tad wearing. So what does that say?

Chris G. That you're a 50 something Terry?

Chris G. Same in New Zealand Mason, spent a month or so out there a couple of years back and for friendliness, and values and politeness, it has be said it was like going back 40 years. Bit of a culture shock calling in on brash Aussies for a few days on the way home though.

Ian H. I'm fine in my village, it's more when I go to Royan a couple of miles away where people are insular. In Wolverton we walked about a lot so we met people all the time.

Chris G. Funny thing I find is that if you walk along the canal or river everyone passes the time of day but you can pass the very same people in the street or Tesco and they don't acknowledge you at all.

Ian H. They are all too busy being busy Chris.

Donna S. Very well put Ian.... I have said before, it's the people that make a community what it is ... no one says hello anymore, no one checks up on an elderly neighbour, I live in a small community in Manitoba and it is very much like we used to have it when we were younger in Wolverton.. but then there are some within our community that keep to themselves, have their own "in crowd" as it were .. it's not looking at things with rose tinted glasses.... it is and was a moment in time and that moment is what made our generation and the ones before who we are today and I'm thankful for that.

Terry L. Ah Chris, I have only been here 8 years that's why I made the distinction, and in my defence I have been brought up the Wolverton way, so try to be ever so nice until some one upsets moi! Perhaps they feel threatened as we have the most family living in the village, but I can't understand why that would threaten people? Perhaps if they dislike one of us, they feel that they should ignore all of us! And no Chris we are not inbred! Lol

Neighbours

John C. I was walking down Victoria Street the other week thinking about 25 years ago when I could name nearly everyone in that street. Now I can't name hardly anyone. Who remembers the names of their neighbours when they were growing up in Wolverton?

Jane B. When we moved into Victoria Street in 1966 we met every single family and knew them all to say hello to. Nowadays Mum only knows a couple of her neighbours - sad sign of the times I reckon!

Terry L. Miss Watson one side and the Thomas's the other.

169

Jean G. Well my two immediate neighbours were the Wilsons, and the Bandys, I remember the Gregorys too, Mrs Canvin, friends of my parents Stuart and Marieann (sorry don't recall surname), also Sid and Min Taylor.

Vivienne B. In St Johns Cres, Price, Woodland View, Barnett, Millard, Haynes. St Georges Way, Lindops.

June L. My neighbours in Victoria St were Mr & Mrs Gill & Mr & Mrs Terry, in Green Lane it was Mr & Mrs Cyril Clark & Mr & Mrs Warner, then after we moved to Raunds (we were only there for 10 months & were desperate to get back to Wolverton) we moved to Oxford St & our next door neighbours were as Terry has already said.

Sylv O. I had Nanna Gill next door when I was born in 62 Victoria street they are my earliest memories. x

June L Mrs Gill was a lovely lady; we lived in no 62 from 1955/56 to 1960, when did you move into there Sylv?

Sylv O. I was born in the house in 69 my brother was born 66. I think I'm getting old now. I can't remember dates. x

June.L I lived next door to Mick Gill he was a close mate of my brother Pete. We were always joking with each other, one of his saying were that I made him blush & could I see him go Red in the face (of course he was Indian) & called my Bruv "Honky" we all use to laugh at it, never thought anything of it.

Vivienne B. After getting married I lived next to the great Clarence Gill, he was on the corner of Windsor Street and I was just around the corner in Western Road, then we both moved to Aylesbury Street West next door to each other. I can never remember the story of how he came to England, but my Dad had something to do with it. Clarence is a Gent and a lovely man, (I miss him as my neighbour).

Brian E. Clarence is one of the loveliest men I have ever met.

Vivienne B. I agree Brian, whenever he is around and my car is on the drive, he calls in to checks that I am ok. He also spoke at my Dad's funeral he said some lovely words, always the Gent. x

Tricia D. Didn't Clarence's family need to get out of their country Vivienne? Weren't Dad friends with a daughter??

Susan B. In Jersey Rd when I lived there (evens), were Herbert's, Lloyds, Fletcher, Amundsen, Mayo Butler, Squires (odds)

McKenzie, Mills, Willis, Ranson, Reynolds and Read, opposite via back alley to Anson Rd Russell, Kemps, Jordan, Collars and Jackmans.

Julie T. June we moved into 62victoria St in 1966 as my brother Peter was born there in May mum is not sure what month we moved there. But we loved Nan Gill, and I used to be friends with Glen Miller who was Nana Gill's grandson. We loved that house and I still remember all the rooms etc.

Hayley D. Windsor Street, one side was a dear elderly lady thinks her surname was Brown, then the Smiths. The other side was Nash then later Grimes/Johnson. Across the road Styles, Timms, Murphys. The house next to the Murphys had several families. Taylors can't recall the names at the mo.

June.L. Yes that was Glen Miller Rita's son who played in the back way with my son Terry, I loved that house it was different to most of the Terrace houses. Do you remember the little room under the stairs? Well my mum had her sewing machine in there & she did all her needle work sthere o she was away from everyone else.

Edith. H. Yes Gloucester Road 40 odd years ago I could name almost all of the people living there.

Julie T. Yes it had the meters in as well. Glen's birthday was the day before mine, 2nd. July 1962, mine was 3rd. I've not seen Glen for years, last time was at CMK. We used to hide in the cupboard that was half way up the stairs and sometimes we would empty the drawers and hide in them. We even had a toilet upstairs in the bathroom and downstairs in the back room but it was really cold in winter and your bum used to freeze.

Terry L Chris Gleadell, I believe our neighbours at 145 Church St. were the Derricuts.

Brian E. I knew some Derricuts, he had his own tipper truck and Mrs Derricut was a teacher.

Chris G. They had the patience of saints that's for sure Brian. They had Terry, me and a few others living next door for a couple of years when we were in our early 20's.

Terry L The Derricuts had two sons one of whom was killed in his Hillman Imp in Gloucester road when it caught fire after a crash in the 70's.

171

Chris G. Remember it well, terrible accident.

Having a flutter

Ian H. Betting was a very common occurrence in my childhood and youth as it is today but a lot different. Men wrote out their betting slips and gave it to a bookies" runner" someone like Jack Squires. A typical bet, and one that my father tried, was a 6 pence each way Yankee. These bets were collected in the pubs and were just about within the law (well maybe not). The Turf Accountants had their customers too with white boards marked out in stencil with the runners name and the latest odds being updated by someone with a coloured marker, all this information coming into the shop through the "ether" and broadcast for all to hear. The "off" was declared and a punctuated commentary was given until the groans of the losers and the cheers of the winners brought the race to a conclusion before the" weighed in" was sounded and the winning tickets were presented to the bookies clerk for payment. Another source of speculation was the football "pools" Littlewoods, Zetters and the like. Coupons were given out and collected to your house before the Saturday 3 o'clock kick offs and then the results of the matches were eagerly awaited on the radio or the Green Un was bought from Muscutt & Tompkins about 6 o'clock.

Bingo was just becoming popular with a book of five games costing two and six in the top room at the club.

The club's weekly "Tote" was drawn each Sunday by a committee member usually Bert Buckingham or Tommy Clarke in my day. This consisted of picking out two numbered balls, if you had been lucky enough to choose the right numbers you won! In all my father's time doing this he never won once nor me!!

Friday night card schools were common too in the club similarly dominoes, most were quite benign, like the "Crib" players but certain of us played Brag and this sometimes got a tad expensive!!

Molly H. Jack Squire was my Uncle, my Mums brother.

Ian H. Hello Molly I was mentioning you a while back on here to Sheila and Jennifer & Lesley! Hope you are well. Often think of the old days, take care.

Molly H. I did send a message to your inbox couple of days ago

Ian H. I didn't see that Molly, never mind I've "seen" you now, do you hear from the Dewicks or the Jones girls? I used to see Brian Bevan when I was living in Potterspury in another life in the 80's. Graham Tomlin told me the tragic story of his brother Alan. How about the Dythams??

Molly H. I last saw Mollie and Betty Dewick at their Mum's funeral. I don't suppose I shall see them again. I haven't seen Brian for years. The Dythams, oh what wonderful memories with my Dad being in Wolverton band.

Lesley W. I remember Greg but I think the others were a lot older than me.

Molly H. You mentioned Sheila, Jennifer and Lesley. Do I know them?

Sheila S. Molly, don't know if you remember me, was Pointer. My daughter lives in Tickford Street in the house where you used to live.

Ian H. What was the youngest Dytham called, not Nick, he scared me to death one day in his car going to Newport Pagnell, think he had been on the "Whacky Baccy" he and Alan Leeson always wanted to be, and did, get in our little click of friends. ...Barbara Bignell, Diane Turvey Geoff Woodward, Eggo, Jim Cobley,Trevor Hobson,Barry Stocker those days up the rec will stay with me forever, wonderful carefree days, wonderful. Were you there that day that Barbara gave Barry Stocker an almighty slap across the face, she nearly took his head off.

Sheila S. Ian, do you remember the bubble car Greg Dytham used to drive?

Ian H. That's him Lesley "Greg Dytham (the one who put the wind up me) good bloke Greg.

Ian H. I remember that scary ride to Newport Sheila how he missed a car by the Rocla works I shall never know, and he did it all with a huge Greg grin, talk about the swinging sixties, rock on !!!!

173

Molly H. Sheila I know your daughter and her husband. I did see you outside but didn't realize it was you. I have been going to that house in Tickford St. since I was 17 years old. They bought it from my ex husband Ray. It was Rudi and I that emptied it. Ray has sadly passed away since then.

Sheila S. We have both changed over the years so didn't realise it was you until Deb said. Rudii knows Ken, small world isn't it.

Ian H. Molly do you see Janet Lichfield, she lived in the pub down Tickford Street?

Ian H. Funny how a topic on gambling finishes up down Tickford Street and not a bookie in sight. Glad to have been of service girls.

Molly H. Ian, I saw Janet at Ray's funeral last August. Sheila it is a small world.

Ian H. My Aunty Joan (Smith) lived just down there in Priory Street on the left. My mother's side is Newport Pagnell. Funny enough my Granddad was a bookies runner too from his pseudo-shop in the high street, quite illegal at that but it gave him a...gave him a good living. In fact my grandfather had a car!! Pity my mother was a bit on the outside of her family as she lost her mother when she was born and was raised by her step mother who was always called Aunty Iliffe, they didn't get on apparently.

Bryan D. Great post Ian. The off topic comments were interesting too.

Premium Bonds

Bryan D.
This is one of my miserable Premium Bonds that has been sitting in a file for almost 50 years, bought at Wolverton post office on August 24th 1963. At that time £5 could have bought you 2 LPs, a packet of fags and a round of drinks for your mates. Instead it has slowly dwindled in value and is practically worthless. Oh, and needless to add, these numbers have not turned up once.

Susan B. Don't cash it in yet Bryan...you just know as soon as you do, it would have won!

Brian E. I think 20 cigarettes cost around 5 bob then Bryan?

Jacqueline G. Bryan, apologies but hahahahahha, next time spend it on wine women and song and just LIVE FAST. chuckle chuckle

3ES 893591

£5

3ES 893595

SERIAL NUMBERS INCLUSIVE

FIVE UNITS

PREMIUM SAVINGS BOND

Issued by the Lords Commissioners of H.M. Treasury under Section One of the National Loans Act, 1939.

NOT TRANSFERABLE

P 31: Old Premium Bond

Bryan D. There's a little bit of Irish in me Jacqueline, so I've pretty much followed your advice. The Premium Bond may be the only legacy I leave to my kids. :-)

Brian E. Do you check your numbers every week Bryan? I suppose it is online now?

Ron B. You can check them on the 4th day of the month Brian, Just put in holders number on the nsandi site

Bryan D. The last time I checked these numbers was about 15 years ago, which shows you how interested I am. I just happened upon them (and other stuff I am posting) in an old folder. If I do win anything the next round is on me.

Ruth E. I have a premium bond for £2 brought for my Patrick 39 yrs ago and like Bryan's it has yielded zilch I did check it last month .

Sue L. I also have various premium bonds to the value of about £25.00 made up of £1.00 to £5.00 ones I had them bought for me in the little post office on the corner of Aylesbury Street West, none of those have ever come up yet either I think Ernie needs to shuffle the numbers into winning ones!!

Plimsolls

Bryan D. I thought these had disappeared in favour of trainers and more advanced forms of shoe technology, but I did a quick Google and there they are in their hundreds. The ones we had at school had a very thin rubber sole and a black canvas upper. They were just about OK for indoor gym use but hopeless on grass and even worse for X country, where they might get buried in a wedge of clay.

Phillip W. My partner and her brother and sister wear them I couldn't understand it.

Ron B. Good for smacking arses though Bryan.

Bryan D. THE SLIPPER!

Brian E. You can buy plimsolls at Maisie's. We wore them for all non-footballing PE activities. They are torture when worn without socks!

Becca H. We had to have a pair of black and a pair of white for different sports as I recall. Also - there was the option of lace up or elastic fronts.

Steve A. Plimsolls there's a great story behind the name Google it when you get chance. The fella helped prevent tragedies on the high seas but his name lives on through the much-reviled footwear.

Bryan D. Becca, you came into that generation that was starting to use technological footwear - as your post illustrates.

Bryan D. Samuel Plimsoll was famous for the "Plimsoll Line" on the side of ships, denoting the maximum safe loading level. Plimsolls were named after him, possibly because he was a pioneering health and safety man and deck shoes of this design would prevent slipping on wet decks.

Ian H. Do you guys remember the pots of whitener for tennis shoes, I used to get covered in the stuff when I put it on.

Chris G. My abiding memory of plimsolls was that when we were seven or eight you could put your own pair on and fit Evill Hands over the top of them because his feet (and his head) were so big.

Ron B. Still got some in the garage Ian, bit hard now.

Bryan D. Keeping them in good shape for smacking arses?

Charmaine M. My abiding memory of plimsolls is the yucky SMELL!

Elaine S. I work in a school where the students have to wear black shoes. If they can get away with black plimsolls they will. In our day we wouldn't have been seen dead in them!

Edith H. They are called daps in Gloucestershire.

Len E. Daps go a bit further west as they are known by that name in Wales.

A bit nippy in Winter

June L. Does any of the older generation remember (before central heating) when our parents always had their Armchairs one each side of the fire & if the fire was glowing & you sat too close you ended up with scorch marks on the side of your legs? mainly women of course, we weren't seen in trousers then.

Pat B. I remember!...Legs would look all red and mottled... As a treat at Christmas we would have roast chestnuts done in the embers of the fire and toast bread on a special toasting fork. Isn't it funny that toast would taste much better done that way.

Nessie J. I remember that well!

Nessie J. Had our crumpets toasted on the fire too!!! Mmmm!!

Terry L. Crumpets and toast still taste better done over an open fire ;)

Ruth E. I always came home from school to toast done on the fire loved it, also thought it was the only way to cook jacket spuds. I was very surprised to find you could do them in the oven lol xxx

Toni B. Ha ha my Nan had those marks. Anyone watch all the soldiers? Little tiny bits of flames.

Terry L. That the only good thing about the winter is to get the fire going..

Toni B. Only like REALLY well done crumpets, because of the coal fires they always got a little over done.

June L. Lovely & Cosy!

Terry L. A battered old three-prong fork with a wooden handle...

Toni B. June yes it was, BUT the rest of the house was bloody freezing. Lol. That's why I can wait for ages till I really MUST go to the loo. lol

June L. Fire Guard, coal scuttle, companion Set & a Fender.

Terry L. Crumpets weren't as nice done on the paraffin heater.

June L. Yes that's right Toni, & the Loo seat was cold to sit on.

Nessie J. Hahaha! Toni it was feckin freeying in that outside lavy!!!!

Toni B. Ohh Terry now paraffin (I love that smell)

Toni B. Ha ha no Ness didn't hang about ay?

Pamela J. Tin bath by the fire side on a Sunday night.

Toni B. Yes Pamela me too - dirty sods 1 a week. x

Ron B. Roasted me chestnuts a few times in front of the fire

Pete B. Much the same as now, armchair with blanket round my legs as the oil central heating is too expensive to turn on.

Pamela J. I was all ways first followed by my Grandad

Toni B. Pamela always had it to myself but it was a smaller1 had to cross my legs.

Sue C. And the tin bath in front of the fire on a Friday night. What fun we had trying to put the fire out with the splashing about! Great memory's, kids today just don't believe it x

Ron B. Sue, I trust you mean splashing????

Sue C. Yes I did Ron i apologise hope the boys don't see that I will never hear the last of it put it down to age Lol .

Maurice H. The boys did too. We had to wear short trousers till we were about 12.

Maurice H. Scorched legs that is.

Margaret C. I had 2 brothers so was always first......that was a blessing,lol..in the tin bath I'm talking about! Ha!

June L. I thought you meant 1st to have scorched legs Margaret.

Margaret C.I did try to clarify it June Ha! but you know how brothers are, didn't want to get in after them! x

Toni B. Life Boy soap.

Margaret C. There was something called Dettol I think!!!!!! Oh this is not nice, I love my brothers. (but still glad I was 1st) Ha Ha !!!!

Toni B. Vosene shampoo, NO conditioner. Ooooch!

Margaret C. And hair spray that was like glue!

Toni B. Ha ha Margaret it did also the wasps liked it too.lol

June L. I'm older than my Brother so I was always before him too Margaret.

June L. Especially if you had a Bird-nest hair do, the wasps use to gather.

Helen P. My Gran used to sit with her legs up on the fireplace, her legs were mottled like corned beef! I can still see her pink bloomers now! She would say 'I'm just 'avin a warm', ha ha. She always had a ciggie in the corner of her mouth and I used to watch the ash get longer and longer. Happy days!

Ron B. Used to love watching the little sparks on the back of the fire. My old uncle used to tell me it was the miners going to work

Margaret C. Yes I'm the oldest June, And do you remember a hairdresser next to the Brighton Bakery in Church St. Thats where I used to get my hair done, I think the lady's name was Mrs Rainbow.

Toni B. Helen was it a woodbine?

June L. Or a Roll-up.

David Wd. That reminds me, must order a ton of coal from K G Smith & Son, but i've missed the summer discount.

Bryan D. It was an eye-opener for me when I went to Canada in 1968 and discovered that people placed their sofas against the wall, rather than in the middle of the room close to the fire. This is odd, I thought, until i discovered that central heating meant that one corner of the room was as warm as another.

June L. I do miss the fire alight, it was the vocal point in the room, like Ron said earlier it was fascinating watching the sparks twinkling on the back where it was black with soot.

Ron B. My old uncle who worked in the brass shop in the works made his own companion set for the fireplace. There was also a horse and rider jumping over a fence. Don't know what happened to them.

June L. We use to put Jacket Potatoes in the Ash under the fire while it was alight & let them cook, best Jackets I've ever tasted with a little salt & plenty of Best Butter, hmmmmmm.

June L. I've still got a open fire in my cottage with the brass scuttle & all the other things but I don't light it because of the work that's involved, couldn't carry the fuel in & out of the garden etc. Pity.

Billy L. Yeah, corned beef leg! Good old Granny Lane!

Vivienne B. I remember arriving at my grandmothers, and there she would be with her back to the fire and her skirt raised up at the back lol . At home we use to do our toast on a three pronged fork in front of the fire, many a burnt piece.

Bryan D. As a kid I loved the heat of the fire on cold winter evenings and the crack of the coal and the dancing blue and orange flames but I hated having to go outside on a damp November evening to fill the coal scuttle. As an adult I have never, ever lit a coal fire in my house. I am sitting in front of a fireplace as I write this and in the 14 years that we have lived here it has never had a fire in it. It doesn't even have a grate!

June L. Oh yes everyone warmed their back side on the fire.

Bryan D. June you're making me feel cold with all this talk of winter fires. :-)

Pamela J. Then you would have mottled legs from getting too close to the fire Happy Days.

June L. Take the plunge Bryan &'light your fire, I bet there are many that envy you having a home fire, they don't even put Chimneys in houses they build these days.

Ron B. Chilblains on your feet, was this caused by warming them on the fire.

Brian E. And of course we had to have draft excluders below every door. Those fires only heated an area up to 2 feet away from the grate. Did anyone ever have a chimney fire?

Bryan D. I wouldn't even know where to go to buy coal these days - and as I said, I have put my coal-scuttle-filling-on-a-miserable-damp-and-foggy-evening times behind me.

June L. Does any of the older generation remember (before central heating) when our parents always had their Armchairs one each side of the fire & if the fire was glowing & you sat too close you ended up with scorch marks on the side of your legs? mainly women of course, we weren't seen in trousers then.

June L. I think it was because it was so cold every where else in all the other rooms with no heating, do people slill get cold feet? I know I don't.

Bryan D. I like history, but some of it I don't want to relive. :-)

Bryan D. Now you're making me remember shivering between the sheets under a stack of blankets when getting into bed.

Brian E. Yes Bryan, going to bed cold, getting up cold.

Bryan D. Wincyette pyjamas! Do they still exist?

June L. Ha! Ha! Sorry Bryan didn't mean to give you the shivers.

Bryan D. I had lino on the floor in my bedroom and it was like stepping on ice, so I had a little rug and used that the scoot across the floor to the landing and thence to the bathroom.

Bryan D. And don't mention the thick frost patterns on the inside of the window in the morning.

Nessie J. Yep i got mine for the winter lol! Well... I have no man to keep me warm, so what's a woman to do? hahhaa!

June L. Me too, Lino was posh some people had floor covering & had to hang their rugs over the washing line & belt them with the back of a brush to clean them.

June L. Bryan you're making me cold now, you'll be talking about icicles next lol.

Toni B. Ohh wincyette sheets striped ones- and a feather eiderdown, plum coloured. You could pick out the feathers - got a right telling off next morning.

Brian E. Lino from Stobies! How I hated those cold mornings, when even the toilet seat was freezing.

June L. Especially if your pipes froze.

Pat F. We lived in the little streets so we had no bathroom just an outside toilet. I remember a tin bath that hung out in the yard and it was brought in on A Thursday night and we took turns to have a bath in front of the fire. It was hideous and freezing and I was glad when at 6 years old we moved to the centrally heated maisonettes on St Georges way. It was nice when mum cooked toast on the fire on a long fork.

Susan B. I remember the wincyette striped sheets, thick eiderdowns and the thick bed spreads on the bed during the winter months

June L. I bet there's not many of you that would remember the flock lumpy mattress before the spring mattress, I didn't have one lol but I remember helping my mum make my Nan's bed, you had to kneed out the lumps with your fingers then put the sheet on top.

Ruth E. We had a bolster pillow x

June L. Yes they were good, the whole width of the bed, better than single pillows Ruth.

Ruth E. We had one of those silky eiderdowns I used to rub it between my fingers to go to sleep x

June L. They were always made of a Satin material & plain colours.

Ruth E. Yeah I can see if now Orange I think

Susan B. I had a dark pink or red one on my single bed

June L. Certainty a bright one Ruth, no wonder you rubbed it with your fingers Ha! ha!.

June L. Do you remember the black & white striped pillows before you put the pillow case on.

June L. Or the Brass knobbed bed frames?

Susan B. The feathers came out as well, do remember the brass knobbed bed frames but don't recall having one in our house

Ruth E. Oh yes the pillows & feathers.

June L. The feathers use to prick when they poked through the material.

Brian E. We had a green iron bedstead with unscrewable brass knobs. And china dogs! And, what we called 'army blankets' dark grey, unyielding things they were.

June L. I know what you mean Brian about the grey blankets. We had them; they were very rough to the skin. You could unscrew my Nan's brass knobs too.

June L. My Nan use to always have a Pumice stone in her butler sink. Do you know what for? Something to do with washing I think!!

Brian E. Umm, June, I still buy pumice. You can get it from Boots, or Poundland!

Margaret C. Brian, my grandparents had a pair of those china dogs. I wish I had them They were King Charles Spaniels, reddish and white. They always sat on the mantlepiece in the front room-- beautiful!!!!

Elaine H. Cooking crumpets over the fire on a toasting fork and `Jack Frost` on the inside of the bedroom windows and liberty bodices. Happy times x

Elaine H. Pumice stones are brilliant for removing hard skin on your heels lol

Jackie N. Does anyone remember "Snofire"?It was a stick of menthol smelling stuff, which I used to have rubbed on my knees in the winter, when they got chapped from the cold (it was the sitting in front of the fire bit that reminded me, because I'd be sitting there having this stuff put on before I went to bed)..........

Vivienne B. Funny when I read these comments on here, that some of these things are still on shops know, eiderdowns, black and white stripe pillow covers (Ticking) and yes, feathers still come through the covers lol

Pat F. OMG I had a liberty bodice and my mum used to buy my school uniform from Masies. It lasted forever unfortunately!!!

June L. I had a liberty bodice too with loads of white cloth buttons up the front, didn't they use to be called Stays?

Elaine H. No I am sure stays are like corsets lol and for the older lady - like we are now lol

June L. That's right Elaine, I remember now, one Christmas I had to share a bedroom with my Grandma & when she undressed & got down to her underwear she had this laced up Corset on with loads of hooks & eyes & yards of laces, it took her ages to undress & when she finally got it off every thing dropped, no wonder your feet get bigger as you get older.

Pat C. June that's enough information please. Don't want to get the "boys" excited coming into the weekend. They can react badly to corsets and suspenders!

June L. Mind you the younger girls today wear Spanks & underwear with false cheeks & other bits & pieces in do they get the boys going too Pat?

Pat C. I think [hope] the young old boys won't get excited by Spanks, but they might get confused between Spanks and a good old spanking!

June L. Ha! Ha! x

Ron B. dribble

Tricia D. I love my coal fires - wouldnt like them quite so much without the central heating as well though!!
June L. Good idea Tricia
Brian E. As ornamental addition yes, but I love central heating. (I had to call Wildens out today as mine chose this cold spell to decide not to work!).
June L. Sounds about right Brian.

Baths

Richie B. Who had a bath in their kitchen we didn't get a proper bath room until my sister moved out when she got married its still there avocado loll
Margaret C. Our tin bath was kept outside in the lean to and brought in once a week and put in the scullery and filled from water that had been heated in the brick corner boiler, then it was eldest down in order of bathing.
Terry L. No we didn't Richie ! You must of been the only one... Loll
Anthony Z. 1966 was the year we got a bathroom
Margaret C. We use to be treated sometimes and went for a bath at the Public Baths on Stratford Road...
Marc H. Yeah 1966 had a bathroom out went the tin bath and Baby Burco water boiler twice a week bath time for me! and that's now LOL
Helen F. We had a tin bath in Buckingham street and a toilet out side. lol
Margaret C. Same here Heather. Loo use to freeze up in the winter.
Helen F. Yes and it was freezing going out there every time you needed the loo.
Margaret C. Can you imagine how it would have been without the chamber pots?
Ian S. Didn't you use that tin bath as a boat Marc at the pond near your house?

Marc H. Blimey Mr Spires you have a good memory! Yes indeed, it was an art to float on a pond in a tin bath

Helen F. I can't remember them we use to live at 76 Buckingham street.

Margaret C. I lived in Creed Street. Going back to the 50's..

Maurice H. Right in front of the fire and listening to the football results. Dad went first, Mum went next, I had to sit in the front room on my own till it was my turn.

Lifebuoy Soap

John R. Anyone remember Lifebuoy Soap? I think the only ingredients were Soap (or whatever it is that makes soap) and Red as opposed to what we have today where soap has herbs, spices, and all sorts of other stuff in it. This was the staple soap in our house growing up and was apparently avoided as much as possible by my brother and myself.

Terry L. Tastes horrible...

Lynnette M. Have you got a Lifebuoy?

Ron. B. Loved the smell of this, and carbolic soap

Chris. G. And Vosene shampoo, a smell that stays with you for life, unfortunately.

Jill. G. I can smell it now.

Lynnette M. We used pears soap in our house.

Ron. B. Ooh! Get you!

Jane B. We used Imperial Leather - and I STILL use Vosene - but yes, the smell is always there!!!!!

Len E. I use Polytar to wash what remains of my hair. It has an old fashioned smell.

Lynnette M. Did anyone have to take milk of magnesia and cod liver oil? My Nan used to lather herself in Nivea face cream - smelled lovely;

Ron B. Surprised you could smell it over the Brut.

Jill G. I love the smell of Brut.

Ian S. Cod liver oil. Splash it all over.

Lynnette M. I liked Ian Spires aftershave cod liver oil. Still smells of it to this day!

Ron B. That wasn't the reason they slapped you to the floor though.

Ian S. It keeps your skin nice. I bet you do get some funny looks.

Brian E. I was thinking of Cod Liver Oil myself today. It used to be standard to give a teaspoon full of it to 5 year olds every day.

Chris G. I tried your oil tip once to impress the girls Spike, splashed it all over, but I slipped off the bus before I got there.

Ian. S. Ha but you always were a slippery customer Chris.

Lynnette M. You stank the rugby club out Ian.

Ron B. When my dad was unwell with shingles on his back, we smeared Olive oil on them. He went downhill really fast after that.

Lynnette M. I have to put olive oil in my ears.

Chris G. Two pints? Don't you spill most of it?

Ron B. She can't hear you Chris. lol

Ian S. That's some cavity you got between your ears Lynette. It must be like a swimming pool of olive oil in there.

Lynnette M. Can't hear any of you.

Alan C. Denim was the stuff, get some of that on you and you had to fight the birds off with a stick... :-)

Ron B. What their white sticks?

Ian S. They used to slip off me Alan.

Brian E. Lifebuoy Soap had that irritating paper label on each bar that never came off, no matter how small the rest of the bar got. You had to take care not to rub the label side against you. Well, I was!

Jackie N. Bought some Pears soap recently, because I used to love the smell of me! They've obviously changed the formula - not the same smell at all, very disappointing.

June L. I liked the bloke that advertised Denim & the one in the Launderette who had clean Jeans. Brut reminds me of my Bathroom when Terry was living at home. I think he overdid it a bit unless he used it as a fresh air spray.

Chris G. Well the advertising told you to 'Splash it all over!' June, perhaps Terry thought they meant the bathroom? Well you know how obedient Terry was as a lad, always doing exactly what he was told. I'd blame Henry Cooper.

June L. I should have given Terry an Ali Shuffle.

Wendy C. Brian the soap with the paper on it imperial leather....

186

Jill G. What about Avon soap on a rope?

Chris G. Marks & Sparks still do football soap on the rope that we seemed to get for Xmas every year 40 years ago.

Jill G. I now know what to get my brothers for Xmas this year.

June L. I never bought them, didn't like balls hanging on a rope.

Ron. B. Nor do I June.

Jill G. Oh you two :)

Ron B. That's why I never played with them clacker thingies

Brian E. I could never get them to clack!

Jill G. Oh them things! I was always whacking my wrists with them. My dad took them off me and put them in the bin.

Noise

Phillip W. Here's a question to all those living in Wolverton in 60s and 70s, what was it like living in Wolverton with steam and diesel trains and shunter engines? And was it noisy with the works?

Andrew L. Traverse sirens, works whistle, Fire siren and trains rattling round Moon's curve are the sound of my youth.

Phillip W. I really wish I had the chance to spend a few weeks in Wolverton in the days of steam but that will never happen

Bryan D. No sound came from behind the wall and once the men had gone inside at 7:43 the doors closed - and silence. Most of the day was punctuated by the rush of passing trains - the noise rose to a crescendo and the, true to the Doppler Effect, immediately fell away. It was a sound we all got used to and largely ignored. There was no road traffic noise and very few cars in the 1950s. In the whole of Windsor St there were four car owners, for example. It was avert quiet place - like a remote country village today.

Phillip W. Does anyone know when the works steam shunters were changed.

Richie B. You can occasionally hear the hi speed trains pass through still but I miss the siren :)

Lesley W. The Works siren. That brings back memories.

Sheila H. The works siren, the rag and bone man, Vic the milkman, The man from the Pru, hearing the trains at night when tucked up in bed under Mum's coats, playing in the street and kicking the leaves in autumn down Marina Drive ..... and many more memories! Wish I could go back for a day :(

Ian H. Me too Sheila ,but as a child.

Sheila H. That's what I meant - as a child.

Ian H. This site is a very good alternative though' and get's better and better.

June L. Terry was a engine driver, can't remember if it was diesel but he always pressed the Hooter (if it was called that) as he came pelting though Wolverton station so I knew it was him late evenings.

Steve A. Living in St George's way in the 60s there used to be a fair bit of noise from Dunlop and Rankin, especially at night. In the summer I used to lie in bed and listen to it, it was quite comforting, you'd hear the 'tea up' shout at about 9.pm

Phillip W. I live in St. Georges way at the moment there is a fair bit of noise that comes from Electrolux and the works shunter when it bring stock in and takes stock out.

Brian E. I can remember Bacals building the electrification pylons. Back then, steam was being phased out. To me, then, steam was old hat, and diesels were a novelty. So I used to hope we got a new diesel when we went on holiday or trips, although it was usually a steamer.

Chris G. Heard a travvy siren the other day walking past the works, not heard one in years.

Phillip W. What was it like living near the works goods yard with the shunters going around

Kathy P. Used to now we were late back to school in afternoon if we heard the " works " hooter going and run like hell to get . and Wolverton was like a ghost town in the 2 week summer shut down, happy days .

Jackie N. One of my earliest memories is lying in bed and listening to the trains (this would be 1950s , so still steam)-and we lived in Oxford Street!-mind you the wind had to be in a certain direction.........

You mean what?

Ron B. Any one else heard people saying the wrong word. My favourite has to be an elderly lady telling me her friend was 94, and she still had all her facilities about her - instead of faculties.

Len E. My other half calls ablutions, absolutions.

Toni B. An old lady saying she wanted a dildo in her bedroom.(she meant dado) aw bless.

Toni B certificate ----- cerstifficate

Pat C. One of my young granddaughters is ballergic to nuts

Ron B. Cafeteria for catheter. My Mum.

Pat C. Heard Steak and Kiddley Pie a few times.

Pat C. Met a chatty fellow in town last week told me He had killed two stones with one bird.

Toni B. Got that imperference-- on my Nan's telly--interference.

Pat C. Many years ago an old man came into the garage and asked me could I fix his front suspenders {suspensions]

Ruth E. My fav one is Arthur Daley "The worlds your Lobster." "Tel and Me take drugs? I don't even take a Paracetatemol."

Wendy C. An old friend of mine used to call my DM's Bob Martins....

Pamela S. Suggestive Biscuits instead of Digestive (ME) ;)

June L. Me & many others say Chimley Pot instead of Chimney Pot.

Penny G. Destruction book Instead of instruction.

Ron B. Statellite, Del boy.

Penny G. Fish that lived in a aquiam ??? never could say aquarium.

Ian B. My granddaughter from a very early age wanted to play on my permuter, sadly now she calls it a computer. They grow up far too fast.

Ron B. I know someone who says plant plot and shracknell instead of shrapnel.

Chris G. I once went out with a Rental Deceptionist

Len E. Worked with a chap who once said he'd had a pint of drought lager.

Jill G. When my son was little he loved the fat controller and when he said it came out f-----gtroller I used to wish the ground to open and swallow me up.

Jill G. My hubby said to our daughter one day would you like a steak sandwich she replied yes please what's in it :)

Elaine S. When we went to London Gareth used to say are we going on the scelalators. In fact we still go on them.

Ruth E. My Patrick's fav one was "Can I have some of those Pillocks on toast Mummy" Pilchards!

Ron B. A bird in the hand is worth one in your bush,

Jill G. Not long ago I was out shopping with Hannah and she said oh look mum beans for blind cooking aint that sweet but how does this help the blind so one had to go get a coffee and explain to her that its not for the blind haha.

Pat C. Over here in Ireland, can I have a hang sandwich please = ham.

Jill G. My sister-in-law in Ireland makes me laugh when she says turkey I can't spell how she says it but pat I am sure you know what I mean.

Ron B. Going somewhat off track, we used to have great fun when setting up exhibitions at the NEC. You could send a note to the Tannoy girls and page someone. Amongst my favourites were. Teresa Green, Hugh Janus and Rudolph Hucker. As you can see, I am easily entertained.

Ruth E. My friends daughter is called Theresa , Ron she is 35 this year and I still call her *Trees are Green* bless her ,xxx

Susan B. Ron, did you also put out calls for Eva Brick and Ivor Biggun?

Ron B. Heh heh Steve, Had a Mike Hunt once though

Elaine P. An old workmate of mine used to call Escalators.... Escalavators !!!!!!!!

Sarah K. When my son was little he used to call the escalator the alligator -we had one in our M & S and he always wanted to go on it :0)

Becca H. When Chris was a toddler he couldn't say Rebecca and the way it came out was "Wee Bugger!"

Jill G. Becca my brother Joe used to call my brother Michael (goggle)

190

Becca H. Years ago my friends 2 year old would really get on her four year old brothers nerves when he was proudly sharing his new skill of counting aloud. She would constantly try to join in and get louder and louder and say "unty fee, leventy one, fitty figh an,........ awl uh numbizz!" It was really comical but would drive her poor long suffering big brother to distraction! x

Nick C. My sister learnt the words to 'Onward Christian Soldiers'...she was only 5 and somehow she thought it was 'with the cross-eyed Jesus' !

Chris G. Can I point out that I could say Rebecca quite clearly, 'wee bugger' was a description after an incident with a plastic hammer.

Terry L. My old granddad went in to Fosters and ask for there finest 3 Piece Suite to wear for a wedding.

Ron B. Try the jacket sir, ooh sofa so good

Terry L. Suite you sir, suite you !

Penny G. When one of my grandchildren was born, she was named Emily. Her big brother was so proud, he said her name was bimbley as he could not say her name. Her nickname is now Bimble.

Ron B. My son used to say Hostipal.

Terry L. My boys are 13 months apart, Stephen called Michael Gweegy and Michael called Stephen Dee Dah as they both couldn't pronounce each others names, and despite them being 18 and 19 now I still call them by these names now and then to their eternal embarrassment...

Susan K. When my son started playgroup with the little girl up the road, he called her NaoNi instead of Naomi, they are now 19 years old and she still answers to Naoni, weirdly everyone else in their friendship group seems to have picked this up :)

Gary C. My daughter asked me "when are you taking the puppies to the vet to have their Michael chips put it?"

Gary C. My Nan once told her friend that I was going down to Essams to buy a pair of Dr Whites!!!

Barbara L. Went to theatre, young daughter saw sign, Stalls. She said we are not sitting on a stool all night mum

Becca H. Same friends daughter as above - when she was 4 started gym classes. Really excited on the phone told her Aunty

191

Becca "Mummy got me a leaping tard. "No sweetheart" said her gently correcting Aunty Bec - "its a L E O T A R D" "No it NOT" said indignant and irritated child. "Its a leaping tard cos you leap up and down in it!" (Said in a very strong Welsh accent" with the customary *int it* on the end!

6 Around the Town

Survivors

Barbara L. Can somebody tell me which shops are still in Wolverton? Maisie's? Summerfield? Any old stores there still? Essams Shoe Shop? Gregory's Fish shop is now what?

June L. Good old Maisie's is there, so is Essams (still exactly the same.) Gregory's is now run by Chinese as a Fish & Chip Shop & very good, cooked beautifully. There's loads of new Take away Shops, don't know how they keep in Business. The Burger Bar still there & does well. I have lunch in there with a mate when we have a day shopping in Wolverton, their food is very good too.

Sharon S. Do you remember Julie Philips on the square and Marisan (I think it was on Church St.) and a furniture shop along the front that used to have bits outside like the little sets for real fires (brush tong and shovels) and fire guards etc

June L. Yes I bought a lot of my clothes from them.

Andrew L. Maisie's moved a few doors along into the old co-op. I believe Essam's shoe shop is still there. Did somebody mention Julie Philips! Wow, I had forgotten that one!

Kevin S. Lived two doors away from Essams back in 1978, my Mum still visits Wolverton to buy shoes from Raymond and I believe the shop is still in some kind of time warp.....

Ian B. My Gran used to live a few doors along from Essams No 68 in the 50's and 60's and maybe even earlier. The curds used to live in the house in between which if I remember right had a shop front but wasn't used as a shop when I knew it.

Kevin S. We lived next door to that as well Ian at no. 80 Church Street which was opposite Eve's (ladies fashions) and which became a number of different shops over the years including Stark Video whose proprietor committed suicide some years later.

Colin T. Mashie started in that shop, Next to that was Nicholson fresh fish, Mrs Curd's son had model airplanes hanging in the window, he use to fly then in the Top Rec.

Ian B. The son was called Brian and there was a daughter as well. The shop may have been an opticians at one time. I remember mum telling stories of her and Mavis working together before they joined the forces.

Bryan D. Some shops have surprising longevity. The jewellers at 28 Church Street has had different owners over 150 years but it is still in the same business. The Candy Box on the Stratford Road was always a sweet shop and has now expanded to take in Pedleys, next door. Pages Garage at 84 has changed a bit but is still essentially a garage. That goes back to the 1930s. Barleys on Radcliffe Street was a greengrocer for about 100 years until quite recently. Lake's of course (and an ironmonger before that) morphed into the Hobby Shop. And good old Raymond Essam, as mentioned, froze time some decades ago. He still has faded packets of metal cleats to reinforce worn leather heels and rubber stick on soles made in 1972.

Brian E. And, although Lakes is now called Al's Hobbies, it is still pretty much the same in appearance, inside & out. They still have the original glass topped counter, and the gates across the front door. It even has the same sixties Keil Kraft old balsa wood aircraft in the front window.

Brian E. On the Square, where Blagroves used to be is still an opticians. And Monty Watts's is still a dentists. And, down at Bradwell, Sid Telfers is still there - how they carry on at their prices is beyond me!

June S. Maises is still there run by her daughter these days, still good for a bargain if you are not fussy!

Penny G. I thought Maises was run by her Son Robert?

Colin T. Good Afternoon Penny. I'm not going to get into a fight over this..........But I also thought that her Son was now running the family shop x

Brian E. Last time I looked, Joan was there

June S. You could be right Penny & Col maybe they own it jointly?

Georgina S. There are two new shops called boutique 77 I think and both sell different styles of clothes really good and very reasonable otherwise Wolverton has gone right down hill in my opinion needs a complete facelift x

Jane B. Regarding Maisie's - it is run by her daughter Joan nowadays. Joan was married to Robert, who ran it with her until they divorced a few years ago.

Penny G. That solved the mystery :) of that then

Pat B. I worked part time in Eve's In Church St. for a while.

Marc H. I still get my shoes from Raymond Essams I am normally there 2 hours while he sorts out the right ones for me one of Wolverton's legends.

Bryan D. Good for you Marc, helping to keep these authentic shops alive.

Ron B. Had a chat to him this morning outside his shop, He's a nice gentleman

Emma P. Stuart Darling [previously Darling & Wood] on Stratford Rd has just closed down

Ruth E. My John gets his shoes there since he broke his leg and ankle only ones that fit him right ,it is like going back 40 yrs when you go in and he is so particular I love it

Maria M. Gregory's along Stratford Rd is now Madira's fish and chips.

Wendy C. That was Rocky's.

David Wd. Hi-Vu Electronics, still exists, but not in its Church Street location where it had been for many years as it is now in a small unit on the opposite side of the road, inside the Agora. Much smaller in size, the shop is now run by Les Payne's son David who still does TV, video and audio repairs.

Essam's Shoe Shop

Richie B. Ooh DMs in Essams window I'm not sure what colour I want !!

Steve A. Richie the sun is shining have a ride over to the factory shop, you'll be spoilt for choice.

Marc H.I am due for another visit there fine service from Raymond.

J. Cato Laces don't forget what size laces

Marc H. And leather laces as well he still does them I imagine.

David W. A chap in our indoor tennis group plays in Dunlop "Green Flash"plimsoles. He also wears immaculate white shorts with "knife edge" creases , a Slazenger top and a hand knitted cable sweater.

Ian H. Like to see it David. It was (is it still?) like that at Stony and Wolverton Bowls Clubs - classy attire.

Elaine S. Anyone know how old Raymond is? His sister Hilary is a few years older than me so he must be ancient.

G. Beales Raymond Essam is the same age as my husband so must be 68 or 69.

Ron B. He is 70.

Chris G. He's never looked any different in the 40 odd years I can remember him has he?

Ron B. No he doesn't seem to change, Such a lovely man

Barbara L. He shoed many a foot in our family. lasted forever, leather soles too.

David W. Raymond is 69 - 1year younger than myself at school in Wolverton.

G. Kelly Raymond's Mum was my piano teacher. Mr and Mrs Essam lived at 96 Victoria St. As a teacher she was very strict but very kind and inspirational - as all teachers should be in my opinion. Raymond's sister Hilary also is married to my Mum's brother - they are a lovely family. Many of you may remember her as Mrs Hunter, who taught at The Radcliffe for quite a while.

Ron B. Told me he was 70 when I met him a week ago

Gurney's

Ian H. Seeing the numbers there 96 & 97 it has got me thinking because I thought the Stratford Road had more "plots" than this up to this spot. I know Windsor Street has more than 200 houses but how many were there in Wolverton pre MKDC say. Reason being I was wanting to know the population when I was a kid and

the number of Works employees. Multiplying each house by say four would give a rough estimate, I'm pretty certain it wasn't 15000 as somebody posted a while back. Maybe that was for the UDC?
Ian H. What was the name of the Greengrocers between Lakes and the Chemist shop? Before it was Barleys that is, was it Ellery's or was that somewhere else.

P 32: Some shops on the Stratford Road

Bryan D. I'm not quite sure what you mean by this. The Stratford Road was numbered from 1 to 101 up to the Anson Road back alley. The Engineer was 1, the cafe 1a. 2-5 were lock up shops. 6-21 took you to Fosters corner, The presbytery was 22.
The greengrocer at No 40 was Keller's. I think its now the Silver Sea. In the late 19th/early 20th C it was a Temperance Hotel, then a coffee house. Barleys (run by Barbers in our day) was on Radcliffe St. Ellery's was on Church St, No 34. I'll look up the population figures.
Ian H. That's it Keller's Bryan ta!! What I meant was that I believed that the Stratford Road had more shops, houses etc with "plot" numbers, clearly from your response and the photo it was

197

shorter than I imagined. No wonder it didn't take long to walk to Stony it was shorter than I thought. If being an Anorak mate is giving some fascinating factual glimpses of our town I am more than happy to call you GUILTY!

P 33: Formerly Gurney's "Monumental Masons"

Tracey S. Gurney's has just been sold again (New City Graphics). Don't know if it is going to business or residential now. Saw a couple of people in there at the end of last week but the windows are all covered up now.

Donna S. What a great picture... you just don't see buildings like this anymore .. the brickwork, the detailing over the doors around the windows... even the railings just gorgeous...

Faye L.I stare at this building every time I happen to walk by , love the bit above the door xx

Ian H. Should have seen it with the gravestones!!!!!!

John C. Was thinking about the shops in Wolverton, The co-op must be the longest serving shop, don't think Wolverton has ever been without a co-op. The second longest serving shop has to be Essams, unless anyone else has a better memory than me.

Bryan D. Not relying on memory John but historical records, Wolverton's oldest shops started on Bury Street in 1840. I won't list them here. Co-op shops started in Rochdale in 1844 and the idea spread. Wolverton's first Co-op started in the late 1840s at the end of Creed St, just before the triangle. I used to think that Billingham's chippy was the remnant of that store, but Margaret Clarke Crew corrected me on that point. Later the Co-op developed shops along Church St and later the Square. The oldest surviving shop (and you are right about Darling & Wood) is the building at 6-8 Stratford Rd, built in 1860 by Charles Aveline - cabinet maker, builder and post office operator. Aveline had one of the first shops on Bury St. The shop which has been dedicated to one function the longest is, I think, 28 Church St., which started as a jeweller and watchmaker in the 1860s and is still a jewellers 150 years later. Raymond Essam's shop was started by his grandfather, who previously had a shop in Bradwell.

Wendy Ch. Maise's

Ian H. Is the monumental masons still there down the front, hardly a shop but still "sell " things??

Natalie J. Me and Mum worked in jersey rd co-op x

Brian E. I know it cannot beat Essam's, but one shop that predates Maisie's is what was then called Lampitt's. Although it was later called Darling & Wood, then Stuart Darling, it is still essentially the same TV rentals shop.

Bryan D. And radio before that.

Andrew L. How long have the two chippies been where they are now? They both pre-date me.

Ian H. What about the "Off Licence" ?

G. Beales Ian, I presume you mean the "Off License" in Green Lane. Sadly it is now an Asian corner shop/halhal meat store.

K. Goodridge I think Mum used to work there. As in the off license, not the halal meat store! : is that right mum? x

Ian H. Any comments on the "monumental masons"? Thanks Gill for the depressing news on my mates home!!!

Bryan D. Gurneys seems to be a photography business at the moment. The fancy exterior has been preserved.

Chris G. Is it still up for sale?

Richie B. Yes drove past yesterday..

199

Chris G. I wonder if it's listed in some way or is bound by being in the conservation area, lot of potential on that corner plot.

Richie B. Could be. I wonder how much it's up for as well? I think its been on the market for ages.

Chris G. Could be wrong but I thought I saw £250k somewhere.

Richie B. Not surprised. Can't see that selling soon.

Ian H. I believe it had a Chapel of Rest?

Chris G. That got separated from the main building a couple of years back Ian, now converted to housing.

Ian H. With all these changes to the place it might be worthwhile for a short video of how it is now for us ex-pats if somebody local could find the time that is. Just an idea that came to my head, much better than thinking about Wolverhampton Wanderers :-(:-(

Wavy Line

Bev P. So who remembers my parents' Wavy Line shop on Cambridge Street? Anyone have any stories about us making tits of ourselves anywhere? My mum was hard of hearing so I'm sure she confused a few along the way. I remember when the money changed from old to new pence. People would pay in old money and get their change in new money. What a nightmare that was because I used to get on the till sometimes even though I was young. I remember the older people not being happy about it.

Chris G. Was Mr Dimmock anything to do with your family Bev? Always knew it as Dimmocks.

Colin H. Yeah me too ... ???

Bev P. We bought it from Mr. Dimmock at the end of 69 and closed it as a grocers in 1975 and moved. Mr. Dimmock had the wooden floors, we made it a self service shop with shelves all around the walls and lunch meat, bacon, and the till in the middle.

Ian H. I remember Dimmocks, I would wouldn't I at my age! Gerald and Pam were their children couple years younger than me!

Chris G. I can remember going in when your family had it Bev, just always thought it had passed down from Mr D.

Ian H. Mr Dimmock always wore a very clean white apron. As a little note of brevity I'll tell you a home truth, my family were poor and so we always got food on the tab, credit that is. When we couldn't pay the grocery bill I went to another shop with a list and got food there. We owed money to all the grocery shops at one time or other including Dimmocks. I'm not proud of this but it is how it was, perhaps for other poor families too. Anybody lend me a fiver?:-)

Bryan D. Undaunted, I chip in my two bits from the past. It was still Byatt's in my early years and I think, as I have discussed with Bev before, he originated the grocery - Byatt and Hopkins. They also had one of the first telephone numbers - Wolverton 2. Dimmocks must have bought it in 1950 or thereabouts. My mother shopped there regularly. I can still recall the smells - loose tea, freshly sliced ham, cheddar cheese, dried parsley. The red bacon slicer was a marvel of a machine which whirred noiselessly while the slab of bacon or ham was pushed back and forth on the table. Ruth Edwards told me the other week that she operated a similar machine at the Maypole grocery and she still has all her fingers! Very little was packaged back then. You bought your biscuits by the quarter pound picked out of a Huntley and Palmer's biscuit tin. Cheese was cut to weight. Tea was loose and kept at home in a tea caddy. My only source of cardboard to draw on or make models in those post war years was an empty corn flakes box. Nice memories, but I'm happy to shop at the supermarket.

Bev P. I used a red bacon slicer when we had it Bryan! It was a wonderful thing!

Ruth E. I remember Dimmocks but just like Chris. Thought it was passed on The Maypole closed in 1971 so I guess your shop had more trade then Bev Pinkerman.

Andrew L. I remember the shop well in the Wavy Line era, I was always curious about that name. It was on our way to the Square so we always passed it on the way to Budgens. I don't know why my mum didn't shop there, it would have meant half the distance to walk. I was sure it was a Mace store after 1975 and I remember it being New City Heating. I made a point of looking at the shop when I went down Cambridge St on Sunday. Not a shop any more, converted to residential and it doesn't look right at all....

Pina R. I remember your shop Bev! Spent a lot of time there with you. Those steps in the back that went up to somewhere, what was that, I can't remember now.

Bev P. It was an attic room. Lynda's room was the one with the ladder that went straight up, mine went up at an angle. Christine Wallace fell down the steps of mine and fractured her skull. I heard years later that her grandmother was still angry and thought it had changed Christine, I wish I knew. It was a great play room, I used to make fires on the wooden floor!

Andrew L. I remember Christine hurting her head, but never knew how. Now I do....

Pina R. I can remember when Christine fell down those stairs & fractured her skull. We'd never heard of anything so serious back then. Christine was still fun loving Christine after that Bev x

Bev P. The cellar there was a creepy place, we pulled out some old serving platters and some Victorian glass baby bottles I wish I still had. After we had our initial hunt down there I don't remember ever going back down.

June L. Pete & I was just married when I shopped in Dimmocks, Pete was in the Coldstream Guards, I was living with my Mum & Dad in Victoria St, I just gave birth to Terry & I use to send my little red grocery book into Dimmocks once a week & my shopping was delivered by the delivery boy on a bicycle in a basket on the front of his bike. When Pete was demobbed we got a home of our own in Green Lane I then shopped @ Vivo's. As it was a bit closer.

Green Lane Stores

Andrew L. Where was Vivo's? Was it the shop at the Osborne St. end of Green Lane?

Chris G. Green Lane Stores? I think Pete had that at one time as a motorbike shop too?

Steve A. Yep the one opposite the Off Licence

Andrew L. In my Bushfield days I would call into Green Lane Stores daily. Then it was run by an Italian, and they had the garlic salami sausages hanging over the counter. I think they had a son who was in my year at Bushfield. Might have been called Cirigiliano.

Chris G. Yep I remember the Italian family, the Dad was a little bald headed man, Pina may know them.

Chris G. Off Licence opposite when we were kids was Marion and Bill Holman, I'm still very good friends with their son Pete.

Pina R. I do know them Chris. Just trying to remember the surname. They were either Greco's or Buscaglia's. Just going to ask my mate Rosa Mulé Buscaglia

Terry L. Greco me thinks.

June L. No, it was on corner of Victoria St & Stacy Ave/ Radcliffe corner (Vivo's)

Colin H. His name was Emilio, and he was married to an English woman about twice his size. He was also the Chef at the Old George and had a Brother called Gino. They were both there when me and Herbie were at the Old George ... Later Emilio opened the Italian next to The Vic on Church Street. Gino went back to Italy many years ago after he got married to an Italian girl and had a baby .... I Think !!!

Chris G. Remember now, Emilio was a partner with Giovanni in the Roman Room next to the Vic.

Pina R. Greco might have been the fathers name & Buscaglia the mothers. just waiting for my mate to get back to me. They were related. I know there was a daughter cos she used to take me for walks in my pram apparently

Andrew L. So Emilio opened the Roman Rooms? Good on him!

Pina R. Emilio's daughter Joanne Romeo was a year below me at school. My mum helped out worked in the Roman Rooms occasionally...clearer upper

Colin H. Yes Chris. The Hairdresser from Cofferidge Close in Stony. That was after his brother Gino went back to Italy. Is the Roman Room still there Andrew ???

Pina R. Think it now one arm bandit heaven, Colin. I heard that the Agora bloke owned it, as he does a lot of Wolverton

Chris G. Yep me and an ex girlfriend got invited one of the first nights when it opened through Giovanni, free booze but the bill still came to £50 which was a lot in the early 80s anywhere never mind Wolverton, good night though that went on late with Giovanni picking up his guitar to sing. He was a better hairdresser.

Colin H. Oh dear Pina .... another memory gone to dust !!

June L. Green Lane stores was top of Oxford St/ Green Lane opposite Off Licence was Marie & Fred that run the shop, their children are Julie & Tracy Magee. Emilio run the shop after them

Terry L. Think Emilio was first Ma xx

Pina R. Maria was Italian too but it was owned by Italians back in the 60s/70s

Pina R. Her mum & dad used to live along Aylesbury st just round corner from oxford st going towards the square, Tony & Margarita, can't remember the surname, its gone out of my head. Tony used to work in the works

Terry L. I think it was 1975 Jackie

Andrew L. Pina mentioned Buscaglias, do I remember right there are Buscaglia twin girls?

Andrew L. Memory might be playing tricks, but I am sure I remember a Rosetta Buscaglia, would be 44/45 now. Always immaculately turned out.

Pina R. Yeah, Rosetta Buscaglia lived few doors down from me in Anson Road, she's lived in London for years now. Rosa Buscaglia lived in Aylesbury St, roughly same age. Their Dads are brothers

Rosa B. Hello. Yes the Green Lane stores was owned by my Uncle, my Dad's brother. Pina is right.

Pina R. OK, back to Green Lane stores. It was owned by the Buscaglias, Greco's lived next door. Emilio bought it off the Buscaglias.

Pina R. Welcome Rosa Mulé Buscaglia x

Pina R. No, Greco's didn't live there, just been put right! they lived in Victoria St.

Rosa B. I Was known as little Rosetta and me cousin was known as Big Rosetta x

Terry L. Yep I second that, welcome Rosa, Benvenuti nella casa pazza.

Andrew L. You Rosetta's were always so perfectly dressed, lots of people used to notice.

Rosa B. Hi Terry grazie millie those were the days Wolverton. Aww really thanks Andrew we were.

Pina R. It was Rosa's husband that used to help me in the chippy x

Rosa B. Yes he did open the Roman rooms Colin does everyone remember the pub across the road from my uncles shop in Green lane, or was it an off licence

Pina R. Off license Rosa!

Rosa B. I know Pina miss them days yes my house is a pazza casa.

Andrew L. That off-license in Green Lane was always open long after all the shops had shut and so us kids were always up there for our crisps and sweets.

Pina R. Best casa pazza I know Rosa Mulé Buscaglia x

Rosa B. Yes I remember buying the glass fizzy bottles and then taking them back and getting what was it 2p

Chris G. Rosa did you used to run the Chip Shop?

Rosa B. Hi Chris I did I helped at Pinas shop a few times but recently I ran Gregory's on church street

Chris G. Yep that's where I recognise you from, Church St

Rosa B. Really yes that's me.

Colin H. Wait till Bev P. sees the threads then ... She just wanted to know if we knew here parents shop on Cambridge St ... And its ended up going all over Europe

Pina R. That made me lol Colin!

Bev P. June, we used the same little red books for customers. One lady lived in an end house somewhere on Southern Way (I can't remember her name but she seemed old so was probably 40 and didn't get around too well). Anyway she wrote her order...in the book and mum read one of the things as frozen chicken, we didn't stock that so I was sent to Budgen, order dispatched. She called the shop laughing her head off because she had written "jar of vicks" and asked how she was supposed to put a frozen chicken on her chest! I remember the handwriting, it wasn't the best.

June L. I did come in your shop when it was Wavy Line Bev, I remember now.

Bev P. It did have a sign on the front that said C & R Food stores but I had to deliver the Wavy Line leaflets all over the place every fortnight.

205

Alice Bremeyer

Ian H. Thought you would have used Alice's shop Bryan , we did.........she gave credit;-)
Bryan D. My Mum popped over the road to Alice's every day, but for tea, bacon, cheese, biscuits and a few more exotic items it had to be Dimmocks. She also used the butcher on the Square (Fred) even though it meant walking past the LCM butcher on Green Lane.

Ron Tuckey

Ian H. Do you recall the butcher? He came from Potterspury, that had the shop that Tuckey took over. I think he farmed as well.
Ruth E. Butchers at Potterspury were Giddings but not sure if they farmed.
Ian H. No, not Giddings I knew him at Potterspury This was in the 50's and he was old to me, then:-)
Bryan D. Butcher prior to Ron Tuckey may have been Button
Ian H. Could be him, his English was a bit dodgy though.

The Square

Terry L. This is on the Square !
Ian S. Nice building
Ian H. No Church Street!! Mr Carroll was the manager.
Terry L. No Ian H. we have been all through this, It is on the Square, previous threads will explain why ! ie Can't get far enough back to take full pic of Maises because houses are in way, sloping road ala the Square, style of brick under eaves herring bone, Masies has door to left, upstairs window lintel to right matches one on square and not Church Street etc etc and also my Nan worked there and I remember vividly visiting her at work. the pictures to prove this point are way back in Oct/Nov on this group page .. ;)

P 34: Co-op Store on The Square

Chris G. Could of course be that the Coop had a standard double fronted shop design they used everywhere and both shops were similar but as Boz, Detective Chief Inspector of Buildings will prove this was the Square.

Ian H. I bow to your superior knowledge Boz (said he grudgingly with a ferocious French like scowl!!). It looked so like the Church St store. For the life of me I couldn't remember the house on the right and when I saw Furniture on the sign I concluded (wrongly said he bitterly under his breath) that it was Church St. I assumed it was where Mr Carroll worked. Well spotted young man but beware I SHALL GET EVEN!!!!

Chris G. Ian wouldn't it be more French like to shrug your shoulders say 'pah' then discount the know all Rosbif to everyone over a Pastis or two even if he was right ;)

Ian H. Boz they must have changed the windows after this photo, do you know the year? The reason I say this is you could do the Harry Worth thing on the square as I did several times and the front of the store wasn't like this then (I think). Chris thought about that but the Wolverton boy in me wouldn't allow me. Je l'aurai :-)

207

Terry L. Non, je ne regrette rien except that in the Co op or in someone's wisdom they decided to change the face of the shop completely, with much knocking about and pebble dash when the original shop was so beautiful. je suis tres fatigue now. lol

Ian H. Young man your French impresses me.............then again I'm easily impressed, however I'm not convinced!! The more I think about it I'm pretty certain the "shop" on the Square didn't sell furniture. Perhaps some of the older posters (Bryan D.,Dorothy Stapleton, Maurice Hunt) could clear this up once and for all ,à bientôt mon ami. Not forgetting Geoff Labrum he might know??

Geoff L. I think Church St. was furniture and the square was clothes but I could be wrong long while ago

Terry L. Ian H. not sure if the Funiture sign is what has confused people, I don't recall Furniture being sold on the Square either, perhaps they had the signage made before they realised it wouldn't fit in there or the 2 Drapery shops were in unison sign wise but one sold the shoes and drapery and one sold the Furniture ! saying that it still does not change the Architectural evidence that one has provided ! I think Dave M.provided a picture of the Drapery on fire in the 1950's this may all so have some baring on the story !

Bryan D. Boz woz absolutement correct to identify this as located on the Square, and he may have been the first to do so. I have seen this photo elsewhere identified as the Co-op Department Store on Church Street and without looking too carefully I also fell into the same trap. Since then I have tried to track the history of the Co-op. There was a bakery on Bury Street and later a Grocery on Creed St - at the south end before the triangle. In the late 19th C. they branched out to Church St., on the south side in the middle of the section between the back alley and Radcliffe St. Now pulled down of course. The Trade Directories suggest that the Co-op examined to the Square at the beginning of the 20th Century and commandeered a block of houses from Aylesbury Street, number 1 to 5. The architecture in this picture is very much Edwardian in style. Clearly this was their flagship store at the time and sold the wares advertised. The Church St shop at 60-64 (now Maisies) was built in the 1930s and they must have moved the bigger stuff, like furniture down there at that time. And this is how we remember it pre-Maisies. Possibly they decided to "improve" the Square frontage at this time. The Co-op was probably in its prime from the 1930s to 1960s, when they had branches everywhere and you could spend your lifetime dedicated to the Co-op - from baby formula to a coffin.

Terry L. Ian H. not sure if the Furniture sign is what has confused people, I don't recall Furniture being sold on the Square either, perhaps they had the signage made before they realised it wouldn't fit in there or the 2 Drapery shops were in.

P 35: Early 20th Century photograph of the Co-op on the Square.

This early 20ᵗʰ century photograph of the south west corner of the square shows the edge of the disputed furniture store. The frontages changed considerably over the century. Ed.

Ian H. Not sure if the Funiture sign is what has confused people, I don't recall Furniture being sold on the Square either, perhaps they had the signage made before they realised it wouldn't fit in there or the 2 Drapery shops were in unison sign wise but one sold the shoes and drapery and one sold the Furniture ! saying that it still does not change the Architectural evidence that one has provided ! I think Dave M.provided a picture of the Drapery on fire in the 1950's this may all so have some baring on the story !

Ian H. Thank you Bryan and a big well done to Boz Snakes , you sir are worthy of being a Wolverton boy. Result Hicko 0 Boz 1. Je vous aurai:-)

Colin T. BUT .....Ian you put up a dam good fight lol xx

I. Spires England 1 France 0 Agincourt

Ian H. Mais c'est que la mi-temps!! On verra, je l'aurai, je promets, à plus tard.

Terry L. Chacun pour soi et Dieu pour tous.

I.Spires Bryan D. for the record the co op also had a sports retail out let on the square near Buckingham st in 75 78 ish my mother managed it for a while

Pina R. I remember the gas shop & Dudeney & Johnsons. What was on the other corner? Was it the coal merchants?

Chris G. Think it was at one time Pina.

P 36: Moreland Terrace, east side of the Square. c. 1920

June L. This is what the Market Square looked like in Wolverton 1915

Linda K. Love this picture. Would love to have seen the Square back then.

June L. Me to Linda, sometimes I think I'd like to have lived back then, but there were rough times too.

Linda K. I agree June. I wouldn't mind living then if I could take today's medical care with me :-). Would quite fancy spending a day in the Wolverton of a 100 years ago.

June L. I live in a cottage & sometimes I try to think what it must have been like to walk to each village as they hardly ever ventured outside their own village.

Faye L. Would be very curious to see what the inside of my mum's house looked like 100 years ago, how it was decorated for example x

Julie W. I love the rainbow effect.

P 37: Cenotaph c. 1970

211

Gary K. Very sad to think that this picture was taken in the midst of World War 1 and that telegrams would have been arriving on Wolverton doormats on a daily basis with news of family members killed at the front. Families lived in fear of the "knock at the door", and very few, if any, Wolverton families would have made it to the end of the War without receiving news of a loved one either dead or missing-in-action. On balance, I think we're definitely better off now, June!

Terry L. No doubt about that Gary, we live in a small village that would have had a small population in the war, yet our local war memorial has an unbelievable amount of local young men killed during the first world war on it.

G.Kelly My relative (59 Green Lane) died on 30 Sept 1918 - 6 weeks before the armistice on his first day at the front. Aged 18. I don't know how these people coped

Chris G. There's some poor chap in the churchyard at Old Wolverton died, probably of wounds, on 18th Nov 1918. After five longs year of war and the relief of all around that it was all finally over, it must have been terrible for his family him succumbing just 7 days after peace had been declared.

Len E. Tragically these "knocks on doors" are still happening :(

June L. I know all about war time Gary, we were in the Blitz and were bombed out twice in fact our house was wiped out totally, my mother & I were evacuated to Wales (my dad did six years service in the army) members of our family & my school friend & her family were killed, a Doodlebug dropped on their house. I could go on but I won't.

June L. I never knew my Granddad Watson (my Dad's Dad) he was killed in the 1914/18 1st world war so was his Brother, my uncle Albert. Dad was only 4 years old.

Pat B. My family too were in the London Blitz and we were bombed out... We were in bed and I can vaguely remember a hole in the roof, but my Mum can still remember grabbing a dressing gown from behind the door to wrap me in. Don't know why we were not in the shelter that night.... Maybe because of the big spiders down there. ...Although quite young some instances stay in your mind. My Dad was in the Bomb Disposal Squad and had some hair-raising times.... I have a telegram...

Faye L. My granddads relation was killed in France in word war 1, they couldn't find his body so he's still over there somewhere, sad he was only 19yrs old

Ron B. My Grandfather was killed in the May of 1918. My Father was only Six weeks old, so he never got to see his Father whose body was never recovered.

Pina R. I remember the gas shop & Dudney & Johnsons. What was on the other corner? Was it the coal merchants?

Chris G. Think it was at one time Pina

Bryan D. Nice to see part of the Cenotaph as it used to be. Why was it replaced. The other corner shop in Buckingham St. was the home of a shoe repairer, John Nichols and the shop sold pots and pans and the like. It was described as "Domestic Stores".

P 38: The Market Square c. 1950

Kim P. I remember the old cenotaph towards the end of its existence, it was all breaking up and falling apart... especially the "steps" where I'm sure we all climbed and ran around as kids, irreparably damaging it for future generations.

Faye L. Is that the square?? didn't recognise it!

213

Chris G. Think it, the old cenotaph, was sandstone or some such and acid rain gradually got it.

Kim P. I was thinking sandstone too, I remember what the cenotaph looked like and I've seen similar damage on sandstone and slate monuments and gravestones here - combination of pollution, physical damage and simple age causes them to "spall", that is they sort of break apart in layers.

Donna S. This is how I remember the square ...

Ian W. Me too

Ian L. And me!! Great pic..

Tricia D. Yes that's how I remember the square too.. and how great it was on remembrance Sunday - felt like everyone used to turn out!!

John C. So nice to see different view of the square

Phillip W. The street may soon be open again

Lynette M. Used to love sitting in the square watching the people it was so busy with some lovely shops. People did go there now as its been spoilt its a shame. The square is one of my most happiest memories of Wolverton.

Becca H. Lynnette If you click on the photo's link at the top, there have been quite a few pics and conversations about the square in the past on here. Most of them will be a nice read, especially ones recalling the shops like Terry's, the Launderette, Davis's, the big Co-op etc.

Geoffrey W. I think that, at one stage, the Square was the centre of our lives due to the amount of shops there. It was certainly part of my life, having lived there for some years. That was when most of the shops in the Square were a Co-op of some sort. In fact, as kids, we reckoned you could live and die in the Square and the Co-op would look after you.

What an amazing group of photos. The aqueduct, I remember we used to walk across it as kids, but on the other side of the footpath for a dare! And 'Terry's', I used to live there with my parents before it became Terry's, and behind our shop, was the Co-op Dairy where they used to bottle the milk and tie up the the dray horses to metal rings on the wall.

214

Bryan D. That's something I didn't know Geoffrey. I always assumed that the bottling took place at Jersey Road, where the horses were stabled.

Geoffrey W. Yes Bryan, the drays used to enter the back way from the top end because it was slight downhill and easier to exit when loaded. As a child living almost next door, and because my dad a lot of milk for his ice-cream making, I got to know those who worked there and would often go and watch the bottling procedure. It was in the days of glass bottles with round cardboard closures which you could make 'fly through the air if you were lucky. I have many, many more memories

Bryan D. Those were the days when the cream rose to the top of the bottle. And on frosty mornings the tops would pop off as the milk froze on the doorstep. Keep 'them coming Geoff. I didn't know your father made his own ice cream. I always assumed it was made by Lyons.

Geoffrey W. Oh yes, it was quite an industry for some years. He had vans touring the villages, and a number of tricycles which were a refrigerated box fixed to a BSA motorbike. He bought people up from Cornwall who needed the work, and at weekends went to motorcycle scrambles and the like to sell the ice-cream. However, much to the disbelief of my friends at the time, I was sick of the stuff !

Bryan D. I had no idea the enterprise was that extensive. I can recall him taking one of these trikes up to the cricket ground and the Recs on a Sunday afternoon in the summer. Back then I wasn't paying much attention to life in the villages. I suppose your father must have retired from the shop about 1960 when Terry Beckwith came on the scene.

Dorothy S. Yes I was right I have just seen this photo above. Mum and Dad's shop was on left corner of Radcliffe St as General Stores then a Mrs Nichols had a shop across the Radcliffe St. A Start's clothes shop cornerwise opposite us too. So the years still move on ....:)

215

Greengrocer on the Square

Kim P. Which was the greengrocers shop on the square in the 70's? Seem to recall it was close to or maybe next to Davies's. Definitely in that corner somewhere, wasn't as far down as the opticians.

Anthony Z. Seem to remember the owners had a couple of sons, names I can't think of at the moment

Vivienne B. There use to be Dudney and Johnsons right on the corner opposite the Large red building, (more like the Co-op)

Bryan D. The Co-op had its green grocers at the south east corner of the Square. Dudeney and Johnston was at the north east corner. I don't recall any other green grocer there.

Bryan D. Dudeney and Johnston were Bedford-based grocers and had a chain of shops across Bdfordshire and parts of Bucks and Northants. They may have had about 20 or 30 shops. I don't know when they disappeared but they we probably gobbled up by Sainsbury's or Tesco.

Keith T. Yes Bryan the Co-op had a green gocers on the square next to Dudney & Johnsons when I started working for them in 1970. When it closed they made it a sorts shop for a few years

Len E. I recall the greengrocers there, very close to if not next to Davies' on the same side does anybody remember Wrights the Insurance brokers in the offices above the chemist, got my moped insurance there 1975

Kim P. Did Wrights have people do rounds to collect insurance premiums? The name rings a bell but I remember my Dad having a bloke (called Jeff, for what it's worth!) come round once a month for "the insurance".

Kim P. Looking at the layout now on Google maps I want to say maybe the Age Concern shop was the greengrocers?

Kim P. I remember the tattoo place was a pet shop around the same time or maybe slightly later.

Chris G. Yep the Age UK place was a greengrocers too at one time Kim.

Lorna W. I think it was run by Mr and Mrs Stokes.

Chris G. Certainly sounds familiar Lorna.

June L. I remember years ago the Co-op had a green grocers & wet fish shop side by side on the square, there was also a Angia Buiding Society, the Pet shop near Davises, Lloyds opticians & Roberts,Dudney & Johnsons on the far corner with the Gas showroom opposite, I shopped in all of these.

Susan B. Also there was Co-op menswear and drapery, chemist Lynsey R.and the co op shoe shopon the square i worked there for 2 years

Lynsey R. Behind the coop was the dairy where they bottled the milk.

Vivienne B. Does anyone remember? there use to be a place in Buckingham Street at the back of Donatos where we use to get orange juice, (I think)

Jackie A. There was definitely a green grocer there, my auntie worked in there but cant remember what is was called

Geoffrey W. The Co-op greengrocers and Co-op wet fish were originally situated in one shop at the top of The Square. Above it, and accessed by a door round the corner of the building was the Co-op hall, where they used to dole out the 'Divi' twice a year. It was often said, at the time, that you could virtually be born and die in the Square, and the Co-op would be able to cater for all your needs !

Ruth E. Think green grocer was Stuart Parker. I think he and his Mum ran it.

Pearks

Jackie N. OOh! I remember Pearks! My Mum collected some crockery from there, getting stamps for it every time she shopped there....I think the crockery was yellow......

Ruth E. I knew Hilda I was born at Yardley and she knew all my brothers and sisters we were Russell's I worked at Pearks and the lady next to her is Hilda Brown and I think Margaret Cox not sure though. When you say was has she passed away?

P 39: Peark's Staff

Maurice W. No she not passed away. She is now Hilda Webb. Sorry for confusion. Mum is still in Yardley.

June L. I was a regular shopper in Pearkes, Pete Neal was manager (he lived opposite me in Cambridge St, still lives there) when I say opposite I mean the back of Oxford St. I can see Joyce in the photo also one of the Fenson twins, which one was your mum Maurice?

June L. I always bought their sausages they were lovely.

Maurice W. Mum is on the left June.

Ruth E. Maurice Webb whew... Well give her my best wishes she will remember me as Ruth Russell.

Ruth E. Well June I must have served you I worked there from 1965 till it closed in 1971.... Know Peter Neal and Pat but he had moved to the Maypole at Bletchley when I worked there.

Terry L. Maurice give her our best to and from the Culleys ....

218

Maurice W. I've just shown these comments to my mum, and the tears started flowing down her cheeks with a smile. Then, she took me to the kitchen to show me a plate that come from pearkes. Mum is now searching more photos..

Ruth E. Ooh how lovely send her big hugs from me she is a sweet lady can you let her know all my brothers are dead now just me and my sister left, sure she would like to know

Ruth E. Well June I must have served you I worked there from 1965 till it closed in 1971.... Know Peter Neal and Pat but he had moved to the Maypole at Bletchley when I worked there.

Terry L. Webb and give her our best to and from the Culleys ....

Maurice W. I've just shown these comments to my Mum, and the tears started flowing down her cheeks with a smile. Then, she took me to the kitchen to show me a plate that came from Peark's. Mum is now searching more photos. Lol.

Ruth E. Ooh how lovely send her big hugs from me she is a sweet lady can you let her know all my brothers are dead now just me and my sister left, sure she would like to know xxxxx

Pedleys

Karen W. My grandpa George taken when he was quite young. Not sure of the date though.

Edward. Q Your granddad cut my hair many many times Karen (Ted Quinn)

Jane B. My Dad used to go there in the late 60's to have his hair cut - I used to be allowed to sit in the vacant chair on the children's seat - thought I was so grown up!!!!!!!

Ron B. Crikey! That's brought back some memories. Shame it can't do the same for my hair

John H. Didn't he also have a helper, I think it was Vic, I remember going there with my dad.

Chris G. Take a look in the background John. Great pic Karen.

Ian S. Eek that's the fella that used to cut my hair (when I had some) it always had that smell of brylcream in the shop.

Doug M. Oh my goodness that picture took me right back. My dad took me in there to get my hair cut. Pedleys right? Had a picture of a Sargent Major saying "Am I hurting you son? I should be I am standing on your hair."

P 40: George Pedley outside his shop c. 1940s

Len E. So smartly dressed.

Terry L. Many visits to George Pedley and Vic as a kid, happy times and hair!

Steve W. Vic cut my ear once, long time since I have been to the barbers.

Terry L. It must have been the stuff coming out of the works chimney that made us all bald; we should consider suing them Steve!

Steve P. That's why I got my own clippers & have never paid for a haircut for over 30 years. When the boys were young had an option of no 1, 2, 3, or 4. Surprisingly enough the girls never took up the option ;-)

Brian E. The Asian barber on Stratford Road next to the Western still only charges £5. And he does eye-brows, ears & nose as a matter of course. Wolverton must have more barbers per capita now than any other similar town?

Jon H. Every 4 weeks without fail my Granddad would take me in there for our hair cut. He would say short back and sides Vic, and so would I. I remember he had a booster seat for me to sit on, and the foot plate of the chair said Usbourn or something. It was ornate metalwork. The hair clippers were not electric either, oh and a haircut was £1 that was 1984 that I recall as I remember reading my football 84 sticker album in the waiting room :-)

Brian E. Back then, short back 'n' sides were the only haircut on offer!

Ron B. And something for the weekend sir?

June L. Pete always went to Mr Cummings in Cambridge St for his hair cut it cost him Half a Crown, then when he stopped cutting hair he got me to do it & I've been cutting his hair ever since. I don't touch the top though.

June L. P.S, nothing for the weekend.

Ron B. Ah Sid Cummings. Went there a few times.

Music Shop

Bryan D. Does anyone remember Anstey's shop on Church St? now pulled down of course. They sold sheet music and records and in the 1950s when EPs and LPs were invented they became Wolverton's only outlet. There was a record shop in Newport Pagnell and I am not sure about Stony. The best selection in those days was in Northampton, a shop on Gold St whose name I can't immediately recall. There they had audio booths upstairs where you could listen to the latest hits - a sort of "try before you buy" policy.

Chris G. The Northampton shop in Gold St with the booths was called John Lever's in the 70's Bryan, not sure if it had an earlier name.

Brian E. John Lever's was my music shop of choice back in the day. I was a regular there, and the staff would often put by a new release in anticipation of my Saturday visit. Bryan, I can't place the shop you refer to, but I seem to recall an electrical shop on The Square - radios and plugs, etc. - that had a few racks of LPs in the

221

shop. I recall getting a Bob Dylan album there, and a Rolling Stones single as soon as it arrived.

P 41: Church Street in the 1950s.

Bryan D. Doesn't ring a bell. It will come to me. My brain is stuffed with information that doesn't always want to come out when I want it. Being a young-un at 50 I'm sure you don't have that problem ;-)

Brian E. Almost 60, if we are counting, Bryan!

Chris G. He means me, 50 on Sunday.

Brian E. Well, Happy Birthday

Ruth E. Remember the Gold St one in the 60's and. How are you Bryan

Bryan D. Bit of an old crock at the moment Ruth. It's a bit hard to lever myself out of a chair. But I'll get over it. It'll teach me not to try walking on air in the future :-)

Diane K. Used to go to Northampton most Saturday mornings to buy a few 45s from John levers then down bridge street to memory lane a second hand record shop used to be able to buy all Motown and soul imports there, the good old days

Chris G. There was also, for us 'youngsters' Spin-a-Disc down towards the cinema in Northampton

222

Ian B. We had a record shop in Wolverton around the mid 60's just along from Foster's, can't remember the name but bought a fair few 45's and LPs in there.

S. Stone Bryan, was Anstey's somewhere between where Joy Willett lived and the Co-op menswear?

Hazel S. In Stony you had Harry Wildman's shop located between Foster & Scott and Hall's Bazaar in the High Street where you could buy records and order sheet music.

Sheila, The Church Street entrance to the Victoria Hotel was exactly opposite Anstey's shop.

Sheila S. That's what I thought Hazel.

Hazel S. Should have been Harry Wildman.

Pamela J. I remember Anstey's used to get song sheets from there on a Friday' pay day.

King's

Phillip W. Kings Bakery.

P 42: King's Bakery on Church St. shortly before demolition

Chris G. Hooray! Didn't think such a thing existed. Well done mate.

Chris G. Many a Wolverton kid sat on that wall over the years picking at the warm crust of the loaf that your Mum just sent you to buy.

Phillip W. it was in a batch of slides i copied a few months ago

Bryan Dunleavy Well done Phillip. This must date from the 70s when the extension was added to the front.

Chris G. Over the road is the side of Eady's, the butchers who I posted an old pic of last week.

Phillip W. Think it was the 70's yeah as it was in with the some slides which had the works time office in

Kim P. Oh wow yes I had forgotten completely but this is where we went before the Agora was built... it seemed like a long walk all the way from Victoria street but I was only a wee one then, no wonder there was no crust left on the bread by the time we got home!!

Susan B. Brings back memories Chris, I was one of those kids eating the warm crust of the bread, cottage loaf was one of my favourites you don't see many of them these days

Len E. That wall was so high to a 3 year old

Chris G. I looked at it in the pic Len and thought surely that wall was a lot higher than that? Perceptions eh?

Andrew L. Wow! This is way back at the very beginnings of my memory, setting off all kinds of linked memories, like opening a box of frogs!

Susan B. I had to walk from the top of Jersey Rd Kim, always picking at the bread

Len E. Never got the chance to pick at the bread on the way home as we only lived a hundred yards away

Katie G. Where abouts was this in Wolverton? Bit before my time! ;)

Len E. Diagonally opposite the Queen Vic in Church St.

Katie G. Ah cool thank u :)

Sheila S. Ask your Dad katie, he will remember it

Pina R. Remember jumping off that wall, it seemed a lot higher back then, lol!

224

Susan B. Yes it did Pina seem much higher back then.

Jill G. Remember coming to Wolverton every Sat to get the bread for the weekend, can smell that lovely bread now :)

Jennifer T. Loved their bread

Margaret C. That's lovely to see, awakened lots of memories and for some reason I thought the wall was higher...

Anthony Z. Malt loaf on a saturday when they delivered

Toni B. mmmm hot bread

Jill G. sometimes i used to break the crust of the end on the way home so mum used to give me some money to get a crusty roll so i didn't do that lol

Margaret Ck. Same thoughts Jill...I can smell that bread baking...Mmmmm.

Ruth E. Been in that bread Queue a few times x great pic x

Colin T. Remember the smell of Fresh Bread Being Baked. Can any one give me a Good Answer as to why this Wonderful place that provided us all near & far with our own home made bread & other bits & bobs is no longer there? Instead we have a HEAP OF CRAP BLOCKING THE ROAD,

Len E. I think they call it progress Colin.

Dorothy Stapleton That is as I remember it as we lived at the back of KINGS THE BAKERS in Buckingham St.b You could always smell the bread baking. :) GREAT very good bread yummmm...

Sue T. Fabulous picture, brings back many memories

Anthony Z. Not far away from you Sue.

Terry L. Fantastic, like others thought we would never see it again, soon as I saw the picture I could smell the bread, and see a little Red haired lady (Mrs King) bless her. I too was surprised at height of wall, we all must of had little legs in the 60's and 70's.....Nice one Phillip !

Steve W. So many memories can smell the bread & yes Terry my legs used to dangle of that wall lol

Mark B. Oh such happy memories of such a great bakers! Cottage loaves oh so tasty! Sitting on the low wall on the corner waiting for my mum to come out happy days

Linda R. I remember standing on that wall every year to watch the carnival. x

225

Gary Crook I can remember running to the end and jumping off straight into the lady who worked in the Gas showroom on the Square. She wasn't best pleased!!, I may have smudged her make up. lol.

Phillip W. I have had this photo in my collection for months. I don't know why it has taken me so long to post it.

Janet B. On Good Friday you had to be early or their wonderful Hot Cross buns were sold out. Nobody made them as good as the Kings.

Andrew L. Shop was long and narrow inside I think, sort of like a corridor?

Edith H. I remembered it as we had steps to climb to get in. I was much younger then.

Ant K. Well Well......lovely comments.

Ant K. My Teddy Bear was buried under this when they knocked it down ;-(.......

Jill G. Poor Ted.

Ian B. The wall in Radcliffe St must have been next to the ovens they were lovely and warm on a cold winters day.

Steve Tw. Allez Mmmmm buying bread still lovely and warm with just a piece of tissue paper wrapped around it and didn't they make little tiny loaves too? It was all so yummy.

Chris G. What year was that Ant?

Ant K. Our family business and home was knocked down around 1975 I think. Lots of stuff was left behind as we had no where to take it. Ted was one, but I had grown out of cuddly toys by 1975!

John Robinson Wasn't there a big Hovis sign painted on the wall on the Radcliffe St side?

Ant K. There was one Golden Hovis Sign on the front of the old shop, before the shop was "modernised" in the late sixties. Not sure what was on the Ratcliffe Street side. The bake house window used to be stored at Stacey Hill Museum.. think it was destroyed in a fire. And I remember the side door into the flour house off Ratcliffe Street and the Bookies further up towards the back alley

Donna S. Mmmmm King's bakers.... there is nothing better than the smell of fresh baked bread. Dad would pick up a loaf on way home from post office , be still warm and we have it with our breakfast... mmm nothing like it.

Jersey Road

Andrew L. Does anyone remember a little shop in Jersey Road, on the Aylesbury Street corner, on the north side opposite the Winsor & Glave shop? I have a faint memory of being allowed to go there to buy sweets when very young as it didn't involve crossing any roads to get there. Could have been called P's or something. Run by 2 older ladies. Would have closed about 1974 or earlier. I need to know if I am imagining this or not.

Chris G. Yep I remember it Andrew, it was one of the shops you could call into on the long walk home from the Juniors or Infants.

Bryan D. It probably was there, although I never registered it as it was not my patch. Before the war it was a stationery and post office run by William Longmore but for some reason he moved the operation to Anson Road after the war. So I presume he left a shop behind that was taken over by your ladies.

Colin H. I remember the shop but not the name ;(..... I used to buy Rainbow Sherbet there and also Sherbet Dib Dabs !!! You could eat the Dib Dab just in time before you got to school at Radcliffe !!! Perhaps Bev P.may know as a former shopkeepers daughter ???

Bev P. I remember a sweet shop there abouts. I think it might be the one people on here have called The Candy Box.

Chris G. It's probably my addled brain but in the summer when the weather was good didn't they put a little table outside with sweets on either side of the school bell to catch passing trade?

Bryan D. I think the Candy Box is at 82 Stratford Road - used to be Bews.

Bev P. Not this one then Bryan, I'm remembering green paint on the outside.

Andrew L. Candy Box was down on Stratford Road/Jersey Road junction next to Pedleys (fantastic shop for under-age firework purchasing). The one I am thinking of shut down but the ladies carried on living there. The other end of Wyvern there was a little

227

general store that was VG stores in the 70s, and it is still open today (I saw it yesterday).

Colin H. I think you are right Bryan ... The candy box was on the "Front" ...

Andrew L. (by "the other end of Wyvern" I mean the Aylesbury St/Windsor St junction.

Pina R. It was Kendall Stores, on the corner of Jersey Road/Aylesbury St. I've mentioned it on here before. oh all those jars of sweeties..mmmm!

Chris G. Yep Smiths or Thorns before it was VG, Mr Thorn also drove the local bus.

Ian H. There was one further up, opposite the Co Op butcher; An odcd couple and the lady's mother . Pearces, we got credit there too:-)

Bryan D. Prior to that, Smiths.

Bev P.I remember them, I wish I could get some of my childhood sweets here!

Andrew L. That Winsor & Glave shop was a little hardware store and we used to get paraffin for our bathroom heater/carbon monoxide gassing device. We paid in the shop and then went to the carpentry workshop at the back, and Frank Atkins would put the Pink Paraffin into your can.

Bryan D. You obviously had good credit everywhere Ian! ;-)

Ian H. No Bryan , just credit ....remember the one on windsor St/church St that one too!!

Chris G. And no racial slight at all as Joe the owner used to call the shop by this name himself, when Joes family from India took the Candy Box over it was know as the Ghandi Box.

Andrew L. Pina, the jars! You've just opened one of my memory cupboards and the contents just fell out all over my brain. That really did it!

Terry L. We must of spent a fortune in the Ghandi box aye Chris, Joe always good to us though, a lovely family...

Chris G. Yep Joe was, and I believe still is, a great bloke. I'm sitting here laughing to myself about some of the stories he told us.

228

Sue L. I remember a shop on the opposite side of the road from the Anson Road post office and i'm sure the man only had one arm? Frightened me to death!

Chris G. That would be Pete Savoury Sue, him and his wife Jean ran it, had sons Phil and Tim.

Chris G. Pete worked in the accounts dept at Aston Martin after they had the shop, he died a few years back, Jeans still alive, saw her in Tesco's the other day.

Chris G. Before the Savourys the Cooks owned the shop 'Fred' Andy C.is on this group.

Sue L. I can remember one bloke from Winsor and Glave at one point he might as well have set up camp in our front garden as he seemed to always be re-glazing our front door when my brother Michael smashed the glass after a few arguments

P 43: Winsor and Glave Workshop

Andy C. Pete Savoury - who bought the shop off my Dad did have one arm (which freaked me out as an 11 year old) but bizarrely was quite a good bowls player from what I can gather. Tried to get my Dad to join the bowls club.

Chris G. Yep he played bowls with my old man for years for Wolverton Town, They were good friends, Jean and Pete, to both my parents.

Sue L. I was only 3 or 4 years old and he was a lovely bloke but it just frightened me for some reason. Not sure if my dad ever played bowls, wouldn't have done for long before he passed away i have some wooden bowls in the loft that he used.

Chris G. What was your Dad's name Sue?

Sue L. It was John Roberts. He was a policeman. We lived in one of the police houses Aylesbury Street West

Chris G. Of course Sue, I forgot you're Mick and Trev's sister. Doh.

Alan Cr. Windsor & Glaves were they not also the funeral directors and also builders?

Ian H. Certainly builders and decorators.

Bryan D. Yes they did that as well.

Ian H. Trevor Glave, where's he now?

Bryan D. Trevor is retired and live in or near Vancouver BC, as far as I know. He worked, as I did, in the Canadian Community College system and taught last at BCIT (British Columbia Institute of Technology). I did have some brief correspondence with him a number of years back.

Chris G. Top of Jersey Road was a butcher one side and grocer the other at one time wasn't there?

Ian H. Sure was Chris as I posted "last night";-)The Co Op butcher run By Mr Richardson in the 40/50's then by Ron ? his assistant, afterwards. Pearce's were opposite an odd Mother with her married daughter called Vera with her husband. A little known fact, Vera took me in her very, very old slow car to Silverstone the day I had to tell my future in-laws that their daughter was "in the club" and not the one along Western Road.

Chris G. Apologies Ian, with all else going on last night I overlooked it.

Ian H. No sweat, last night kept my mind off the Wolves :-(

Ian H. If you missed my post about the butchers I'll recant a bit, Mr Richardson wore these lovely black leather gaiters around his lower legs. When he skinned a rabbit in front of this little lad, who always went shopping, *see notes about credit* :-) the way he pulled the skin off over the head to reveal a bald headed staring Ray Wilkins lookalike animal never ceased to amaze me. I used to ask for a nice piece of topside for six shillings please, weekends that is, or a breast of lamb, or some scrag-end for mutton stew or a leg of lamb, knuckle end for the same six shillings. If you bought a piece of beef he invariably put a big chunk off lard on it, gratis, for the basting. Ron helped him lift the carcasses and "butcher" them up. At closing time they dragged metal across the wooden chopping blocks to scrape off the residues of meat then give it all a good scrubbing with brushes and hot Water. I liked Mr Richardson;-)

John R. I remember Phillip Windsor and Roberta Glave - I think they were some of the Windsor and Glave kids.

Ian S. Jackie Steensel I was playing snooker with Paul Butcher Fri evening.

Ian H. Roberta lived up the top end, Marina Drive or Gloucester Road.

Sylvia A. I remember at little corner shop at the top end of Jersey Road and another opposite the little post office on Anson road. Don't remember one at bottom end of jersey road must admit.

Smiths

Bev P. I remember the shop on Windsor Street too. You'd think I wouldn't have gone in them since ours was basically the family larder!

Becca H. Thorns had a daughter called Tina

Bryan D. Smiths was the first and last place I spent a farthing.

Ian H. A licorice twig?

Bryan D. Whalley's. I used to go in there with David W. and Mr Whalley's moon face would come out of the back room to watch our every move in case our fingers got too light.

Prices in 1964

Pat B. Here is an even earlier Lampitts advert. Wolverton Express. April 1964. Cost 3d.

John R. The washing machine costs 65 GNS. I wonder how many people even know what that is these days?

Len E. Wasn't 1 Guinea = 21 Shillings? 20 old Shillings to £1.00?

Ian S. Winsor and Glave remember them ?

Andrew L. Remember Winsor & Glave? Their yard was my playground, they spent more time clearing up the sand I chucked everywhere than they did building anything.

Pat B. There are loads of old advertisers in this paper and quite a few wedding photos.

The Old Market Hall

Chris G. On the right Eric Olthwaite with his brand new shovel!
Steve A. Trying to work out the aspect Chris.
Elaine P. One word Chris............ W O W !!!!!!!!! x
Terry L. On the right was the Sweets man from town, and Lawson's had the stall on the left, if that helps !
Terry L. or vice versa
Steve A. So are we looking down towards Stratford road from the side entrance?
Terry L. I think we are looking away from Stratford Road !
Chris G. Yep that's what I thought too.
Jane B. Where the moustachioed man is on the left is where my desk was !!!!! I worked there when it was the Travel Organisation - so yes, it is from Stratford Road looking towards St Georges Institute
Jane B. I meant on the right - DOH!!!
Terry L. Didn't know you worked for the Travel Org Jane.

Jane B. Oh yes - I was PA to 2 of the Operations Manager - and stand in PA to the Operations Director when his was away - enjoyed the work and it was within easy walking distance of home!!!!

Terry L. What was the woman's name on reception, was it Barbara?

Bryan D. Family album coming out tonight Chris? This may be a photo from the first time the old school was used as a Market Hall. Therefore 1908.

Chris G. From the Bucks County Archive Bryan.

Terry L. Boy's got same cap on as the cottage picture so could be similar date!

Jane B. Boz - when I was there the receptionist was called Kim and she came from Wokingham in Berkshire - which was an awful long commute I thought - but hey ho, each to his own I suppose !!!!

Terry L. Hmm, the people who I worked for used to make a fortune from Travel Org, sending stuff all over the place by courier... Sorry Bryan I wasn't asking if Barbara was in the picture but I can see how it looked, even made me laugh. How do you spell Barbara ?

Helen P. Wow, that is a brilliant picture! Brings back a lot of memories, those lamps for example!

Chris G. I'm slow today Bryan, hey I'm slow everyday...

Brian E. I think we are looking towards Church Street? Isn't the stall on the left the butcher who had the "Pleased to meet you meat to please you" pig's head as a centrepiece?

Barbara L. Do you remember Wolverton market, bought a pint of winkles, prawns jellied eels etc, proper market traders, calling out to customers loudly, to sell their wares, hated smell of fish, even rabbit sold too

Brian E. Scroll back through photos here Barbara, there are a few pics of the market there. The shellfish man had his stall round the back. Cockles and winkles were sold by the pint. The upstairs toy stall opposite the butchers was a favourite of mine. They sold clockwork tin-plate trucks, always Bedford's. The kind of toy that had sharp edges, and if you poked your finger in the works it came out bloody!

Sheila S. Remember the faggots from the market, never had such good ones since.

June S. Oh yes Barb I remember it well, we used to live right opposite in the 'little streets' & I remember going round with my 'proper' pram, I loved the smell of the pork pie man in the corner! Ah happy days :-)

Brian E. The fish-cakes were excellent too, best I ever had.

Ian H. The shellfish seller always had an impeccable white overall and a neatly clipped moustache, sold his wares in pint and half pint glasses!!

Brian E. And he drove around in a Morris van, stopping every so often to step out and bellow "fishooh!"

Pat B. There was also Botteral's (not sure of spelling) of Northampton. Fruit and Veg. and Tony Sweet with his fabric stall.

Margaret C. Just inside the steps into the market in Creed Street was the shoe stall. Just as you went into main market hall...

Ruth E. I worked on Barleys fruit and veg stall in the. 70's

Terry L. Who remembers the material man from Northampton,

Ruth E. I remember Sweets think he sold coats as well seem to remember getting a maxi coat from his stall.

Terry L. I worked for him for a while, used to have to get there early and lug all the rolls of fabric into the market hall, and then go back later and lug it all back into the van!

Celia R. My late husband use to help Tony sweet I often got my material off him. My husband did the afternoon sometimes in the mornings

Stephen G. I used to like the black pudding, used to sit in the office in the works on an afternoon and eat the lot.

Ian H. Mr Sweet's 'gofer" in my day was Billy Sharman from the Little Streets.

Janice M. They always had good stuff at the fish mongers on Church St. years ago, hated the smell but good stuff in there

Kim P. I remember the sweet stall with the hard sweets that came in a long stick like square rock, broken up with a small hammer for sale by weight. Some of it was little more than dust (especially if you got one of the mixed bags they made up by mixing all the leftovers together) while other bits were so big you could hardly

235

get them in your mouth. Clove was my favourite, to this day the smell of sweet cloves takes me back there.

Donna S. Rock...mmmm there something I cant get anymore ... anytime anyone went someplace for holiday was always brought back rock.

Donna S. humbugs loved humbugs...

Kim P. I still have an unopened slab of Romney's Kendal Mint Cake in my freezer from my trip home last year (got it at the MK museum gift shop!). All the fudge and coconut ice is long gone though

Janice M.I loved the rhubarb and custard hard candy

Donna S. I haven't been back since 77... with exception in 2004 went to Scotland, had my fill of irn bru, tizer,curly wurly's etc.. brought back Turkish delight for my dad . and what was the dark chocolate one with white filling ... oh forget name of it but I like it

Kim P. Oh yes, I liked rhubarb & custard too, also the big cough candy twists... the colour always reminded me of lucozade. Fry's Chocolate Cream! I bought a bag of Curly Wurlies at the Co-Op to bring home but I got sick on the plane on the way home and I was kind of in and out of it for a few hours. When I came round properly I found my daughter had got into the bag and eaten most of them!!

Donna S. My hubby likes them too. My aunt in Scotland sends them to me each year on my birthday I have to hide them ... remember they used to be oh at least 6 inches long, a good inch wide and thicker good thing they sell them in multi packs.. what was name of comedian that promoted them terry something or other ... dress up like a schoolboy... love curly wurly.... can get over here in some English food shops but so darn expensive

Janice M. I usually come back with a bag full of junk I can't get here, especially Bombay mix, revels, minstrels.

Little Streets

Bryan D. Here's a view from the then new (probably unfinished) Gables Tower showing the "Little Streets" in process of demolition. Creed Street on the left, Ledsam Street down the middle, and Young Street and part of Glyn Square (original Glyn Square) on the right. — with Training School.

The "Little Streets" under demolition in the 1960s.

Bev P. Corner fireplaces, that's different.
Terry L. Great picture, I remember playing in these houses when they were empty, and David Shaw threw a roof slate at me which caught me right in the corner of my eye, and I still have the scar to this day!
Pina R. David married my mate Lynne, they later divorced......
Steve A. Great picture that I haven't seen before Bryan, I took the liberty of tagging a couple of landmarks.
Bryan D. Good idea Steve. The Fish and Chip shop was Billingham's btw. I've just put up another post about it.

Steve A. Cheers Bryan, I've got a picture somewhere of my dad sitting on a bulldozer atop a pile of rubble that was Billinghams.

Julie K. It amazes me how they got so many houses on that bit of land, it didn't seem that big when I worked at Able Jacks. Little houses all squeezed together.. ..

Diane K. Memories, what great pics.

Margaret C. I wished I had seen these photo's earlier they bring back so many memories. My maiden name was Clarke and we lived in Creed Street right opposite the church gates.

Bryan D. Margaret. I wish I had been able to make contact with you when I wrote my book on the Little Streets. I worked mostly from 19th century records but could have done with a bit of first hand information. There were 5 units on your section of Creed St - on the Church St corner a bakery, then a butcher, then a house that was always private, the shop which became Billingham's, then the larger house on the corner, which was always associated with the shop. Which one were you

Terry L. I have got your book Bryan and it's very good !

Margaret C. I think if you were to stand by the church gates dead opposite was my home No 49 to the right was I think what was a shop can recall it had larger glass windows, to the left just a couple of houses before the fish and chip shop. Do you recall Bill Callow he lived further down Creed Street opposite the Market?..

Bryan D. Margaret. I've just figured out that you must have been in the end house at Number 49. It was originally the living quarters of the people who ran the shop next door - a grocery for about 60 years. I'm just going to put up the only photo I have, taken from Ledsam St.

Margaret C. Spot on it was the last house but not the end, I am sure the shop was the end just before the triangle...My house was split level you went down some wooden steps from the back (living room) to the scullery/kitchen then down a step out into the backyard. To get upstairs there was a door in the corner of the back room.

Bryan D. If you take a look at my photo of Billingham's which I put up some time back you can probably see the outline of your staircase.

238

John R. I sort of remember a little garden area, sort of a semi-circle with a brick surround holding up the flower beds. I can't ever remember seeing any flowers but it was the area where all of the kids gathered to play. I was opposite St. Georges where a couple of the streets came together.

Margaret C. We called it the triangle..

Pauline M. I lived at No 70 Ledsam Street. I was Pauline Tindle then.

One more conversation

Faye L. Glad to see this group is doing better than the others.............. not that I am competitive or anything lol x

Brian E. Why, what others are there?

Donna S. Well Faye. Wolverton is the only one I can really comment on. I hardly ever went to Stony... and only went to Bradwell to see my Gran or my cousins... and my memories of Wolverton are pretty cloudy at best of times... so for me this is the better site...and its ok to be competitive ..lol

Terry L. I think this site is by far the best. I also think it is something to do with Wolverton people that makes this group so successful, and maybe because our Town was the hub for work, education, and travel. I know one of the sites has a similar group and people just hated to live there, and it's posters are all people that have moved away and say they are glad not to be there any more as they hate the town, which is very sad and makes me cherish even more the fact that I Grew up in Wolverton !!!

Richie B. I never hung out in Stony mainly due to the Saunders and other riff raff that lived there had enough trouble staying out of their way at school lol so I don't really have a lot to comment on that site. I think I can count on 1 hand how many times I've drank in a pub there and two of them times were at wakes .Do love Stony High St. though, has more going for it than the main road in Wolverton. I think we have some lovely towns and villages around us but I don't feel the need to be on a site for every one of them lol ..and as for the people that hate Wolverton half or more of them wouldn't have been here if it wasn't for WOLVERTON works providing jobs for their parents to bring them into the area .

Terry L. Richie, the town that I referred to as being hated by ex residents is Towcester. I haven't heard anyone slag Wolverton off with the exception of one person who thought the shops in Church St weren't up to their standard, but I think they have paid for that now! This Group has made me realise how lucky I was growing up in Wolverton, and the time (70s - 80s) was in my humble opinion was just the best two decades to be a Wolvertonian. I look at my two teenagers now, and think to myself My God, by the time I was at your stage of life I had done so many things, adventures, travel, countless groups I had socialised with. Jobs you could just walk into and then walk out or move on if you didn't like it. I Joined the Army at 16 and left after basic training as I missed Wolverton and my mates, worked in London for 2 years on shifts, but missed the gang at the Galleon, so transferred to the works. Groups of us travelled and holidayed together. Weekends in Yarmouth and Henley. The Rugby Club Discos etc etc. Also you wasn't the only one to have to run the Gauntlet of the Saunders boys and others. I had a girl friend in Stony for sometime and was caught and attacked by one of them a few times, but it made me a stronger person and it was all apart of growing up !

Terry L. See what you done now Faye Elizabeth Lloyd, you have got me ranting ! lol x

Ian H. Excellent post Terry; however I would add the two decades before were equally as formative. In my humble opinion of course.

Faye L. You don't need me to start ranting lol. Well I think the 90s were the best for me, growing up playing in the streets and climbing trees x

Ian H. I've been contemplating Terry's post while having a stroll down the fish port here. Now I'm not sure what the population of Wolverton was after the war, I seem to think about 4000, but it really was very much self sufficient. With the exception of a swimming pool and a theatre (not withstanding the local pantomime shows and singing/music organisations (both available with a short United Counties bus ride away) I can't recall what was missing. As for someone's comment about Church St. shops I wouldn't mind betting most people would welcome the quality and service you got In Essam's (shoes) Chown's menswear) Lawson's (toys magazines etc) today. You name it we had it and not a supermarket to be seen. Did you know you could get cockles winkles and whelks (measured in a half-pint glass on the market every Friday. Wonderful town back then.

Faye L. Er my mum ate cockles lol. . . gross x

Ruth E. I remember the fish stall I worked at Barleys Stall. It was so cold and there were gas lights even in the 70's..... And the veg people from Northampton were so rude to a young 20yr old Ruth. They used to delight in making me blush - no easy feat now ! Lol...

Ian H. Browns Pork Butchers too..........tasty dripping from them, good on King's toasted bread!!!

Ruth E. Oh yes my staple food growing up lol....

Ian H. ..Not forgetting the local girls!! Stunning, all of them. ....and us blokes for the girls!!!!!!!!

Chris G. Ha-ha Ruth, remembering you from Stony - the Stony days of 20 odd years ago that did make me smile, I can't imagine anyone ever making you blush! ;)

Ruth E. Chris it's not an easy task now but was then a shy 20yr old just married...... Lol...

Jackie S. Ian, cockles, winkles and whelks in a pint mug. Love seafood. (Well any fish really) Lucky if they're measured in an egg cup now.

Last Words

I loved this Dirty Old Town of Wolverton - and I say that fondly as you would, about favourite old slippers or Granddads" old chair.

I grew up there and although life at times was difficult, I remember it now with so much fondness; for what I missed with family, I made up with those special memories and friendships that carry me back there whenever I close my eyes.

I remember the simple things, like the Works' siren, playing up the back alleys and sharing sweets, Summer holiday fishing and conkering in the Churchyard; sniggering in School assemblies and singing *All Things Bright and Beautiful* - I remember that all those people I met and spent time with no matter what age, helped to shape me into who I am. I read of all the changes that have happened to Wolverton in these past 30 years; and I can tell you now that what was so special about Wolverton then exists now, still. What made Wolverton special, was the people, the diversity of ages and the interaction of the young and the older residents. It was in the laughter and the story telling and in the ability to care and empathise and share sorrows, when they came.

From an almost old Wolvertonian, I can see demonstrated on a daily basis that all is well in Wolverton and the laughter, humour and humanity that I knew, resonates still in the people of Wolverton and with the magic of the internet, I revisit those old haunts and catch up with familiar faces and share memories and walk those familiar streets again.

Jacqueline Grey

Index of Contributors

Here is a list of those who contributed their thoughts and comments to the text. In the book they are represented by first name and initial to improve readability.

Jackie Abbott   Jackie A.
Toni Adams   Toni A.
Steve Adams   Steve A.
Lynn Adamthwaite   Lynn A.
Angie Ainsworth   Angie A.
Alan Ainsworth   Alan A.
Sylvia Airs   Sylvia A.
Karen Andrews   Karen A.
Kath Atkinson   Kath A.
Deborah Bader   Deborah B.
Jane Bailey   Jane B.
Jane Baker   Jane Br.
John Baker   John B.
Pam Baker   Pam B.
Ron Baker   Ron B.
Steve Baker   Steve B.
Julie Barnes   Julie B.
Geoff Baron   Geoff B.
Mark Baxter   Mark B.
Pete Beale   Pete B.
Gill Beales   Gill B.
Dale Becks   Dale B.
Julia Bennett   Julia B.
Vivienne Bennett   Vivienne B.
Susan Blackwell   Susan B.
Kazza Bomble   Kazza B.
Ian Bowers   Ian B.
Ritchie Bowers   Ritchie B.
Christian Bowler   Christian B.
Mark Boylan   Mark Bn.
Andrew Bromley   Andrew B.
Dave Brown   Dave B.

Lorraine Bruce   Lorraine B.
Pat Buller   Pat B.
Donna Burbidge   Donna B.
Stan Butler   Stan B.
Wendy Carpenter   Wendy C.
Nick Carter   Nick C.
Jackie Cato   Jackie C.
John Chapman   John C.
Wendy Chapman   Wendy Ch.
Stephen Claridge   Stephen C.
Vince Clinton   Vince C.
Gary Cook   Gary C.
Andy Cook   Andy C.
Margaret Cook   Margaret Ck.
Eleanor Cooper   Eleanor C.
Ed Corney   Ed C.
Alan Cosford   Alan C.
Sally Cox   Sally C.
Deborah Creedy   Deborah C.
Ralph Cresswell   Ralph C.
Margaret Crew   Margaret C.
Alan Cribbett   Alan Cr.
Gary Crook   Gary Cr.
Pat Crowley Snr   Pat C.
Simon Croxall   Simon C.
Sue Croxall   Sue C.
Deborah Davey   Deborah D.
Sarah Day   Sarah D.
Jane Deeks   Jane D.
Jenny Denton   Jenny D.
Andrew Dix   Andrew D.
Tricia Downes   Tricia D.
Hazel Drinkwater   Hazel D.
Brian Eakins   Brian E.
Len Eccles   Len E.
David Emery   David E.
Heather Brown   Heather B.
Pam Farmer   Pam F.
Helen Fisher   Helen F.
Shell French   Shell F.
Pat Fryatt   Pat F.
Jill Garrett   Jill G.

Penny Glasgow	Penny G.	Susan Kirton	Susan K.
Chris Gleadell	Chris G.	Andrew Labrum	Andrew Lm.
Stephen Godfrey	Stephen G.	Geoff Labrum	Geoff L.
Katie Goodridge	Katie G.	Andrew Lambert	Andrew L.
Lin Goodwin	Lin G.	Ian Lawson	Ian L.
Roy Green	Roy G.	Sue Leacock	Sue L.
John Grey	John G.	Barbara Levitt	Barbara L.
Jacqueline Grey	Jacqueline G.	June Levitt	June L.
Patsy Griffin	Patsy G.	Pete Levitt	Pete L.
Gareth Griffiths	Gareth G.	Terry Levitt	Terry L.
Jean Grogan	Jean G.	Brian Lewis	Brian L.
Molly Hagan	Molly H.	Billy Lisle	Billy L.
Sarah Hampshire	Sarah H.	Faye Lloyd	Faye L.
Mark Hampson	Mark H.	Mike Lloyd	Mike L.
Gaynor Hancock	Gaynor H.	Graham Lloyd	Graham L.
Susan Hay	Susan H.	Julie Locke	Julie L.
Eddie Hayes	Eddie H.	Lynette Mallows	Lynette M.
Colin Hayle	Colin H.	Doug Marshall	Doug M.
Rebecca Hemmerman		Elaine Martin	Elaine Mn.
	Becca H.	Stephen Martin	Stephen M.
Ian Hickson	Ian H.	Jane Maxey	Jane M.
Sheila Higginbotham		Julie Maxey	Julie M.
	Susan H.	Ian McKenzie	Ian M.
Jenifer Hobbs	Jennifer H.	Elizabeth McMillan	
Debbie Hodder	Debbie H.		Elizabeth M.
Lisa Holman	Lisa H.	John McSherry	John Mc.
Edith Holyhead	Edith H.	Maria Miceli	Maria M.
Elaine Hudson	Elaine H.	Dave Millard	Dave M.
Maurice Hunt	Maurice H.	Clare Moody	Clare M.
Trevor Iles	Trevor I.	Mason Moore	Mason M.
Natalie James	Natalie J.	Pauline Morgan	Pauline M.
Nahida Kassam	Nahida K.	Elaine Morley	Elaine M.
Bob Kelly	Bob K.	Andy Morris	Andy M.
Danny Kelly	Danny K.	Rosa Mule Buscalgia	
Gary Kelly	Gary K.		Rosa B.
Julie Kelly	Julie K.	Janice Myers	Janice M.
Sarah Kelly	Sarah K.	John Myers	John M.
Diane Kent	Diane K.	Susan Nicholson	Susan N.
Linda Kincaid	Linda K.	Andrew Norton	Andrew N.
Ant King	Ant K.	Jackie Nott	Jackie N.
Susan King	Susan Kg.	Donnah Oakey	Donna O.

David Old	David O.	Ian Smith	Ian S.
Sylv Olver	Sylv O.	Graham Smith	Graham S.
Chris Owens	Chris O.	Andy Smith	Andy S.
Constance Owens	Constance O.	Pamela Johnstone	Pamela J.
Kathy Paice	Kathy P.	Ian Spires	Ian S.
Julie Palmer	Julie P.	Sheila Stanbridge	Sheila Se.
Steve Palmer	Steve P.	Dorothy Stapleton	
John Parker	John P.		Dorothy S.
Helen Paton	Helen P.	Jackie Steensel	Jackie S.
Kim Pavey	Kim P.	John Stephenson	John S.
Dave Phillips	Dave P.	Tracy Stephenson	Tracey S.
Elaine Pilcher	Elaine P.	Sheila Stone	Sheila S.
Bev Pinkerman	Bev P.	Lee Ann Styles	Lee Ann S.
Gary Pooley	Gary P.	Elaine Sullivan	Elaine S.
Jon Pooley	John P.	Paul Swannell	Paul S.
Cate Prescott	Cate P.	JulieThompson	Julie T.
Craig Preston	Craig P.	Keith Tilley	Keith T
Lee Proudfoot	Lee P.	Sue Timms	Sue T.
Emma Pullen	Emma P.	Jennifer Todd	Jennifer T.
Edward Quinn	Edward Q.	Graham Tomlin	Graham T.
Lynsey Rainbow	Lynsey R.	Liz Toomey	Liz T.
Del Ratcliffe	Del R.	Ian Turner	Ian T.
John Reed	John Rd.	Colin Twisleton	Colin T.
Lynn Reeves	Lynn R.	Steve Twisleton	Steve Tw.
Diane Richards	Diane R.	Mandy Udhus	Many U.
Pina Ricioppo	Pina R.	Shirley Vickers	Shirley V.
John Robinson	John R.	Lesley Waite	Lesley W.
Celia Robinson	Celia R.	David Watcham	David Wm.
Alan Robinson	Alan R.	Stephen Watson	Stephen W.
Matty Rogers	Matty R.	Sam Watts	Sam W.
Linda Rowlinson	Linda R.	Steve Watts	Steve W.
Donna Scott	Donna S.	Karen Waugh	Karen W.
June Scott	June S.	David Weatherhead	
Darren Seaber	Darren S.		David Wd.
Georgina Sherwood		Phillip Webb	Phillip W.
	Georgina S.	Maurice Webb	Maurice W.
Sharon Sherwood	Sharon S.	Heather Webberly	Heather W.
Martin Skinner	Martin S.	Dean West	Dean W.
Kevin Slaymaker	Kevin S.	Ian Whiting	Ian W.
Hazel Smith	Hazel S.	Peter Whiting	Peter W.
Janet Smith	Janet S.	Elvia Willems	Elvia W.

247